PROVOCATIONS

JEFF SPARROW is a writer, editor, broadcaster and Walkley award-winning journalist.

He is a columnist for *Guardian Australia*, a former Breakfaster at radio station 3RRR, and a past editor of *Overland* literary journal. He is the author of *Crimes Against Nature: Capitalism and Global Heating*; *Fascists Among Us: Online Hate and the Christchurch Massacre*; *Trigger Warnings: Political Correctness and the Rise of the Right*; *No Way But This: In Search of Paul Robeson*; *Money Shot: A Journey into Porn and Censorship*; *Killing: Misadventures in Violence* and *Communism: A Love Story*; the co-author, with Jill Sparrow, of *Radical Melbourne: A Secret History* and *Radical Melbourne 2: The Enemy Within*; and the co-editor, with Anthony Loewenstein, of *Left Turn: Essays for the New Left*.

He is a lecturer at the Centre for Advancing Journalism at the University of Melbourne.

'Jeff Sparrow's writing makes me think, laugh and shake my fist at the sky with rage. He explains and critiques and illuminates our messed-up world with moral clarity and humour, allowing even a dum-dum like me to get my head around what the hell capitalism is doing to us all, and why it must be stopped.'

Tom Ballard

'Jeff's writing is not always comfortable, but it's absolutely necessary, peering into the cracks too many of us pass by, and revealing them for the chasms they are. But what sets him apart is the unflinching hope he offers at the same time. Jeff shows us the world, our world, can be so much better if only we were more willing to face it as it is now and fight for what it could be. Drench yourself in his words and find your cause.'

Amy Remeikis

'Jeff Sparrow has a profoundly thought-provoking way of presenting the truth.'

Thomas Mayor

'Reading Jeff Sparrow is always like having a conversation with the smartest person in the room. He's essential.'

Chloe Hooper

'Jeff Sparrow is a critical voice for justice in an increasingly sparse field. As mainstream journalism teeters between commercial clickbait and dreary stenography, take a moment to celebrate the determined independence that he brings to his work. This is a timely retrospective, balancing a sharp eye for domestic political dynamics with an internationalist worldview; fresh, fierce and uncompromising.'

Scott Ludlam

'Sparrow is the most effective and consistent communicator of left-wing thought to a mainstream Australian audience of the past twenty years.'

Sydney Review of Books

'Sparrow is one of Australia's leading public intellectuals.'

SALIFE

'He's one of Australia's most crucial political thinkers.'

Saturday Paper

PROVOCATIONS

NEW AND SELECTED WRITING

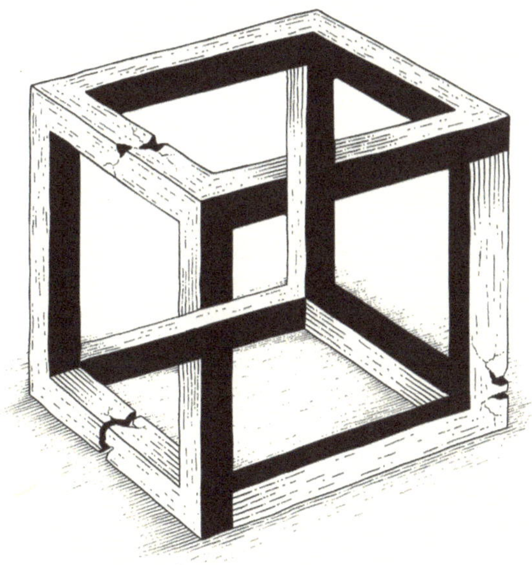

JEFF SPARROW

NEWSOUTH

A NewSouth book

Published by
NewSouth Publishing
University of New South Wales Press Ltd
University of New South Wales
Sydney NSW 2052
AUSTRALIA
https://unsw.press/

First published 2022

10 9 8 7 6 5 4 3 2 1

NATIONAL LIBRARY OF AUSTRALIA

A catalogue record for this book is available from the National Library of Australia

ISBN 9781742237510 (paperback)
9781742238463 (ebook)
9781742239361 (ePDF)

Internal design Josephine Pajor-Markus
Cover design and illustrations Sam Wallman
Printer Griffin Press, part of Ovato

UNSW SYDNEY

Contents

Introduction

'This is a little bit of my life; I will give it to you.'

So said the bushranger Ned Kelly as he handed over the document now known as the 'Jerilderie Letter' to men he'd bailed up in a New South Wales country town.

Every writer understands what Kelly meant.

This book compiles decades of my work for newspapers, magazines and online outlets, pieces that analyse, in Ned's words, 'the occurrences of the present, past and future'.

It's a large bit of my life.

In the digital age, opinionating demands more justification than bushranging ever did, given the hot takes, concern trolling and clickbaiting clogging up the internet. Amid the churn of social media outrage, we instinctively sympathise with the advice the Roman emperor Marcus Aurelius gave himself in his *Meditations*.

'You don't *have* to turn this into something', he says in Book Six, almost as if he were peering dubiously at his Twitter feed. 'It doesn't have to upset you.'

Most op-ed writers feel a sneaking admiration for the

column published by the American journalist Bob Considine in 1973.

It simply read: 'I have nothing to say today.'

Yet the stoicism of Marcus Aurelius ('Things can't shape our decisions by themselves') distilled a particular social logic – and not necessarily an admirable one. He could counsel detachment because he believed in predestination, confident that the universe itself mandated his rule over a vast, cruel empire. The slaves in the imperial palace might not have shared Marcus's faith that everything could be left to happily work itself out.

In any case, the Romans inhabited a very different world to the one we've inherited. The cascading disasters of the 21st century inevitably inhibit those who would float serenely above political contentions. You might not care about climate change but climate change certainly cares about you, as each passing season demonstrates.

George Orwell once said that, after his experiences in the Spanish Civil War, he wrote as a deliberate intervention, a literary blow directed against Stalinism, fascism and the other evils encapsulated in that conflict. 'It seems to me nonsense', he said, 'in a period like our own, to think that one can avoid writing of such subjects.'

According to the best available science, the next few years will determine the fate of the entire planet, with the decisions made (or not made) permanently affecting human, animal and plant life on the one inhabitable world we know. With the fire spreading, how can anyone be indifferent to its flames?

In the same article, Orwell explained that he saw his writing as a personal contribution to socialism.

For more than thirty years, I've also been a socialist, sharing HG Wells's opposition to an order in which 'a small minority [...] dance on the faces of everyone else.' In some nations, socialism remains an unexceptional feature of the political landscape. Not, however, in Australia. As a political writer, I've usually found myself tremendously isolated, one of only a handful of socialists contributing to the mainstream media with any regularity. That's partly because the deep structures of the media facilitate the status quo.

If you're repeating an argument that everyone already accepts, you can do so in a few lines or a snappy soundbite. The more you walk well-trodden paths, the faster you can advance. If, however, you oppose the consensus, you can't take anything for granted. You're forced to argue each point almost from first principles, like a mountaineer hacking steps into a summit.

That shapes your writing.

Of necessity, I make my influences overt, explaining, as best I can, the traditions that have shaped me, in the hope that others will find them equally useful.

In Australia, a tradition of anti-intellectualism means that journalists, most of whom are highly educated and erudite, often adopt a persona of ocker larrikinism, fearing they'll alienate readers unless they pretend they've never read a book in their lives.

But a disdain for philosophy and theory doesn't make ideas any less significant. Even (or perhaps especially) 'common sense' comes from somewhere. When the pundits of the populist Right work themselves into a rhetorical lather, they are, as the economist John Maynard Keynes put it, 'distilling their frenzy from some academic scribbler of a few years back'.

This book's title shouldn't be taken as an endorsement of culture war contrarianism. There's nothing particularly interesting or admirable about *épater le bourgeois* provocations. The superficial outrage ginned up by trolls barely impinges on the truly powerful, who understand how late capitalism can recuperate cultural transgressions, as today's edgelord becomes tomorrow's social conservative.

Genuine radicalism provides hope. It provokes through a scandalous insistence that life can be otherwise, that we aren't doomed to economic and environmental decline, and that we can make our future better than our past.

The pieces in this book are classified (very loosely) thematically, rather than chronologically. I've selected the essays that retain their relevance, articles in which the arguments still matter, even outside their original context.

Words, in and of themselves, rarely change the world, despite what writers often imagine. Ned Kelly composed his tract as an apologia and a manifesto, urging authorities to restrain a brutal police force terrorising north-eastern Victoria.

'Neglect this', he concluded, in an unpunctuated rush, 'and abide by the consequences, which shall be worse than the rust in the wheat in Victoria or the druth of a dry season to the grasshoppers in New South Wales I do not wish to give the order full force without giving timely warning, but I am a widows son outlawed and my orders must be obeyed'.

They weren't, of course. The astonishing, apocalyptic prose of the 'Jerilderie Letter' made no difference to Kelly's fate or to that of his friends. When Kelly walked to the scaffold a few years later, all the other members of his gang were already dead.

History gets made by the actions of real men and women, not by words alone. That's something journalists, in particular, would do well to remember. The Canadian columnist George Bain described writing an op ed as akin to wetting your pants while wearing a blue serge suit. You get, he said, a brief warm feeling but no-one else notices.

Yet sometimes – just sometimes! – the right lines find the right person at the right moment. A phrase sticks; an argument resonates; an idea clicks into place.

These pieces were a part of my life. I hope they mean something in yours.

HEROES AND VILLAINS

Today, politicians of all stripes laud Martin Luther King almost as a secular saint. Yet, in 1968, the year of King's assassination, opinion polls recorded 75 per cent of Americans as disapproving of a man who had denounced the Vietnam War, urged massive expansion of public services, and joined striking sanitation workers on the picket line.

Something similar might be said about the equally beloved Nelson Mandela, who – almost unbelievably – remained on the US State Department watchlist as a terrorist until 2008.

The recognition that both men eventually obtained never comes to most activists, who remain, at best, anonymous and, at worst, actively persecuted.

Political heroism looks nothing like the antics in a comic book franchise. The people who make change don't wield special powers and are not anointed by prophecy. History moves when ordinary men and women screw their courage to the sticking point and say no to matters that revolt their conscience.

For the most part, their actions don't bring them acclaim but rather the opposite.

Villains, by contrast, rise depressingly often to the top.

In a letter to his friend Karl Marx, Friedrich Engels once suggested that Australia would become 'an astonishing example of what a state of unconcealed blackguards can do in the way of miracles ... Carlyle will see his aristocracy of rogues established in full glory'.

One could – as you'll see in the essays that follow – adduce considerable evidence to suggest that his prediction duly came to pass.

Australia's not alone in that respect, of course. Ours is the era of unconcealed blackguards, a global scoundrel time, in which the gulf between the few and the many has grown to proportions almost impossible to comprehend.

According to one calculation, Amazon's Jeff Bezos makes US$3715 per second – nearly four times as much as the average American worker gets from a week's worth of labour. Similarly, between April 2020 and April 2021 Elon Musk received, on average, US$383 000 000 each and every day.

Both Bezos and Musk pay minimal tax as they preside over unparalleled exploitation. Yet, like many of the tech tycoons, they obsess over space travel and the colonisation of Mars. As the grip of environmental crisis tightens around Earth, the super-rich – like so many cartoon super-villains – quite literally plan how they might blast off to other planets.

We're often told we shouldn't harbour enmities, that we should rise above crude hatreds. The 19th-century poet and critic Heinrich Heine scorned such a view. 'I am the most peaceable of men', he explained. 'All I ask is a humble cottage with a thatched roof, a good bed, good food, fresh milk and butter, flowers before my window and a few fine trees at my door; and if the dear Lord wants to make my happiness complete, he will grant me the joy of seeing some six or seven of my enemies hanging from those trees.'

He then added the sage maxim: 'One must forgive one's enemies – but not before they have been hanged.' Capital punishment is barbaric but, in a purely metaphorical sense, there's definitely something to Heine's sentiment.

The late political journalist Alexander Cockburn, for

whose newsletter *Counterpunch* I wrote occasionally, told a story about welcoming interns who worked with him on the *Nation*, the American radical magazine. On their first day, Cockburn would approach them and ask: 'Is your hate pure?'

The query, he said, provided a perfect test. The opportunists, careerists and conciliators – Cockburn specifically mentioned the future Labour leader Ed Miliband – would stammer something about trying not to hate anyone. Only a feisty minority understood what Cockburn meant: that politics meant struggle, that the stakes were high, and that the leaders of the other side were out-and-out enemies whose defeat was a precondition of any social progress.

The pieces in this section focus on different kinds of heroism and villainy, some of them real and some of them imaginary.

I wrote the first article here specifically for this collection after reading in Terry Smyth's book *Australian Confederates* a passing mention of a proposed slave state in northern Queensland. I knew a little about so-called 'blackbirding', but the centrality of slavery – that most villainous of institutions – to colonial history astonished me. As the essay argues, it seems to me now that you simply can't understand Australian federation without discussing what took place in the tropical cane fields.

Bushrangers – simultaneously admired and decried – have always occupied an equivocal place in Australian culture. The story of Captain Moonlite queers that ambiguity, encouraging us to think about the white masculinity of the bush in a very different way. It was a fun piece to write, not least because it meant embarking on a road trip on a bushranger's trail and talking about homosexuality with a National Party politician, both activities that I wouldn't normally undertake.

I wrote the article on the refugee Omid Sorousheh very quickly, at a time when it seemed likely he would die on his hunger strike on Nauru. Fortunately, he started eating again in hospital after his body nearly collapsed. He was eventually released and now lives in Sydney with a relative.

The final piece in this section – a polemic about global inequality – appeared in the *Guardian* in 2013. Since then, the figures have changed, with the disparity between rich and poor increasingly significantly. The argument, I think, retains all its validity.

A slave state

In July 2021, Jack Dempsey, the mayor of the town of Bundaberg, delivered an official apology for Northern Queensland's past reliance on the indentured labour of Pacific Islanders, many of whom were kidnapped (or 'blackbirded') and forced to work on the state's cane plantations. 'To say sorry', explained Dempsey, 'is a start in the healing and the hope for a better relationship going forward'.

The emotional response – equal parts sorrow and relief – from the local Islander community confirmed the gesture's importance. 'I'm thinking about my mother and my brother and my aunties who have all passed on', said Aunty Coral Walker, the president of the Bundaberg South Sea Islanders Heritage Association. 'It would have meant a lot to them because they were a part of that era where they knew about blackbirding.'[1]

But if the Bundaberg apology began a healing, it by no means completed it. On the contrary, the statement highlighted the inadequacy of Australia's reckoning with its past.

That's because the practice Dempsey described – sometimes known as 'sugar slavery' – was not a minor or incidental phenomenon. On the contrary, it was so important to plantation owners that, to defend it, they briefly contemplated separation from the rest of the colony, with Townsville mooted as the capital of what many observers dubbed a 'slave state'. This 'scheme for the extension and perpetuation of the slavery system' showed, one journalist claimed at the time, that Queensland had become 'what the United States were before the Wars of the Secession'.[2]

Similar references to civil war occurred again and again during the debates prior to the federation of the Australian colonies. Slavery and its consequences – both in Queensland and in the American South – obsessed Australia's founders, and fundamentally moulded the country they created. Australia's first prime minister, Edmund Barton, explained, quite accurately, that the 'limited slavery' of the cane fields had agitated 'the whole of Australia' and so was 'a question which belongs to the Federation we have succeeded in establishing'.[3] He also outlined the shocking philosophy upon which he considered Australia based:

> I do not think either that the doctrine of the equality of man was really ever intended to include racial equality. There is no racial equality. There is basic inequality. These races are, in comparison with white races—I think no one wants convincing of this fact—unequal and inferior. The doctrine of the equality of man was never intended to apply to the equality of the Englishman

> and the Chinaman. There is deep-set difference, and we see no prospect and no promise of its ever being effaced. Nothing in this world can put these two races upon an equality. Nothing we can do by cultivation, by refinement, or by anything else will make some races equal to others.[4]

It's impossible to understand that speech – and Barton's conviction that, in dismissing racial equality, he spoke for the nation – without thinking about the sugar fields of Queensland and what was done there.

The French historian Ernest Renan described forgetting as 'an essential factor in the creation of a nation', since patriots do not want to remember the 'deeds of violence' at the origin of all political formations.[5] In the Australian context, a strange contradiction contributes to the ongoing amnesia about slavery and its consequences.

From the very beginning, enslavement shaped white settlement in Australia – and so, too, did abolitionism. That paradox, a peculiar entwinement of two ostensibly antagonistic impulses, makes for a complicated narrative, one that cannot be grasped simply as a local version of the better-known American story.

But if regret is to bring change, we must comprehend what we're apologising for and why. The great abolitionist Frederick Douglass, a man who had escaped enslavement in 1838, described the past as a mirror that could, if used correctly, convey 'the dim outlines of the future' and, perhaps, 'make them more symmetrical.'

With that in mind, let's talk about Australian slavery.

*

In 1788, England remained the most important slaving nation in the world, a country that, from the 17th century until 1807, conveyed a dizzying 3.25 million people out of Africa and into bondage.[6]

The planners of the new convict colony in New South Wales drew directly on logistical skills acquired through Britain's long involvement in the slave trade. They contracted the Second and Third Fleets to one of London's biggest slaving firms, the merchants Calvert, Camden and King, who duly showed the same care for British convicts as they did for African slaves.[7] Some 25 per cent of prisoners died on the voyage; 40 per cent succumbed within six months of arrival.[8]

In New South Wales, the men and women labouring on the settlement were officially described as 'in servitude' until they became 'emancipated', a vocabulary taken directly from the Atlantic trade.[9]

Yet if slavery pressed on the colony, so too did anti-slavery.

Britain required New South Wales because, after the American War of Independence broke out in 1775, the English could no longer dump its criminals in the American territories. The same colonial uprising that disrupted transportation to the New World also turned public sentiment against slavery, an institution tainted by association with the ungrateful Americans.

That was why, in the month that the First Fleet sailed from Portsmouth, evangelical Christians in London launched the Society for Effecting the Abolition of the Slave Trade –

an organisation that would eventually succeed in rendering slavery illegal in Britain.[10]

A few years later, the Haitian revolution – perhaps history's greatest uprising of the enslaved – would intensify respectable concern about the dangerous instability of slave societies. The visceral fear of black revolt induced merchants enriched by trading Africans to consider the new opportunities of the factory system, shifting Britain's economy away from plantation agriculture to manufacturing and other, more modern, industries.[11]

All of that affected the Australian colony. The more far-sighted members of the British elite had no desire to replicate the American disaster – and they most definitely did not want to found a new Haiti in the Pacific. So, before the First Fleet even departed, its commander, the 50-year-old naval veteran Captain Arthur Phillip, explicitly eschewed any intent to allow enslavement in the settlement.

'There can be no slavery in a free land', he declared, 'and consequently no slaves'.

In 2020, with Black Lives Matter protests spreading globally, Prime Minister Scott Morrison took a question from a radio host about the removal of colonial statues. In response, the Prime Minister defended the European settlers as relatively enlightened men, committed to ideals of freedom in New South Wales.

'It was a pretty brutal place', he concluded, 'but there was no slavery in Australia.'[12] The comments brought widespread condemnation, and the Prime Minister quickly acknowledged that 'hideous practices' had indeed occurred.[13]

Yet Morrison's initial point was not entirely wrong.

Phillip had, indeed, promised a free colony. So how did his pledge affect the 'hideous practices' the PM described?

In 1788, mainstream abolitionism was not especially radical. The evangelicals, with their concern for human souls, considered chattel slavery – the legal ownership of one man by another – a denial of the personal agency so central to Protestantism. But, as moral campaigners, they also approved of punishing sin – and in the late 18th century there was plenty of it to punish.

In Britain, the enclosure of the English commons had driven impoverished rural populations into cities like London. Swelling unemployment meant crime and rebellion. To control the desperate and the jobless, the authorities passed harsh new laws, a legislative program designed to quell disorder and ensure a pliant workforce for the factories. The Riot Act banned public disorder; the Combination Act made trade unions illegal; the Workhouse Act forced the poor to work; the Vagrancy Act turned joblessness into a crime. Eventually, over 220 offences could attract capital punishment – or, indeed, transportation.

As we have seen, convict transportation – a system in which prisoners toiled without pay under military discipline – replicated many of the worst cruelties of slavery. Yet, rather than fostering opposition to the forced labour of transportees, mainstream abolitionism helped justify it.

Middle-class anti-slavery activists expressed little sympathy for Britain's ragged and desperate, holding the urban lumpenproletariat responsible for its own misery. The men and women of London's slums weren't slaves. They were free individuals – and if they chose criminality, the abolitionists reasoned, they brought their punishment on themselves.

That was how Phillip could decry chattel slavery while simultaneously relying on unfree labour from convicts. The experience of John Moseley, one of the eleven people of colour on the First Fleet, illustrates how, in the Australian settlement, a rhetoric of liberty accompanied a new kind of bondage.

Later in life, Moseley claimed to have been employed as a 'tobacco planter in America'. By that he almost certainly meant that he had been enslaved on a plantation in the Tidewater region of Virginia and Maryland.[14] How had he washed up in Sydney?

Like several of the black First Fleeters, Moseley fought for Britain during the American Revolution. That was because Lord Dunmore, the last British governor of Virginia, had offered liberty to 'all indented Servants, Negroes, or others ... that are able and willing to bear arms' against the insurrectionists.

Moseley, and others like him, chose freedom – and then faced recapture when Britain surrendered. One slave later said that the success of the revolt 'diffused universal joy among all parties; except us who had escaped from slavery and taken refuge in the English army'.[15] Desperate to evade their old masters, the formerly enslaved begged the retreating British for passage to London. Those who were successful remained free – but also, for the most part, unemployed, struggling in a strange and harsh city without friends or family.

Loyalists could, in theory, claim compensation for fighting in the revolutionary war. In practice, the authorities generally rebuffed pleas from ex-slaves, on the cynical basis that emancipation constituted sufficient reward.

'Instead of suffering by the war, he gained by it', wrote an official about one claimant, 'for he is in a much better country where he may with industry get his bread, where he can never more be a slave.'[16]

Moseley, like so many others, struggled in the harsh city to get his bread. When he eventually turned from industry to criminal fraud, the contrast between British liberty and American slavery provided the ideological justification for the treatment he received. He was a free man; the court held him responsible for his own dishonesty and sentenced him to death. The eventual commutation of a capital sentence to transportation meant that armed guards marched a black ex-slave, chained once more by the neck and ankles, to the *Scarborough*, on which he sailed to New South Wales.

Phillip's prohibition on chattel slavery was, on its own terms, genuine. But we need to understand what those terms were. For John Moseley, the 'free land' of New South Wales brought only a replication of that captivity he'd endured in Virginia.

His experience was not unique. As the poet and playwright Bertolt Brecht might say, throughout the settlement, the old strode in, disguised as the new. In years to come, colonial opposition to slavery would co-exist with, and even facilitate, various kinds of bonded labour – and nowhere more so than in Queensland.

*

From the very start, the Australian sugar industry demonstrated how formal and real freedoms might collide.

In Tascott in New South Wales, you can still find a plaque celebrating the man who gave the town its name: a certain Thomas Scott, who, we are told, 'arrived in the colony in 1816 [and] pioneered the sugar industry in Australia.'[17]

The Tascott memorial neglects to mention Scott's background in the slave trade. Yet that was how he developed his familiarity with sugar. As a young man, he assisted an uncle buying and selling Africans, before he began managing slave labour on his family's plantation in Antigua.

Scott came to Port Macquarie in 1823, where Major Frederick Goulburn engaged him for an annual salary of £250 to grow sugar in the strange climate.[18] Historians now agree that he failed miserably.

'How many times did you try to make sugar at the settlement before you made anything like it?' a contemporary mocked him. 'What you made yourself was not fit for dogs to eat before the poor black man shewed you the way.'[19]

That 'poor black man' was another Antiguan, James Williams.

Where Scott was an ex-slaver, Williams was an ex-slave. He had somehow escaped to England, where, like Moseley, he resorted to crime. Sentenced to seven years transportation, Williams arrived in Sydney in 1820. Another theft saw him banished to Port Macquarie. In that town, a full year before Scott's arrival, he established a viable crop from eight joints of cane, using the 'knowledge of the growth of that Plant' he had acquired as a slave.

Despite the successful production of 'very good Sugar and Rum', Williams never adjusted to life in the colony, spending the rest of his days in and out of various forms of custody. By contrast, Thomas Scott, confident the rival claims of a 'poor black man' would not be heeded, basked in an entirely undeserved reputation as the father of Australian sugar, even receiving an annual pension for his supposed achievements. In that foundational moment – an ex-slaver exploiting an ex-slave – the racial dynamic of the industry was already visible.

When the American Civil War broke out in 1861, many Europeans in Australia sympathised with the Confederates, particularly after the Unionists briefly seized the *Trent*, a British Royal Mail steamer. The Melbourne *Argus* anticipated war between Australia and the northern American states, arguing that that 'as a matter of sound precaution, citizens of the United States now resident in Victoria should be placed under surveillance.'[20] Some of the gun emplacements still visible in Sydney Harbour date back to that fear of invasion by the Yankees.

In the context of that widespread enthusiasm for the South (the welcome extended to the Confederate ship *Shenandoah* in Melbourne in 1865 led one of its officers to conclude 'the heart of colonial Britain was in our cause'), Queenslanders dreamed of building a 'second Louisiana.'[21] They could, they thought, capitalise on the disruption of the international cotton and sugar trades, if only they could establish a viable local crop.[22]

But how might they emulate agriculture from a slave state?

Attempts to attract English workers to Queensland did not succeed. The men that came found the conditions unbearable, something the colonists attributed not to the innate unpleasantness of cutting cane in the sticky heat but to the racial unsuitability of white labour to the tropics. So, in 1863, the shipping tycoon Robert Towns (the man who gave Townsville its name) tried another approach.

Towns knew that, back in 1847, an entrepreneur called Benjamin Boyd – another man with a background in Caribbean slavery – had scandalised the colony by transporting men from the Pacific Islands of Tanna and Lifou to supply his cattle station with labour. The 'signatures' on the documents that indentured them were thumb prints from illiterate men who had never before seen cattle; their 'contracts' bound them to work for a pittance however Boyd commanded. Some of the labourers revealed their genuine feeling by fleeing as soon as they could; the others demanded to be sent home. Boyd's business collapsed and he decamped to California.[23]

In Boyd's inauspicious venture, Towns glimpsed a solution, a means by which he might recreate Louisiana in Queensland. The insatiable demands of the textile industry meant, he thought, that cotton plantations would be far more profitable than Boyd's cattle stations. Accordingly, Towns chartered a ship called the *Don Juan* and sailed it to the New Hebrides from where it returned crammed with Islanders destined for Towns' huge property near the Logan River.

The Civil War ended before Boyd could prove his experiment a success. But though peace dashed prospects for a Queensland cotton boom, a planter called Louis Hope realised that cotton fields could also be used for sugar, a commodity always in demand. He duly sent out ships to obtain indentured labour of his own.

That was how it began.

Between 1863 and 1904, 62 000 South Sea Islanders were transported to Australia, landing in Brisbane, Maryborough, Bundaberg, Rockhampton, Mackay, Bowen, Townsville, Innisfail and Cairns. Most indentured labourers arrived from the New Hebrides, with a substantial proportion taken from the Solomons, as well as smaller islands. By the 1890s, Pacific Islanders constituted 85 per cent of the workforce for Australian sugar.

Some came willingly, accepting – as desperate people do – unknown hardship to escape grinding poverty. Some, equally clearly, did not. Faith Bandler, the much-loved civil rights activist and hero of the 1967 Indigenous rights referendum, was the daughter of one such sugar slave. As a child, she'd listened to her father, Peter Mussing, describing his youth. He told Faith about 'when he was kidnapped and taken into the boat by the slavers, and what it was like in the boat coming over from his island Ambrym in the New Hebrides, and how rough it was and how they were all held in the hull and how sick they were and those who died would be thrown overboard and how it was when the boat would arrive in Australia and how strange everything seemed to him.'[24]

Paradoxically, such experiences – so reminiscent of the Middle Passage endured by slaves brought across the Atlantic Ocean – coincided with a hardening of official hostility to slavery throughout the British Empire. In 1833, the parliament in Westminster had officially legislated abolition, with enslavement thereafter disdained as contrary to English principles of liberty. The politicians allocated an extraordinary sum of £20 million (about 40 per cent of Britain's total income) to restitution: an amount granted not to the slaves but to their owners, compensation to them for the loss of their 'property'.[25] The records of those disbursements include a remarkable number of colonial Australians.

Judges, statesmen, bankers, even the poet Adam Lindsay Gordon: the upper echelons of Australia society contained many men who had either personally kept slaves or belonged to families that did.[26]

In the bigger population centres, the beneficiaries of enslavement generally distanced themselves from their less than reputable past. The tropical north, however, was different. There, those with a background in Caribbean slavery could recreate something of their old ways.

Louis Hope, for instance, set himself up (according to one biographer) 'as a landed aristocrat', with a grand mansion at Ormiston, an estate akin to those his slave-owning relatives occupied in the Caribbean. He was not alone in his affectations. A visitor to Queensland in the late 1870s and early 1880s described the planters living along the river at Mackay:

> Their houses as a rule, are extremely comfortable, and very well furnished, and the gardens of many of them are paradises of beauty. In good times, they make tremendous profits, and their occupation

> chiefly consists in watching other people work, in the intervals of which they recline in a shady verandah with a pipe and a novel, and drink rum-swizzles. Most of them keep a manager, so that they can always get away for a run down south, or a kangaroo hunt up the country.[27]

The men did not merely adopt a lifestyle associated with New World slavery. They also relied on its techniques and its personnel.

Hope, for instance, acquired his sugar plants from the old slaver Thomas Scott. He hired supervisors from Jamaica and Barbados, looking for those with experience driving plantation slaves. To obtain the men for his fields, he turned – just as Boyd had before him – to a certain Captain Lewin, a notoriously shady character.

The Royal Navy's Commander George Palmer described Lewin's vessels as 'fitted up precisely like an African slaver, minus the irons' and noted that, 'I heard of him [Lewin] at every island I was at as a man stealer and kidnapper'.[28] Lewin escaped conviction for a rape committed on one of those ships when a Brisbane court held that his 13-year-old victim could not give evidence since 'she was not a Christian, and there were no courts of law in her country', ignoring the testimony of the Islander witnesses who described the girl's screams.

Between 1863 and 1868, this was the man responsible for 'recruiting' nearly half the Islanders who arrived in Australia.[29]

*

The uncontrolled growth of blackbirding eventually spurred the Polynesian Labourers Act, an attempt by the Queensland government to enforce some sort of regulation. The law required recruiters to get a licence; it mandated certain minimum standards on voyages where previously passengers had often simply been imprisoned in the holds.

Yet conditions did not necessarily improve. In general, the treatment of Islanders in Queensland depended less on legislation than on how desperately the planters needed labour at any given moment.

Some young men found indenture quite bearable, so much so that when one contract ended, they signed on for another, before eventually returning to their homes with cash in their pockets. Yet when the sugar boom of the 1880s fostered a scramble for cutters, the cruelties intensified.[30] On occasion, recruiters – desperate to fill their quotas – travelled to islands where blackbirders had never previously visited and simply grabbed whomever they could find.

In 1884, at the height of that demand, a vessel called the *Hopeful* opened fire on Islanders who resisted being stolen, killing at least thirty-eight people and possibly more. Its crew faced trial for kidnapping and murder; a subsequent Royal Commission found that only nine of the 480 people 'recruited' by the ship had understood the supposed agreements they'd signed. The commission described the *Hopeful*'s expedition as 'one long record of deceit, cruel treachery, deliberate kidnapping and cold-blooded murder'.[31]

The sailors were subsequently released, after 'public indignation [about their convictions] in Brisbane and the coast towns waxed to fever heat' and some 28 000 people signed a petition calling for clemency.[32]

The massive support for the *Hopeful*'s crew needs to be understood in the context in which indentured labour was advocated. Hope, and the others like him, did not see themselves as recreating slavery. On the contrary, they declared their opposition to the practice. The Islanders were not, they said, chattels. Rather than being bought or sold, the men were employees, hired like any other workers. They received money in return for the contract; when their term expired, they could leave.

This was not altogether untrue. Legally, the Islanders were never enslaved. Unlike the slaves in America, they were not officially classified as property. Some managed to improve the terms of their engagement, winning better wages and less brutal conditions. By the 1890s, many were engaged in something more like wage labour.

Nevertheless, the reason the sugar barons wanted Islanders did not vary: they understood that white men could impose upon indentured non-white labourers a discipline that Europeans would not accept. They could pay them less (and sometimes not at all). They could beat them and belittle them and abuse them, confident no law would intervene, and they could work them relentlessly under regimes that regularly proved fatal.

Queensland was not the Americas. What was done in Australia was different and needs to be understood on its own terms. The historian Emma Christopher suggests that, rather than being imagined as analogous to Atlantic slavery, the trade in the Pacific might be thought of as one of its illegitimate offspring: a forced labour both reminiscent of and distinct from the practices of the New World. Nevertheless, a legal case in Rockhampton in 1868 illustrates the aptness of the term 'sugar slavery'.

In January that year, a man called John Tancred faced charges under the Master and Servants Act after a conflict with one Arthur Gossett over an Islander boy identified only as 'Towhey'. Though bound to Gossett, the child had fled his employment to join men from his own island who were labouring for Tancred. Their teary reunion provoked a legal dispute between two white men about the 'lawful ownership' of Towhey (known by a quite different name among his own people) – a matter settled when Gossett proved his claim by identifying a brand on the boy's leg.

'The advantage', explained the *Rockhampton Bulletin*, 'of the branding these intelligent islanders who cannot speak English and who make crosses to their agreements, has been made very manifest by this case, and, perhaps, it may not yet be too late for the Assembly to insert a "branding" clause in the Polynesian Laborers Bill'.[33]

The Assembly did not adopt that suggestion. It did, however, accept an amendment proposed by Hope himself (who became a member of the Queensland Legislative Council in 1862), which decreed that if an indentured labourer 'absent[ed] himself from the place of employment for a greater distance than one mile [...] without a pass from his employer', he would be 'liable to apprehension and punishment' – a clause justified by the need for 'the employer to retain control over his laborers'.[34]

The Australian press described the Islanders as 'kanakas'. In its original, Hawaiian context, *kanaka* meant 'free man'. In Australia, it signalled the opposite, as no less an authority than the Governor General confirmed.

Like many of the planters, Sir Anthony Musgrave had come to Australia from the West Indies.[35] Like them, his family had owned slave-run plantations – and so he knew enslavement when he saw it. In Australia, he privately described the recruitment of Islanders as 'a system & arrangements wh. are as much like slavery & the slave trade as anything can well be wh. is not avowed as such'.[36]

By 1884, the annual mortality rate for Islanders in Queensland had climbed to 147 deaths per 1000 people. Everyone knew why: as the Brisbane *Courier* reported, the causes of mortality were 'indisputably plain; the islanders were being killed mainly by overwork, insufficient or improper food, bad water, absence of medical attention when sick, and general neglect'.[37]

The harshness was not accidental. '[Islanders] must be treated with firmness', explained the planter JW Anderson, 'they do not expect much leniency and would take advantage of it. Above all, they must not be treated too well, according to our notions ... for their minds are so constituted that they do not appreciate such treatment'.[38]

Anderson's belief that Islanders were innately predisposed to appreciate brutality illustrates how Queensland sugar depended on the most pernicious ideological legacy of the Atlantic slave trade: modern racism.

*

The philosophical underpinnings of slaving might seem obvious. The perceived inferiority of Africans enabled, we assume, merchants to buy and sell them as commodities. But that's quite wrong. Africans weren't enslaved because they were black. They were black because they were enslaved, with the vast profits in Atlantic slavery giving rise to entirely novel forms of classifying humanity.

Slavery existed in the past, of course. But in the ancient and medieval worlds, enslavement related typically to conquest or religion rather than 'race' – a concept that didn't really exist as we know it today. Anyone could become a slave after a battle; slaves could sometimes free themselves by converting to their masters' faith.

Slavery was not, in other words, a condition attached permanently to a certain type of person so much as an unfortunate fate that might befall anyone.

The system imposed in the Caribbean and the Americas was different. The immensely profitable cultivation of cotton and sugar required vast quantities of labour, not least because the plantations often proved fatal to the men and women toiling in them. Begrudging any cessation of production, planters in the New World did not release converts; they deemed the sons and daughters of slaves to inherit their parents' status.

Accordingly, slave owners developed a different rationale for their system, one under which the skin pigmentation of the enslaved – previously an entirely incidental feature – defined them, as an indelible quality that marked men and women as suitable for servitude. The French philosopher and mathematician Nicolas de Condorcet pointed out that the new theories made 'nature herself an accomplice in the crime of political inequality.'[39] Indeed, the identification of 'blackness' with inferiority corresponded with an equally novel claim about the superiority of 'whiteness', one that provided a legitimation for the spread of British power.

From the very start, such ideas had underpinned the establishment of the Australian colonies.

The 'natives', Phillip complained soon after landing, were 'far more numerous than they were supposed to be.'[40] Their abundance mattered because it undercut the legal foundations of the entire colony. Phillip, like everyone else on the mission, knew perfectly well that international law forbade a nation claiming sovereignty over territory inhabited by others.

The settlers resolved the jurisprudential problem by ignoring it. The colony might have been illegal, but race theory allowed the colonists to believe themselves committed to universal law, even as they more or less entirely excluded Indigenous people from its remit.

That provided the pattern for everything that followed. In theory, Indigenous people enjoyed all the protections of British subjects. In practice, they were often treated as animals – or, indeed, slaves.

As late as 1899, a Select Committee of the South Australian Parliament received grotesque testimony about the sexual slavery to which Aboriginal women were subjected. One policeman explained that the rape of 'lubras' (a racist term for Indigenous women) was commonplace.

'If half the young lubras', he said, 'now being detained (I won't call it kept, for I know most of them would clear away if they could) were approached on the subject, they would say that they were run down by station blackguards on horseback, and taken to the stations for licentious purposes, and there kept more like slaves than anything else. I have heard it said that these same lubras have been locked up for weeks at a time – anyway whilst their heartless persecutors have been mustering cattle on their respective runs. Some, I have heard take these lubras with them, but take the precaution to tie them up.'[41]

A few years later, persistent accounts of abuses in Western Australia led to a Royal Commission in that part of the country. Under its auspices, Walter Roth, the former Chief Protector of the Aborigines in Queensland, produced a lengthy document chronicling the proliferation of forced labour.

'Here at our own doors', said the *Melbourne Advocate*, '... we have had revealed a system of slavery so revolting in its brutality, and so inhuman in all its details, as to equal all the horrors that have been alleged against the slave owners in America and the military expeditions in Central Africa.'[42]

The activist and historian WEB Du Bois once described America as 'built upon a groan.' Something similar might be said about the colony of Australia, at least as far as Indigenous people were concerned.

White Australians tend to imagine frontier violence largely in images derived from first contact: a matter of sharp, almost accidental, clashes as European and Indigenous worlds collided. In fact, the worst depredations were considerably more deliberate, and they escalated as the settlers established themselves. The increasing independence of the colonies during the second half of the 19th century reduced the humanitarian influence exerted by London and allowed the settlers to bring to the frontier techniques of dispossession refined through bloody experience.[43]

The European occupation of Queensland took place later than in other states. As late as 1850, the state contained only about 8000 white settlers. Thereafter, a rapid influx of Europeans unleashed horrific violence against an Indigenous population of about 200 000 people, in a process the colonists considered both necessary and inevitable.

'We should be sorry to see the natives treated with cruelty and oppression', explained a Queensland cabinet minister to parliament in 1861, 'but that the settlers will increase and the colony expand, is a result which the rules of nature render positively certain'. The whites could not and should not be prevented from taking the land and 'if the inferior race suffers in the process, that is only what has happened in all such cases, and will happen again until the end of time'.[44]

In reality, his government was less a passive observer of 'cruelty and oppression' than a key facilitator. The authorities established the Queensland Native Mounted Police in 1855, equipped its members with high-powered rifles, and paid them to 'disperse' any Indigenous people they located. As another parliamentarian acknowledged, the euphemism 'dispersal' meant 'nothing but firing into them'.[45]

The Mounted Police were, in contemporary terms, death squads – and some historians estimate they eventually killed as many as 40 000 Aboriginal men, women and children.

As late as 1880, the liberal *Queenslander* described the slaughter on the frontier, noting that the Indigenous inhabitants of territory into which Europeans moved were 'treated exactly in the same way as the wild beasts or birds the settlers may find there ... Their goods are taken, their children forcibly stolen, their women are carried away, entirely at the caprice of the white men. The least show of resistance is answered by a rifle bullet; in fact, the first introduction between blacks and whites is often marked by the unprovoked murder of some of the former—in order to make a commencement of the work of "civilising" them.'[46]

That article provoked a year-long discussion, in which the *Queenslander*'s contributors demonstrated how the genocidal campaign against Indigenous people had normalised measures unthinkable in any other context.

A writer styling himself 'Never Never' called, for instance, for a speedier genocide, urging the 'exterminating force' of the Native Police to work more 'thoroughly and effectually'.

'Is there room for both of us here?' he asked. 'No. Then the sooner the weaker is wiped out the better, as we may save some valuable lives in the process.'[47]

Others, like a certain 'Outis', argued for what he saw as a more liberal solution. He suggested that, rather than being murdered, Aboriginal people should be treated like 'rogues and vagabonds', and forced to work so that 'they will have no time to hatch mischief'.

Outis noted how planters were bringing 'large numbers of South Sea Islanders to Queensland' under laws that forced them to work as directed by their employer. He argued the same policy could be applied to Indigenous people forcibly removed from their land:

> Only get the blacks out of their own district and it would rest with the employer to make them work; some harshness would no doubt be necessary (as I am told is also the case with Kanakas), but I firmly believe that firmness combined with kindness, and the low rate of wages that the blacks would be paid, would make the employment of aboriginal labor a payable speculation.

For Outis, officers from India or Ceylon could enforce the necessary discipline – so long as they were 'untethered by red tape'. A policy of enslavement rather than murder would, he said, remove 'the present blood guiltiness that weighs upon us each individually as colonists', and so would be worth whatever it cost.

'Is there no member of Parliament who will take this question up?' Outis wondered, 'Are all so overburdened by the cares of the squatters, or diggers, who comprise their constituencies that they cannot spare the time to consider and devise a remedy for "the poor old nigger"?'[48]

As it happened, at least one MP did share his enthusiasm.

On 21 October 1880, the Queensland Parliament debated the role of the Native Police. In the discussion John Douglas (who would later become premier) argued that the distinction between Islanders and Aboriginal people was not so great to extinguish 'the hope that some use might be made of the latter'.

He pointed to Western Australia where 'the natives had been ... in some cases captured, and as prisoners of war had been compelled to submit to a period of pupilage, afterwards becoming useful settlers'. Queensland, Douglas said, might follow suit by taking 'the natives prisoner, instead of shooting down and killing them.'

He did acknowledge the legal difficulties in a policy 'by which these people, taken in open warfare, might be kept in a state of captivity' but stressed it would 'be a more benevolent process than shooting them down and taking their lives.'[49]

The chamber did not embrace Douglas's 'benevolent process' (which would, of course, have been entirely illegal), though some years later a correspondent to the *Adelaide Evening Journal* reported that the Native Police were, in fact, selling into slavery the children of Indigenous people they had massacred.[50]

The willingness of Queensland parliament to ponder the relative merits of enslavement over murder provides a particularly repellent example of the moral desensitisation arising from colonial dispossession. Amid the cruelty inflicted on Indigenous people, the indentured labour of Islanders could seem entirely unremarkable.

*

The relationship between sugar slavery and the foundational racism of a colonial settler state makes an intuitive sense. We understand that the planters who built fortunes from forced labour were infused with a sense of their own biological superiority.

We might not grasp that those who denounced slavery were often even more avowedly racist.

In the Queensland parliament, the Liberal politicians attacked the planters' reliance on Islander labour almost as soon as indenture began. They did so by objecting to the sugar barons polluting the colony with, as the Liberal MP Charles Lilley said in 1869, 'men of an inferior race'.

'The British people are the possessors of this soil', Lilley declared. 'We hold the land in trust for our countrymen alone not for Polynesians or Chinamen.'[51]

The parliamentary argument about the sugar industry was not a debate between racists and their opponents but a contest between different visions of whiteness.

The Conservative Premier Sir Thomas McIlwraith, a man with personal interests in the sugar industry, expressed the perspective of the planters. He wanted, he said, a Queensland both successful and white. Economic prosperity depended on cane, a crop he thought Europeans racially incapable of harvesting. Hence the necessity for a subservient caste of Islanders, who could ensure Queensland remained 'a white man's colony, influenced by white men and owned by white men'.[52]

His Liberal rival Samuel Griffith, on the other hand, argued that the importation of Islanders would foster the 'degeneration which we have seen whenever the black and white races have endeavoured to mix'. If whites depended on slavery, they'd lose their racial consciousness and accept widespread immigration. Accordingly, Griffith advocated a purely European colony based on the rigid exclusion of all non-whites – in essence, attacking the proponents of sugar slavery for being insufficiently racist.[53]

When Griffith won the 1883 election, his victory threw the sugar industrialists into panic. Politics in Queensland, the Sydney *Evening News* explained, was 'fast narrowing itself down to the very simple issue – sugar versus slavery', since 'sugar plantations cannot be worked in Queensland without slave labour in some form or other'.[54]

Fearing the collapse of their estates, the sugar barons contemplated secession. Seeking to marshal all those benefiting from the industry, they presented a vision of independence. They would, they declared, form their own colony, where they could employ on their plantations as much Islander labour as they saw fit.

In April 1885, a Northern Separation convention in Townsville attracted delegates from eleven towns in the region. A petition for secession gathered some 10 000 signatures, a not insignificant number in a population area of perhaps 19 000 European men.[55] In parliament, Maurice Hume Black – a representative of the sugar interests – openly warned that North Queensland wanted to go its own way, while the planters John Ewen Davidson and Sir John Lawes argued their case to the Colonial Office in London.

For a while, it seemed entirely possible that Northern Separation – a movement led by some of the wealthiest and most influential people in the region – might prevail. In his book *A Land Half Won*, historian Geoffrey Blainey suggests that, had that occurred, northern Queensland 'would probably have remained outside the new Commonwealth of Australia ... [becoming] a version of Rhodesia or the old American confederacy of cotton states'.[56]

Many people at the time, with the American Civil War fresh in their minds, thought the same.

'If tropical Australia is politically severed from the South', warned the *Brisbane Courier*, '... we may leave to our children such a legacy of evil as that from which America only rid herself by the most terrible fratricidal war which the modern world has seen.'[57]

That didn't happen because, with their dream of Northern Separation and sugar slavery, the planters faced two powerful opponents.

Overseas, Britain reacted to the petitioning Queenslanders with unabashed horror. If anything, London's concern about the social instability of chattel slavery had only increased since in 1788. In the wake of the civil war in America, British diplomats regarded the prospect of a new antipodean Confederacy as disastrous. As the *Times* noted, England bluntly informed the planters and their supporters that it would 'not permit the establishment of a slave state in Northern Queensland.'[58]

At home, the separatists confronted a different problem. After the gold rush, Chinese immigration had become the focus of racist agitation all over the colony. As early as 1855, Victoria had passed 'an Act to Make Provision for Certain Immigrants', which imposed a discriminatory tax on the Chinese. Other states followed. In 1857 Europeans physically attacked Chinese miners in the Buckland River gold fields; similar riots took place at Lambing Flats in 1860 and 1861.

Many leaders of the newly-formed trade unions blamed the Chinese for driving down wages and so called for racial exclusion, a policy famously expressed in the slogan used by the pro-labour *Bulletin*: 'Australia for the White Man.'

Politicians agonised over whether a colony reliant on a non-white workforce would remain sufficiently British. Many saw the Queensland plantations as a dangerous wedge, a crack in the white wall through which other races might insinuate themselves.

In the days of Arthur Phillip, anti-slavery had legitimised transportation. It now served an even more perverse cause, providing a moral justification for those demanding complete racial exclusion.

The Rockhampton-based *Daily Northern Argus*, for instance, attacked sugar-growers for their 'extraordinary persistence' in agitating for a cause that had already been defeated in the southern states of America. Yet the editorialist's loathing for what the paper described as a 'slave colony' culminated in a lurid vision of the sugar industry facilitating a Chinese takeover.

'The Mongolianisation of North Queensland', the *Argus* declared, 'is only an advance operation of the Mongolianisation of all of Australia.'[59]

The advocates of Northern Separation denied, again and again, any intent to create what the press referred to as a 'black state'. Again and again, they were attacked on precisely that basis, with secession decried as a pretext for slavery, and slavery as a threat to whiteness.

In 1885, Griffith announced that he would prohibit the importation of Islanders within five years. His declaration promised to end the whole controversy, committing Queensland to the Liberal vision of a racially pure nation, rather than the Conservative plan for apartheid. But before the plan could come into operation, the Great Depression of the 1890s struck, threatening the state with economic ruination. Baulking at the prospect of closing the sugar industry in such desperate times, Griffith united with his former rival McIlwraith to delay the ban.

The prevarication by 'the Griffilwraith' (as the press dubbed the unlikely alliance) transformed the sugar debate in Queensland from a local dispute into a national issue, one of the major controversies preoccupying colonial politicians as they planned an Australian federation.

*

The present location of Canberra, halfway between Melbourne and Sydney, echoes arguments made by Queensland secessionists.

In 1886, John Murtagh Macrossan, a prominent Northern Separationist, had proposed establishing the capital of the new Queensland state away from existing population centres so as to minimise regional jealousies. The logic later prevailed with the creation of Canberra.[60]

Even though the Queenslander Samuel Griffith played a major role in drafting a national constitution, the unresolved tension over indentured labour limited the participation of his state in the federation debates. The representatives of the other colonies might have been divided over the merits of free trade versus protectionism, but they shared the goal of an entirely white Australia.[61] That was, indeed, a major motivation for unity: as Alfred Deakin later explained, only federal legislation could prevent the discrepancies between different laws that constituted 'a half-open door for all Asiatics and African peoples.'[62]

With the national project at odds with the planters'

continued hopes for some form of indenture, a divided Queensland did not attend the 1897/98 constitutional convention. It was only in the following year, when the sugar industry had been placated by the offer of federal compensation, that a pro-federation referendum narrowly succeeded in the state – a victory that signalled majority support for racial homogeneity.

In the *Westminister Review*, TM Donovan explained the triumphant Liberal perspective: 'Federation will bring us statesmen, an honest democratic franchise, and will, no doubt, in a short time rid us of the Asiatic and coloured labour curse. Under the federal flag a piebald race will be an impossibility. ... [T]otal exclusion alone can save Queensland from the coloured problem of the United States.'[63]

His reference to America expressed a common perception that the legacy of slavery had polluted that country, in ways that young Australia, with its commitment to racial purity, needed to avoid. When Prime Minister Barton introduced the Immigration Restriction Bill by declaring non-whites to be fundamentally inferior and their exclusion something to be greatly desired, he did not consider the statements at all controversial.

The intensity of the discussion that followed (the Hansard account runs to nearly half a million words) was not the result of any programmatic disagreement among the speakers. On the contrary, the Leader of the Opposition George Reid declared unanimity on the aim that 'the current of Australian blood [...] not assume the darker hues'; the Protectionist Samuel Mauger cited 'expert' opinion that bringing 'the white man into contact with the black [would] suspend the very process of natural selection on which the evolution of the higher type depends'; and Labor's James Ronald explained that Australians objected to 'inferior races' because 'they are repugnant to us from our moral and social standpoints.'[64]

The debate centred not on the desirability of a White Australia (for on that the MPs were as one) but on how it might be obtained, after four decades of indentured labour had brought so many Islanders into the country. That was why slavery in the United States featured so heavily in parliament's deliberations: it was invoked again and again as a cautionary tale of racial pollution.[65]

America was, explained the Liberal MP HB Higgins, undergoing 'the greatest racial trouble ever known in the history of the world' and so Australians should 'take warning and guard ourselves against similar complications.' Foolishly, white Americans had failed to expel their former slaves. America would, he continued, 'have been ten times better off if the negroes had not been left there. There are no conditions under which degeneracy of race is so great as those which exist when a superior race and an inferior race are brought into close contact.'[66]

A supportive press concurred. 'The Australian Commonwealth,' explained Queensland's *General Advertiser*, 'at the outset of its career has the golden opportunity of preserving to its citizens the purity of race. The great American commonwealth had not quite such an advantageous opportunity, insofar as long before it was founded the negro race had partly become rooted in American soil.'[67]

Local parliamentarians pledged not to make the same mistake, congratulating themselves on the superiority of their constitution over the one ratified by the United States, on the basis that its Section 51 (the so-called 'race powers') allowed them, as Prime Minister Barton had explained, 'to regulate the affairs of the people of coloured or inferior races who are in the Commonwealth.'[68]

Attorney General Alfred Deakin went so far as to boast that 'our Constitution marks a distinct advance upon and difference from that of the United States.' Its passages explicitly permitting racial discrimination enabled parliament to pass the Immigration Restriction Act (to keep non-whites out) and the Pacific Islands Labourers Act (to deport those Islanders already in Australia).

'The two things go hand in hand', Deakin explained. Stopping the 'lesser races' from arriving (with Islander recruitment ceasing in 1903) and expelling those who were currently resident: these were 'the necessary complement of a single policy – the policy of securing a White Australia.'[69]

The new nation thus signalled its birth by doing what the United States did not dare: ethnically cleansing its former slaves.

*

The deportations began in 1904.

By then, the Islanders resident in Australia numbered perhaps 10 000. Many had built lives for themselves after their terms of indenture ended: finding jobs, building houses, raising families. Some barely remembered the places from which, decades earlier, they'd been taken. They were incredulous they were expected to return. 'Is it really true that white people want to send all boys back to islands?'

asked an Islander in Mackay. '[W]e been work well in this land for white people, then why they want to turn us out?'[70]

From the start, they resisted. In 1902, more than 300 Islanders signed a petition that they presented to Queensland's governor and, via him, to the king. It pleaded for an end to a policy 'contrary to the spirit of English common law and of freedom, justice and mercy', a scheme that would 'induce for hundreds, if not thousands of us, misery, starvation or death.'[71]

In Mackay in 1904, a man called Henry Tongoa organised a Pacific Islanders Association. The association held meetings across North Queensland, where speakers explained that white men had refused to work in the cane fields and had been 'glad to get us to do so.' The planters had become rich on Islander labour, they said, 'with good homes, buggies, horses, pianos, sewing machines and all sorts of other good things which they could not buy or have before we came to the country and worked hard for them.' Yet, despite that, 'these people want to hunt us out of the country.'[72]

The protests – and persistent fears by Queensland planters about labour shortages – forced a 1906 Royal Commission into the program. The Commission recommended exemptions, including for the elderly, for long-term residents, those who could prove themselves in danger, and people who had married others from outside their own islands.

But the expulsions were not halted.

In desperation, Tongoa sailed to Melbourne with another petition, this time for Alfred Deakin. The signatories begged for citizenship for those who wanted to stay. They even offered to remove themselves to a reserve somewhere in the north, a place where, they said, they would pose no competition to white men and could put their 'long experience of tropical cultivation to use'.[73]

Deakin remained unmoved.

After the 1902 petition caused a stir in London, he'd responded by emphasising parliament's unanimity about racial purity (as well as slandering the signatories as 'ignorant savages unable to read and write').[74]

He'd also resorted to the old trick of legitimating repression by fulminating against enslavement. In reply to British humanitarians in London, he expounded on the brutality of the blackbirders, the recruiters' trickery, and the cruelty of the planters.

Slavery was an abomination, Deakin said – and the government was shutting it down.

A supportive press chided the Islanders for the petition, with the *Telegraph* dubbing them 'ill advised' for resisting measures so obviously necessary. The paper invoked the experience of America, where, it explained, 'the negro was emancipated ... but he was left in the country'. That, the *Telegraph* explained, was a disaster not to be replicated.

'Now he lives and multiplies. The presence of about 10,000,000 negroes in America, without civil rights, is a great danger. It might be a greater danger if he had civil rights.'[75]

The purported opposition to slavery slid, once again, into a justification for tyranny, legitimating a rhetoric that became, at times, almost fascistic.

When, for instance, Deakin's government accepted the Royal Commission's recommendations – including the exemption for married men – the *Bulletin* published a call to make miscegenation a crime punishable by hard labour so as to avoid a race war similar to one being fanned by ex-slaves in America. Its correspondent concluded by proposing the boiling in oil of 'nigger-loving legislators [...] who recently voted in favor of non-deportation of those Kanakas married to white men' – a suggestion to which the magazine's editor added his endorsement.[76]

The novelist Christopher Isherwood once described broadcasts of Hitler as conveying a sense of a man dancing up and down on the tips of his toes while he spoke. The shrill, mad voices in the *Bulletin* and elsewhere give the modern reader a similar impression.

In that ideological environment, the deportations continued. By 1908, only 2500 Islanders remained: a few of them because they successfully hid and the others because they'd been exempted. Most, however, were herded on to boats, in a ghastly process that separated lovers, friends and relatives from each other and from the country for which they'd toiled for so long.

In an extra act of bastardry, the government defrayed the expense of a process that was meant to be funded by employers, instead using money from the Pacific Islanders Fund – a trust established to remit wages owed to deceased labourers.

The Queensland *Evening Telegraph* recorded the understandable bitterness of the deportees, voiced once they were beyond the reach of the police on the wharfs and the jetties.

'Goodbye you white —,' they yelled, 'and your — white Australia!"'[77]

*

What might an apology for sugar slavery address?

What was done in in the cane fields was not merely the responsibility of the planters who benefited directly from it. Its centrality to politics in Queensland and, later, to Federation, implicated the men most responsible for Australia's foundation.

To be clear, the big names in colonial politics – Deakin, Griffith, Barton, Watson and others – did not defend slavery in the manner of, say, those Confederate leaders whose statues still mar towns across the American south. On the contrary, most of them railed against the practice, competing with each other and with state politicians in Queensland to make their disdain known. '[T]his government thinks', explained Barton bluntly, 'that the traffic in itself is bad and must be ended.'[78]

Yet, almost without exception, politicians used their hostility to slavery to legitimate a generalised racism, which they then presented as the foundation of a new state. Barton, for instance, introduced the Pacific Islanders Bill as embodying 'the policy, not merely of the government, but of all Australia, for the preservation of the purity of the race.'[79]

'Let us keep before us', urged the Labor MP James Ronald during the debate, 'the noble idea of a white Australia – snow-white Australia if you will. Let it be pure and spotless.'[80]

Instead of facilitating justice, opposition to sugar slavery enabled institutionalised discrimination, a policy its advocates grotesquely draped in the garb of abolition.

The differences between indentured labour in Queensland and chattel slavery in the American south did not prevent Australian parliamentarians from comparing the two. In their discussions of the federation they were building, American slavery provided a constant referent. A past reliance on African labour had left, they said, the United States a piebald nation, subject to the mongrelisation that a white Australia would avoid. Racialised anti-slavery justified the expulsion of Islanders, an ethnic cleansing necessary for Ronald's 'pure and spotless' society. As Deakin explained, White Australia meant 'the prohibition of all alien coloured immigration, and more, it [meant] at the earliest time, by reasonable and just means, the deportation or reduction of the number of aliens now in our midst'.

With the passage of the Pacific Islands Labourers Act, the founders explicitly sought to control not just sugar slavery but also its historical legacy. That was the point. The law meant, they said, that white Australians – unlike their American cousins – could avoid the descendants of those they'd enslaved. The exclusion of the Islanders would excise an awkward history, with the slaves expelled from Australia's border and its memory.

For a time, it seemed like they'd succeeded. The deportations marginalised the Australian Islander communities, with those who remained often forced on to the margins of white society, usually alongside an equally oppressed Indigenous population. Like African Americans under Jim Crow, Islanders faced segregation in schools, shops, theatres, swimming pools, workplaces and just about everywhere else. A raft of laws forbade them from working in the cane fields, with an industry that had relied overwhelmingly on Islanders in 1902 using nearly 90 per cent European labour by 1908. The resulting impoverishment was exacerbated by their exclusion from the welfare system – they could not, for instance, claim the old age pension until after 1942.[81]

Yet, despite the best efforts of white Australia, the Pacific Islanders survived – and they did not cease fighting to reclaim their past.

The ceremony in Bundaberg came as the result of prolonged lobbying from Islander organisations, part of a campaign that is forcing official recognition of blackbirding and sugar slavery. 'The full truth needs to be told', explained Emelda Davis from the South Sea Islanders Association to the *Guardian* back in 2017. 'It's inaccurate not to talk about the trade in people that built this part of Australia and there's a lack of knowledge about what happened. Our people are left out of the narrative.'[82]

That remains central to justice: an acknowledgment of the victims and what was done to them. But the reckoning cannot end there.

In 2019, on the 400th anniversary of enslaved Africans arriving in Virginia, the *New York Times* launched its '1619 Project', a series of essays, events and podcasts intended to place the consequences of slavery at the centre of American history.

'America', explained Jamelle Bouie, one of its contributors, 'holds onto an undemocratic assumption from its founding: that some people deserve more power than others.'

What might we say, then, about the assumptions fostered through the founding of Australia on 1 January 1901?

Unlike in the United States, slavery was always illegal in Australia. From the colony's first days, enslavement was understood as both a crime and a sin. No-one called himself a slaver, not even the overseers.

That hostility to a practice still widely accepted elsewhere helped define the settlement and the nation it became, as the composer Peter Dodds McCormick recognised. 'Australian sons, let us rejoice', his lyric for a future national anthem urged, 'for we are young and free.'

The line hinted at the ideological work that freedom performed, then as it does now. McCormick's invocation of 'youth' defined the nation in opposition to its Indigenous people and their ancient culture, identifying the country with its European invaders. His song implicitly excluded the Aboriginal population from the rights of citizenship, calling on Australian sons to celebrate a liberty they denied to others. By 1878, when McCormick wrote 'Advance Australia Fair', sugar slaves had been toiling in Queensland for more than a decade.

Australian politicians today praise a 'national character' defined by tolerance and laconic egalitarianism. They recall a past exemplifying those traits, a chronicle of good-hearted larrikinism quite distinct from the depravities associated with other countries. Yet the record shows something different.

'We have decided', declared Prime Minister Barton, 'to make a legislative declaration of our racial identity.'

Australia's first leader explicitly understood the ethnic cleansing that followed slavery (along with racialised restrictions on immigration) as definitive, a policy central to the nation's self-perception.

In the process of federation, Queensland's peculiar institution served as the grit around which Australia cohered, a persistent irritant that gave the new nation its shape.

That's a point on which Australians should ponder. The history of sugar slavery highlights a national obsession with racial purity, a corollary of the dispossession that white settlement entailed. The treatment of Pacific Islanders built upon the treatment of Indigenous people, the great weeping sore of antipodean history.

In thinking about that, we might also consider the contemporary use of self-congratulatory humanitarianism and the ways a very Australian rhetoric of fairness continues to legitimate official cruelties. When our politicians explain the indefinite detention of those fleeing persecution as a policy to prevent refugees drowning, their words echo previous invocations of morality in service of bondage, a tradition stretching back to 1788.

The American scholar Richard White once described history as the enemy of memory. 'The two stalk each other', he said, 'across the fields of the past, claiming the same terrain.' That encounter matters, not simply because of the abstract virtue of truth prevailing over delusion but because an acceptance of history might enable a different future to be built.

The story of Queensland sugar highlights a particularly degraded notion of freedom, one in which liberty for some justifies oppression for others. But that's not the only way to understand the concept. The philosopher Jean-Paul Sartre, for instance, once described freedom as 'what we do with what is done to us', a definition that aptly describes the long struggle by Pacific Islanders, and many others, to build something better in Australia.

The past cannot be altered. But it can, perhaps, inspire a different future.

A queer bushranger

I first learned of Captain Moonlite from the historian Graham Willett. In *Secret Histories of Queer Melbourne*, a book Willett co-edited, Moonlite features 'as the bushranger most likely to qualify as queer'.

Andrew George Scott – George to his friends – was born in 1845 (some records say 1843) to a wealthy family in Ireland. He emigrated with them to New Zealand in 1861, where his father served as a clergyman and magistrate. Arriving in Australia six years later, the young Scott, too, became a lay preacher, before turning to crime. In 1879, he held up a cattle station in New South Wales. Two of his associates were killed when the police arrived, as was a constable – and Scott was hanged in Sydney at the start of the following year.

But it was Scott's relationship with James Nesbitt, one of his gang members, that attracted Willett's attention. 'Nesbitt and I were united by <u>every</u> tie which could bind human friendship', wrote Scott (underlining and all) during his final incarceration. 'We were one in <u>hopes</u>, one in <u>heart</u> and <u>soul</u> and this unity lasted until he died in my arms.' Awaiting execution, Scott wore a ring made from

Nesbitt's hair, and pleaded with his gaolers to bury him with the younger man in the graveyard at Gundagai.

'I long to join him where there shall be no more parting', he wrote.

The request wasn't granted, of course, but Willett's account concludes by explaining how, in 1995, 'a group of [Scott's] admirers persuaded the government to surrender Moonlite's body to be re-interred in the Gundagai cemetery'.

That struck me as entirely remarkable. Exhumation requests are seldom granted. Given the context, I'd assumed Moonlite's 'admirers' to be queer agitators. One of them was a woman called Christine Ferguson, who was definitely an activist – but her activism centred on the National Party, of which she'd been federal president until earlier that year.

What was going on? Why had a leader of a staunchly socially conservative party gone to such trouble to re-bury an executed murderer next to the man he loved?

I found the phone number of the cattle and sheep station Ferguson runs near Gundagai. Oh, yes, she said, she'd love to talk about Moonlite.

When Scott landed in Victoria in 1868, he may well have been fleeing a scandal concerning his military service in New Zealand. Regardless, the Bishop of Melbourne offered the well-spoken newcomer a plum post as a lay preacher in the Bacchus Marsh settlement. At the time, worshippers there were still gathering each Sunday in a building known as the Iron Church, one of many pieces of prefabricated infrastructure imported during the Victorian gold rush.

In archival photos, it looks like a corrugated-iron shed, unflatteringly supplemented with a steeple.

Such was the colony at the time: a still-fluid society in which the stone certainties of Anglicanism were replicated with ersatz materials entirely inappropriate to the local climate. The setting suited Scott, who emerges from Paul Terry's authoritative biography *In Search of Captain Moonlite* as charming, self-centred, and almost entirely amoral.

The Reverend WH Cooper of Bacchus Marsh presented the recruit to his flock 'as a young warrior who now has a firm grip on the sword of righteousness'. And, at first, Scott justified Cooper's faith. The archivist at Bacchus Marsh's present-day Holy Trinity Church showed me a weathered ledger where Scott's beautiful copperplate signature repeatedly appeared alongside the number of parishioners he attracted – generally, close to 100 each week.

But in early 1869 a man called Robert Crook faced the Bacchus Marsh Court House accused of breaking a neighbour's fences and stealing his cattle. Scott had ingratiated himself with the Crook clan, one of the grandest families in the parish, and obligingly provided the young squire with an alibi. Unfortunately, it was immediately contradicted by one of his Sunday school students, who swore she'd seen Scott and Crook loitering near the crime scene.

Naturally, the court believed a churchman over a teenage girl. But the acquittal did not quell the Anglican hierarchy's unease about its lay preacher, who was abruptly banished to the isolated mining town of Mount Egerton.

The remains of the Iron Church were sold for scrap in

the 1870s to make way for a stone chapel, but the archivist directed me to a decaying house on the corner of Waddell and Graham streets where pieces had been dumped. In the knee-high grass of the backyard I found rusted slabs of iron – remnants of the church – now crudely fashioned into a garden shed. Wasps were nesting on one panel; there was a strong smell of rot coming from inside.

It felt, perhaps fittingly, like a crime scene.

*

In dusty Mount Egerton, Scott befriended the few respectable people he could find, including a 17-year-old banker, Ludwig Julius Wilhelm Bruun, and the town's schoolteacher, James Simpson.

On 8 May 1869, Bruun told authorities that a masked man had forced him to open the bank's safe and hand over its gold. The intruder left a note: 'I hereby certify that LW Bruun has done everything within his power to withstand this intrusion and the taking of money which was done with firearms.'

It was signed 'Captain Moonlite.'

The whole implausible story was probably a fabrication, a scam cooked up by Scott, Bruun and Simpson. Their friendship, however, had soured, and Bruun said he recognised the gunman as his former friend, tying Scott to the Moonlite moniker. Scott hotly denied the charge and threw the blame back at Bruun and Simpson, who were sent to trial (and later acquitted); Scott departed hurriedly, taking himself to Fiji and then to Sydney, where he began spending the wealth he'd mysteriously acquired.

In late 1870, he was arrested for passing bad cheques. Confined in Maitland Gaol, he feigned madness and was transferred to the more comfortable Parramatta Lunatic Asylum, where the medical registry described him as a 'civil but ... unprincipled fellow without a spark of honour or decency to him.'

Upon his release in 1872, Scott was charged with the Mount Egerton robbery. While on remand, he dug through the brickwork in his cell and scaled the walls of the gaol. He was quickly recaptured. Redmond Barry (the judge who later sent Ned Kelly to death) sentenced Scott to ten years in Melbourne's Pentridge prison for the robbery, adding one for his attempted escape.

As a criminal, Scott was always more urban hustler than highwayman. But he was handsome and athletic, had reportedly seen heavy combat in the so-called Māori Wars, and was a skilled rider and crack shot. The Captain Moonlite sobriquet, with its irresistible hint of midnight romance, took on a life of its own. His attempted escape further popularised the reputation of the bold and dashing Moonlite. 'Brave to the verge of recklessness', a journalist wrote, 'cool, clear-headed and sagacious, and with a certain chivalrous dash, he is the beau ideal of a brigand chief'.

The press thought him a bushranger – and a bushranger he would become.

It was a long drive from Bacchus Marsh to Gundagai. The spring rain had left the wheatfields a deep green and those of canola garishly yellow. The landscape tramped by George

Scott and James Nesbitt and their four young companions, in drought-stricken 1879, must have been very different.

Scott met Nesbitt – a petty criminal from Carlton – in Pentridge, where the younger man was once disciplined for 'taking tea to Prisoner Scott.' As biographer Terry says, it's an affectingly tender infraction.

Upon Scott's release in March 1879, the men shared a rundown house in Fitzroy. But how would they live? Scott tried lecturing on prison reform but, though he drew huge crowds, theatres often refused to book him, particularly with the press linking the notorious Moonlite with every unsolved crime. Police warned potential employers against him; he was dragged in for questioning about the most preposterous allegations.

Scott resolved to walk to New South Wales in search of work and a new start. He took with him a coterie of young men from the slums of inner Melbourne. Like Nesbitt, Thomas Rogan was 21. Frank Johns, Graham Bennett and Augustus Wernicke were in their teens. Exiled from polite society, the 34-year-old Scott basked in the admiration of these youths, to whom, as an urbane intellectual, he seemed like a visitor from another world.

The journey proved an utter disaster, a weary trudge along a hot and inhospitable track. The privations were exacerbated by constant police harassment.

'As long as our money lasted', Scott explained later, 'we bought bread, and when our money was gone we sold our clothes and bought bread, with what we obtained for them. We tried to get work, but could not, and we fasted day after day.'

They'd been living on damper and tea and koala meat – and then no food at all – when they approached Wantabadgery Station, near Gundagai. The property was known for its hospitality but, unbeknown to Scott, it had recently changed hands and the new owner harboured little sympathy for itinerants.

Abruptly ordered to leave, Scott snapped.

'Misery and hunger produced despair', he wrote later, 'and in one wild hour we proved how much the wretched dare'. He retreated into the bush and then returned with gun in hand – transforming, at last, into the persona that had been created for him.

The men with Scott had never previously left the city, let alone ridden a horse. Suddenly, though, they too were bushrangers.

Scott acquired nothing of value at the station. Instead, he demanded food and drink. Leaving his men, he then bailed up the Australian Arms Hotel and detained everyone inside before forcing them back to Wantabadgery: he was more concerned about playing the gentlemanly host than planning an escape.

Inevitably, the police arrived; inevitably, a gunfight ensued.

Scott and his small gang then decamped to a nearby farmhouse, which was soon surrounded by troopers. 'Come and fight!' Scott yelled, even though the rest of his gang could barely hold a rifle. Poor Tom Rogan spent the whole shootout hiding under a bed.

Wernicke was mortally wounded. 'I am only fifteen', he cried. A short time later, Nesbitt was shot in the head.

A journalist of the time described how, as Nesbitt died, Scott 'wept over him like a child, laid his head upon his breast, and kissed him passionately'.

In the exchange of fire, Senior Constable Edward Webb-Bowen took a bullet in the spine – his subsequent death sealed Scott's fate. The surviving 'bushrangers' were tried for murder. With the Kelly Gang still at large, the court set an example, handing down death sentences to all. Johns and Bennett received an eventual commutation on the grounds of their youth; Scott and Rogan (who hadn't even fired a shot) walked to the gallows on 20 January 1880 and were buried at Sydney's Rookwood Cemetery.

I drove to Kimo Estate, about twenty minutes from Gundagai, where a troop of dogs romped up to greet me. A minute later, Christine Ferguson roared into view on a ride-on mower. She was wearing a pullover emblazoned with a Captain Moonlite logo.

'G'day', she said, wiping clean her hands. 'You find the place all right?'

Kimo's house dates back to the 1870s, and is pleasantly weathered. In spite of recent renovations for the bed-and-breakfast trade, Kimo is still a working farm. We sat in a lounge room crowded with books and framed photos, and talked about the exhumation in 1995.

Ferguson confirmed that disinterring a corpse wasn't easy.

'We were actually the first people who weren't relatives or the state to get a body exhumed. The only reason it was possible was because of Moonlite's last letter, in which he wished to be buried in Gundagai next to his friends.'

But why had Ferguson gone to such trouble? 'Here you are putting money and time into re-burying a convicted murderer who seems to have been involved in a same-sex relationship. It does seem, well, a bit strange.'

'Well, it was really only after the whole event that people raised that he might be gay', Ferguson explained. 'For a long time, we said, "Look, we believe they were just good mates, good friends". Just recently Sam Asimus, my partner in crime in the whole affair, told me she'd done some more research and she thinks Scott might have been bisexual. But who knows?'

As well as exhumation approval from the state, the women needed permission from the Anglican Church – eventually, both were granted. Ferguson's team enlisted a local undertaker ('He was terribly excited!'), and they brought an ornate horse-drawn hearse to Gundagai on the back roads. The pallbearers wore period costumes.

'The locals here aren't terribly excited about anything much', Ferguson said, shrugging. 'But when it was all done and it didn't cost them any money, they did get into the swing of things. We had people lining the roads to watch.'

I still wanted to talk about sexuality. I'd learned about Moonlite from Willett and other gay historians, I explained. 'Here was someone saying in those last letters, "I love this man, I want to be buried with him".'

'He actually didn't say that', Ferguson said, then corrected herself. 'Well, he did say it – in a way. But it was a long time ago, and mates were mates. We don't know if he was gay or not. It comes down to your interpretation of "mate" and what "mateship" would have meant at the time.'

Fair enough. But mateship was a lot queerer than most people thought. In his 1958 book *The Australian Legend*, which popularised the concept as a national trait, Russel Ward suggested that, in the masculine environment of the frontier, the typical bushman satisfied his libido with sex workers and Indigenous women, then assuaged his 'spiritual hunger' with 'a sublimated homosexual relationship with a mate, or a number of mates'.

Was that how to think about Scott? In Bacchus Marsh, he seems to have been involved with a woman named Mrs Ames, who felt strongly enough about Scott to visit him regularly before his execution. Yet she barely registers in Scott's death-cell writings, in which he returns again and again to Nesbitt.

'He died in my arms', Scott wrote. 'His death has broken my heart.'

That didn't seem sublimated.

In one of his letters, Scott ended his plea for burial alongside Nesbitt with a quotation:

> Now call me hence by thy side to be:
> The world thou leavest has no place for me.
> Give me my home on thy noble heart,
> Well have we loved – let us both depart.

The lines came from a Felicia Hemans poem entitled 'The Lady of Provence'.

'The original was about the feelings of a woman for

her dead lover', I mentioned to Ferguson. 'So here's Scott including what seems to me clearly a love poem to a man.'

'Well, that was never brought up at the time', she said. 'But, again, we don't have the evidence. Do homosexuals now write poems to each other? It's an odd thing to do, writing poems – not something people do these days.'

Until quite recently, I'd been the editor of *Overland*, a literary journal that regularly publishes poetry. Nevertheless, I took the point. The more I read about sexuality in the 19th century, the more it seemed both strikingly familiar and disconcertingly strange.

During Scott's criminal career, the police in Victoria had been led by Chief Commissioner Frederick Standish. He was a gambler and libertine, who, at one notorious dinner, decorated the room with naked women seated on black chairs to better show off their white bodies. When Prince Alfred, the second son of Queen Victoria, toured Melbourne in 1867, Standish acted as royal pimp, escorting the prince to Sarah Fraser's brothel in Stephen Street.

But, as Willett says in *Secret Histories of Queer Melbourne*, the commissioner was also infatuated with men – in particular with Frank Hare, another policeman chasing the Kellys. 'It was almost pathetic to see ...' wrote one of their contemporaries, 'how restless and uneasy [Standish] became were Hare out of his company. I have seen Standish on the top rail of a fence watching anxiously for Hare's return from a short ride.'

And then there was the story of Edward Feeney, who, eight years before Scott's execution, was put to death at Melbourne Gaol for his part in a bizarre suicide pact.

In March 1872, Feeney had accompanied Charles Marks into Melbourne's Treasury Gardens, where, according to a pre-arranged plan, they attempted to shoot each other. Feeney's gun fired; Marks's didn't. This left Feeney on trial for murder.

Feeney refused to offer any explanation. But the court heard that he and Marks exchanged letters about their passionate love for each other. A bar owner testified that they regularly cuddled in his premises, sometimes laying their heads on each other's laps. In her article about the case, historian Amanda Kaladelfos points out that while the proprietor believed their behaviour unusual, 'he expressed no malice toward Marks and Feeney; nor did he give evidence that he ever asked them to stop showing their affections in his place of business'.

'Men often slept together in the same beds', historian Clive Moore explains in his study of sexuality on the frontier, 'without raising the slightest suspicion that they were involved in what we would call a homosexual affair, were physically affectionate, had romantic crushes, wrote lovingly to each other and fretted when they were apart ... For most of the 19th century there was no clear social, medical or legal concept of homosexuality; homosexual acts were recognised, particularly sodomy, but not a personal disposition or social identity'.

Today, of course, matters are very different.

'Is there a gay community in Gundagai?' I asked Christine Ferguson.

'Hmm. I know one who's come here, used to be with Qantas and he's here ... I've only met him once but I know he's here. A couple of others in town who are probably bachelors but most people say they are [gay]. But that's about it.'

'Do they have a hard time?'

'No, I don't think so. You really wouldn't know. They're not openly living with a bloke or anything. Gundagai is conservative but I don't think it's really bothered by homosexuality.'

'Would the town be open to the tourist potential of Moonlite as a gay icon?'

'No, I don't think Gundagai would be into that', Ferguson replied. 'A lot of the old people want to keep Gundagai how it is and how it has been in the past. They don't see ... they're not very progressive.'

She told me that she and Samantha Asimus had wanted to establish a bushrangers and police museum in the old gaol, when a property there became available. They'd had plans for holograms; they'd spoken to the Justice & Police Museum in Sydney about borrowing exhibits.

'We thought it would be fabulous for the town. But no, no one was interested.'

We talked for a little while about politics in general – Ferguson is close friends with Tony Abbott and struggled to sound enthusiastic about Malcolm Turnbull – and then she showed me through the station.

'I like to have a project', she said. 'I like to keep myself busy.'

And that, it seemed, helped to explain her involvement in the re-burial, a cause she'd taken on almost *because* of its inherent difficulty.

In his cell, Scott had described the headstone he wanted:

> [A] rough unhewn rock would be most fit, one that skilled hands could have made into something better. It will be like those it marks, as kindness and charity could have shaped us to better ends.

The words were now carved into a suitably craggy stone located at the very edge of the North Gundagai Cemetery.

In some ways, the sentiment seemed less apposite for Scott (who, in his early life at least, had scarcely been deprived of opportunities) than for the slum kids who died with him.

Ever since I stumbled upon Edward Feeney and Charles Marks's story, I'd been thinking about the inner-city origins of Moonlite's unhappy gang, and the strange visual connection between the past and present. Before Marks and Feeney went to the Treasury Gardens to kill each other, they'd posed for final portraits in a Bourke Street photographer's studio. The resulting images are utterly compelling. In one picture, they're holding hands – and, with their bushy whiskers and cloth trousers, they look disconcertingly contemporary. You would not blink an eye to see them strolling in Fitzroy or Carlton today.

On the scaffold, Feeney had issued a statement denying he'd been 'improperly intimate' with Marks. The doctors who dissected his body inspected his rectum for signs of sodomy. In that posthumous indignity, we can detect, Amanda Kaladelfos says, the beginning of the modern science of sexuality, which in the decades to come would establish 'homosexuality' as a distinct and all-consuming pathology.

A second photo of Marks and Feeney depicts them with pistols against each other's breast. The photographer had suggested they pose as 'bushrangers', a comment that made me wonder if, by the 1870s, the life of the outlaw gang was seen as representing a kind of male intimacy that the cities were beginning to exclude.

Was Feeney gay? Was Moonlite? In one sense, asking such questions is almost silly, the projection of contemporary categories on to a past where they do not belong. Yet, in another sense, the rediscovery of men who loved other men (as both Feeney and Moonlite clearly did) matters a great deal.

I'd also asked Christine Ferguson whether, in today's Gundagai, men who wrote love poems to other men would be welcome in the local pub.

'Yeah, they probably wouldn't go to the pub', she replied, amused at the thought. 'The pubs in here are pretty blokey.' She didn't drink in them much herself, and nor did many women.

Surely that was the value of the Moonlite story. It revealed the traditional masculinity enforced in public bars, sporting clubs and other bastions of heterosexuality to be neither innate nor eternal.

Scott had designed his own epitaph. He'd wanted it to read 'This stone covers the remains of two friends'. He'd then written Nesbitt's name and his own, with Nesbitt's death listed as the date the pair were 'separated', and his own execution recorded as when they were 'united by death'.

The exact location of Nesbitt's body in this cemetery is no longer known. When Scott's body was re-buried, the tombstone noted that he had been 'laid to final rest near his friends James Nesbitt and Augustus Wernicke who lie in unmarked graves close by'.

The inscription diffused Scott's passion for one man into a more conventional friendship with two.

The morning was starting to warm, but Scott's grave was pleasantly shaded by a beautiful old gum tree. Its slight separation from the rest of the cemetery gave it an unmistakeable prominence – a gesture that the always-vain Scott would have liked.

The threshold of another trembling world

'I am standing on the threshold of another trembling world. May God have mercy on my soul.'

With that diary entry in 1981, IRA prisoner Bobby Sands launched his famous hunger strike in a British prison. But the words might equally have come from Omid Sorousheh, the Iranian asylum seeker near death in Nauru after forty-five days without food.

Has Omid kept a record of his ordeal? We don't know, since Nauru remains largely off limits to journalists. Last week, the *Age*'s Michael Gordon hiked to the perimeter fence, where he witnessed scores of asylum seekers raising their arms as if manacled and chanting, 'We want freedom' and 'Don't kill refugees'. But he didn't manage to speak to Omid – and neither has anyone else from the press.

In other words, though the British government detained Sands in the notorious Maze ultramax prison, the public remained far better informed about his protest than Australians are about Nauru where, according to the Refugee

Action Coalition, Omid is paralysed and no longer taking fluids.

The writer Hannah Arendt once noted how the treatment received by the oppressed in the 1930s had been largely determined by their oppressors.

'Those whom the persecutor had singled out as scum of the earth—Jews, Trotskyites, etc.—actually were received as scum of the earth everywhere', she wrote. '[T]hose whom persecution had called undesirable became the *indesirables* of Europe.'

That's precisely what we see today. Omid fled the dictatorship in Iran. He's no longer suffering at the hands of the Iranians. He's dying in an internment camp run by Australians, as if the clerical regime had outsourced its policies here.

For Arendt, the refugee – that symptomatic figure from both the thirties and today – posed a radical test for nations that called themselves civilised. Yet, she said, the supposedly inalienable 'Rights of Man' seemed to collapse when those who espoused them found themselves confronted by people with no other political claims on which to fall back.

'It seems', wrote Arendt, 'that a man who is nothing but a man has lost the very qualities which make it possible for other people to treat him as a fellow-man.'

Or, as the philosopher Giorgio Agamben put it in his gloss on Arendt, 'When the rights of man are no longer the rights of the citizen, then he is truly *sacred*, in the sense that this term had in archaic Roman law: destined to die.'

The Irish nationalists traced their hunger strikes back to the pre-Christian tradition of *Troscadh* or *Cealachan* where a wronged person would fast outside the home of the transgressor, relying on strong indigenous traditions of hospitality to force justice.

Australians claim to be hospitable, too. But charity only applies to people – and Arendt's argument implies that refugees are no longer understood in that category.

Certainly, in most discussions now, asylum seekers feature not as wronged parties entitled to redress but simply as a problem, a burden unfairly foisted upon innocent Australians. Hence the increasingly punitive response. Refugees have fled unimaginable suffering. But they are not received as victims. They are seen, on the contrary, as oppressors – and it is white Australians who are being persecuted.

The cruel measures imposed duly become their own justification.

Writing about the slaves of the 18th century, the philosopher Montesquieu famously concluded that 'it is impossible for us to assume that these people are men because if we assumed they were men one would begin to believe that we ourselves were not Christians'. Australians might be led by an atheist but the same principle applies. If we allow ourselves to think about the evil places to which the so-called 'refugee debate' has taken us, we might begin doubting our core self-beliefs. Better, then, to all agree: the refugees deserve to languish in camps on Nauru.

There's an old joke from the Irish struggle that captures the sentiment precisely. A British soldier has bayoneted a rebel, and as the Irishman slowly dies, the Brit kicks him again and again. In his last moments, the rebel gasps, 'Why do you hate us so much?'

The soldier looks down and says: 'You bastards – we will never forgive you for what we've done to you.'

Sands died and so did nine of his comrades. But their unimaginable suffering spurred a major political crisis for the British government. In his agony, Sands became, for millions, recognisable not merely as an Irish figure but a universal one, a representative of oppression struggling against injustice.

Omid's not alone standing on the threshold of another world. Australia's reached the edge of something very dark with refugee policy. But it's not too late to turn back. Omid does not have to die; we don't have to go down this path. There's still time. But it is quickly running out.

Today's elites are gods

In a 2013 article for the magazine *Salvage*, the novelist and academic China Miéville warns progressives against adopting the cynical savviness so characteristic of mainstream punditry.

'Becoming a radical critic of capitalism', Miéville writes, 'involves a process of disenchantment, the dying of surprise at the system's depredations; but being one, a long-term witness to those depredations, is to repeatedly discover that we can be shocked by what no longer surprises us.'

That's something to bear in mind when reading the latest Oxfam report into inequality in the global economy, a document that reveals that sixty-two individuals now control more wealth than the bottom half of the planet's population.

Such statistics should come as a shock: not necessarily a surprise, but something more like an electrical jolt, awakening us to the global order we've constructed, now, in its everyday operations, demonstrably more unfair than any previous society in human history.

In the ancient world, the rulers lived in a luxury denied to their subjects, so much so that they often imagined themselves deities. But there were material limits to their delusions. Rich or poor, noble or commoner, everyone on the Nile Delta or the fertile crescent of Mesopotamia suffered alike from disease and natural disaster and the other privations of a low-tech society without medicine or science.

In 1844, Marx discussed the super-wealthy of his own time, explaining how they took on the properties of the money they possessed:

> I am ugly, but I can buy for myself the most beautiful of women. Therefore I am not ugly, for the effect of ugliness – its deterrent power – is nullified by money. I, according to my individual characteristics, am lame, but money furnishes me with 24 feet. Therefore I am not lame. I am bad, dishonest, unscrupulous, stupid; but money is honoured, and hence its possessor. Money is the supreme good, therefore its possessor is good.

To update that list, add everything made possible for the wealthy by the almost magical technology of the 21st century. Once you do, it's clear that today's elite don't need to imagine themselves gods. By every meaningful measure, that's what they are. They have absorbed, via their wealth, all the attributes that religion traditionally attributed to divinities, even as the world's poorest still endure conditions familiar to the labourers who constructed the pyramids.

Back in 1999, Adrian Peacock entitled his book on globalisation *200 Pharaohs: Five Billion Slaves*. More than twenty years later, all that's changed is the ratio.

Some will argue that income equality doesn't matter,

that we should concern ourselves only with absolutes. Between 1990 and 2010, they remind us, the number of people classified as enduring extreme poverty fell by a half. Economic growth in China and India lifts all boats – and, if some vessels have floated rather higher than others, at least they're all rising.

But life in poverty (rather than extreme poverty) still means a deprivation unimaginable to the wealthy. How, then, does one morally justify a distribution of resources that allocates so very little to so many and gives a tiny few more than they can ever consume?

According to Oxfam, the wealth of those richest sixty-two people grew by more than half a trillion dollars since 2010, even as the wealth of the bottom half of the world dropped by 41 per cent. That, mind you, took place in the period after the global financial crisis, during the years of supposed recovery.

In other words, inequality increased massively when the economy was growing, with most of the new wealth created going to the rich rather than those who needed it most. As the report explains, 'in almost all rich countries and in most developing countries, the share of national income going to workers has been falling'. In contrast, 'the owners of capital have seen their capital consistently grow (through interest payments, dividends, or retained profits) faster than the rate the economy has been growing'.

In the key scene in the Orson Welles movie *The Third Man*, Holly Martins (Joseph Cotton) confronts Harry Lime (Welles) while they ride the Vienna ferris wheel. He accuses Lime of selling penicillin on the black market: essentially, risking the lives of the sick to enrich himself. Lime scoffs at Martins' concerns.

'Look down there', he says, pointing at the revellers way down on the ground. 'Tell me. Would you really feel any pity if one of those dots stopped moving forever?'

Lime's question illustrates the implications of the Oxfam figures, extending well beyond economics. What, for example, can democracy possibly mean in a society resting on such disparities between the blessed and the damned?

'All men are created equal', explained the United States Declaration of Independence. At the time, Thomas Jefferson's slaves might have found that assurance rather hard to swallow. Nonetheless, by the mid-20th century, the social equality upon which genuine democracy necessarily rests seemed at least vaguely possible, with the American poor able to imagine themselves (as Steinbeck put it) not as a permanently exploited proletariat but as temporarily embarrassed millionaires.

Today, though, the notion that our god-kings can be in any way constrained or controlled by Joe and Jane Citizen dropping their votes in a ballot box is too ludicrous for serious contemplation. On the contrary, the multibillionaire relates to the pauper as a predator does to its prey, with the vast human flock simply a resource that, in the poet Alexander Pushkin's phrase, can be 'either slaughtered or shorn'.

The billionaire Warren Buffett puts it like this: 'Sure there is class war, and it is my class, the rich, who are making it and we are winning'.

Again, let's emphasise that the Oxfam study describes developments since the world recovered from the global financial crisis. Today, we can all hear the Chinese economy sputtering and misfiring, and the reassurances from politicians sound (to borrow an old gag) rather like the *Titanic*'s captain announcing: 'Nothing to worry about, ladies and gentlemen – we are merely stopping briefly to take on some ice.'

The poor missed out during the boom: what do you suppose is about to happen to them during the coming slump?

In an era such as ours, it's easy for progressives to develop a protective layer of cynicism, an ironic detachment predicated on the conviction that nothing can actually be changed. But we can't afford that now. It's way past time to rediscover some anger.

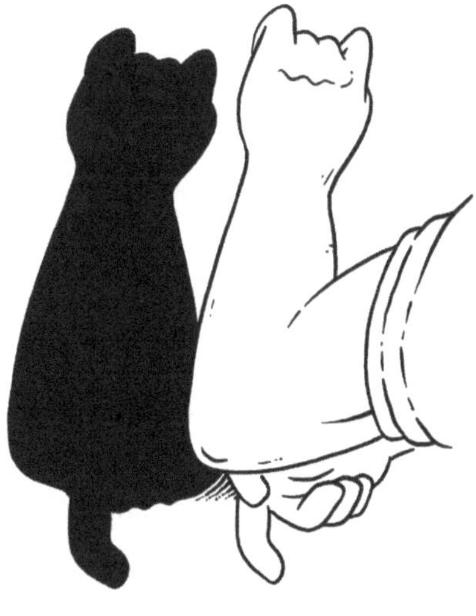

CULTURE IS ORDINARY

Many years ago, I helped organise an Australian tour for the Afghan parliamentarian Malalai Joya.

Joya had campaigned for women's rights under the Taliban. But after the US invasion, she became equally appalled at the Western forces propping up warlords and human rights abusers.

At that time, the press still regularly ran pieces in which so-called progressives enthused about how the West was freeing Muslim women from feudal oppression. Joya's meetings provided a rare opportunity for Australians to hear a feminist for whom the occupation of Afghanistan was not an airy abstraction but a daily reality. In her presentation, she painted a bleak – and, as it transpired – entirely accurate portrait of what the invasion meant, scoffing at liberal claims about American humanitarianism.

The new Western-backed government did not, she said, constitute a liberation from the Taliban so much as a continuation of their oppression, in that it relied upon men who shared the social views of the old regime but differed from them in their willingness to cut deals with the Americans.

I went with Joya to the filming of the ABC's *Q&A* program, at which she'd been invited to speak. As we sat down in the Green Room, my bag fell open and she saw I was reading *The Gadfly*, a melodramatic novel written by the British author Ethel Voynich in the late 19th century.

Her eyes widened in surprise.

'This book changed my life.'

She explained how, in the refugee camps in Pakistan, where her family fled during the civil war, she'd read and re-read the novel, and then watched repeatedly a tape of the old Soviet film adaption.

Perhaps the coincidence wasn't quite as startling as it seemed. *The Gadfly* had circulated widely in both China and the former Soviet Union; its narrative about a revolutionary confronting the Catholic church and the Italian state in the years prior to the 1848 uprising contained obvious parallels for a teenager surrounded by religious authoritarianism.

Nevertheless, the conversation stayed with me afterwards, an illustration of how cultural artefacts can travel through time and place, carrying their message to settings that their authors never could have imagined.

I've written a lot about culture, particularly (though not exclusively) books.

In 2018, the *Sydney Review of Books* commissioned me to write on Behrouz Boochani's *No Friend but the Mountains*, a book that had been widely acclaimed but (in my view) entirely misunderstood. My review essay, in which I tried to bring out the radicalism of Boochani's project, won the Pascal Prize for Arts Criticism at the Walkleys that year.

I first read *What Days Are For* when I interviewed Robert Dessaix on breakfast radio. In the book, Dessaix – one of the most sophisticated and elegant writers in the country – says 'Enid Blyton ... shaped me in a way no other writer or book ever did'. I thought about that a lot, especially after finding, in a junk shop, a huge collection of books by WE Johns, whom I'd loved as a child. Later, I wrote about Dessaix, Blyton and Johns for my *Guardian* column.

The piece on Len Lawson – artist, sociopath and murderer – emerged accidentally, as many articles do, from research into something quite different. I'd been trying to understand why, during the Cold War, both the Left and the Right loathed comic books when I stumbled upon the bizarre and horrible story of the monster behind the nation's most popular comic.

Despite lacking any sense of direction at all, I've always loved maps. The decision by Geosciences Australia to cease printing its topographic surveys thus provided a pretext for an essay about mapmaking past and present, a subject that proved even more fascinating than I expected.

The Irish tell a joke about Bono, the tax-dodging front-man of rock band U2, pausing between songs to harangue the crowd about world poverty.

He begins clapping his hands, slowly and dramatically.

'Every time I clap,' he says, 'a child starves to death in Africa.'

From somewhere in the audience, a voice shoots back, 'Well stop fucking doing it then!'

The gag was already old when, in 2014, U2 signed a deal with Apple that pushed out one of their albums to every iPhone in the world. In response, I wrote a brief piece for the American magazine, the *Baffler*.

In 2015, the *Guardian* asked for an article to mark the centenary of Norman Lindsay's *Magic Pudding*. Lindsay was a racist and an avowed reactionary, whose serious art hasn't dated at all well. But few books make me laugh as much as his comic novels – and, as I tried to show, the Pudding remains one of the great characters of Australian literature.

The final pieces refer to two quite different fads.

The *Pokémon Go* craze didn't last long. Still, you might

remember how, for a few months in 2016, the game brought everyone on to the streets, so that when you walked through the city you encountered people chasing invisible monsters. I couldn't decide whether this was appalling or inspiring, and so I wrote something about it.

The brief fashion for blending literature with pulp horror has also come and gone, but I retain a fondness for my review essay on it, not least because an inspired *Age* subeditor gave it the title 'Fangs for the memories'.

In Australia, right-wing populists often present the arts as signifiers of elitism, an exclusive preoccupation of inner-city know-it-alls. The doughty folk of suburbia, we're told, cleave to political conservatism and traditional values, with no interest in snobby culture.

It's simply not true. The most recent study from the Australia Council found greater participation in the arts than in sport. For instance, nearly three-quarters of the population read for pleasure, with nearly half regularly enjoying novels. People care passionately about books, about music, about films, about games and much else beside.

'Culture is ordinary', argued the great Welsh socialist Raymond Williams. 'An interest in learning or the arts is simple, ordinary and natural.'

That doesn't mean we should ignore how exclusionary artistic institutions can be. The very ordinariness of learning and the arts makes gatekeeping more grotesque, with the same people who hoard life's other pleasures determined to control culture, too.

We should argue for culture; we should argue about culture. These are some of my attempts to do both.

A place of punishment

In his astonishing book *At the Mind's Limits: Contemplations by a survivor on Auschwitz and its realities* (1980), Jean Améry devotes a chapter to intellectuals in the Nazi camp. An essayist and novelist himself, he focuses on how writers made sense of their incarceration. 'Did intellectual background and an intellectual basic disposition help a camp prisoner in the decisive moments?' he asks. 'Did they make survival easier for him?'

The answer, he decides, was no. Those whom he described as 'cultured' found that culture a hindrance. The liberal intellectuals, with their commitment to reason and rationality, could not explain Auschwitz, a place where, as a guard once instructed writer Primo Levi, 'there is no why'. Furthermore, they discovered that imprisonment stripped of its power the literature to which they'd devoted their lives. Améry recalls being marched back from the IG Farben work site on a freezing winter evening and reciting to himself a verse from the poet Friedrich Hölderlin, silently mouthing lines that, prior to his arrest, had moved him profoundly. 'But nothing happened', he explains. 'The poem no longer transcended reality. There it was and all that remained was objective statement: such and such, and the Kapo roars "left", and the soup was watery, and the flags are clanking in the wind.'

One hesitates to invoke Auschwitz in a discussion of Australia's asylum seeker detention regime, a system that, for all its horrors, does not implement genocide. But Behrouz Boochani's *No Friend but the Mountains* – a book about, among other things, the power of writing – invites the comparison, as a text self-consciously positioned within a broader literature of incarceration.

The narrative begins with Boochani leaving Indonesia on a decrepit boat, a voyage that culminates in his arrival on Australian territory (specifically, Christmas Island). There, as the asylum seekers learn of their imminent transfer to Manus Island, they're told to change into new clothing provided by the guards:

> A grim-looking officer gives a set of clothes to anyone who passes through the strip-and-search stage, even though the clothes don't match the size of the person in any way whatsoever. There is no choice. We have to wear whatever they issue ... Yellow polyester T-shirts – they transform our bodies, they utterly degrade us.

The vignette is immediately recognisable as a key generic element of the prison narrative. Compare, for instance, a passage from Alexander Berkman's classic *Prison Memoirs of an Anarchist* (1912). 'Humiliation overcomes me', writes Berkman, 'as my eye falls, for the first time in the full light of day, upon my striped clothes. I am degraded to a beast'. Berkman was imprisoned for attempting to assassinate the industrialist Henry Frick during the great wave of anarchist terrorism in the 1890s. Boochani is incarcerated in a contemporary refugee detention facility. Yet the scene is almost identical.

The French novelist and revolutionist Victor Serge explains in *Men in Prison* (1930) why the first encounter with prison uniform so consistently features in narratives of gaol:

> Man imprisoned differs from man in general even in his outward appearance. Prison marks him from the very first hour ... He feels as if he has been stripped of part of himself, reduced to an impotence inconceivable an hour before. His clothes hang loose, with nothing to fasten them, constantly in the way. His shoes yawn open. He is disheveled from head to foot.

The uniform externalises the transformation of the detainee. In civilian clothes, he's a citizen; in the ill-fitting costume of the gaol, he becomes a prisoner.

This is a crucial aspect of Boochani's project: to understand Manus Island first and foremost as a place of punishment, where 'waiting is a mechanism of torture used in the dungeon of time'. Throughout *No Friend but the Mountains,* he pointedly refers to the facility in which he remains contained, not by its official description as a

'Regional Processing Centre' but rather as 'Manus Prison', a characterisation that universalises his account.

Serge again:

> All men who have experienced prison know that its terrible grasp reaches out far beyond its physical walls. There is a moment when those whose lives it will crush suddenly grasp, with awful clarity, that all reality, all present time, all activity – everything real in their lives – is fading away while before them opens a new road onto which they tread with the trembling step of fear.

Boochani's book chronicles how the road unfurls for detained refugees: specifically, how they're gradually and systematically destroyed. 'I am a piece of meat thrown into an unknown land', he writes, 'a prison of filth and heat.' The overcrowding in a crudely built camp leads to what he calls 'a confrontation of bodies, a confrontation of human flesh.' That flesh then begins to rot in the tropical heat of Papua New Guinea. Again and again, Boochani shows how the camp transforms living people into decaying flesh. The decomposition reaches its logical and grotesque apotheosis with self-butchery as inmates carve away at their own bodies. 'When someone cuts themselves', Boochani explains, 'it elicits a form of respect among the prisoners. However, the criterion pertains to the depth of the slit, the severity of the wound. The more terror inflicted, the greater the credibility. It is unwritten and cryptic – but it is real.'

The prisoners themselves become 'pieces of meat in a

metal pressure cooker'. But the camp also stinks of other bodily odours – in particular, human shit:

> This soul-destroying prison is made with a mix of lime and dirt. Everywhere, fine white sand sticks to one's feet, particularly to the plastic flip-flops. From one of the camps to the other drainpipes protrude from the kitchen and bathrooms. They create a potion of rotten excrement ... the stench of sludge, a multicoloured spread laid out for both microscopic and mammoth mosquitoes which linger regularly around the troposphere above the drains.

The untreated sewage spilling out around the facility produces a 'smell ... so vile that one feels ashamed to be part of the human species'.

The inability of prisoners to attend to basic needs with dignity ensures that they no longer feel part of the civilised order, a point Boochani illustrates by the fate of a detainee known as the 'Prime Minister'. The man – once an engineer and businessman – earns his nickname by his gravitas and character. 'His kindness is unconditional', says Boochani, 'and he is generous. He is a man of virtue'. Acutely conscious of his dignity, the Prime Minister plans his routine so as to obtain some privacy in the camp's squalid toilets. One day, however, the need to defecate overcomes him when the queue is at its longest and so he must rush off to relieve himself in public. In his own eyes – and the eyes of the other prisoners – he's forced, quite literally, to shit all over his own principles and reputation. The attendant humiliation drives him to accept the offer of return to the country he'd sought to escape. 'The prison dictates', Boochani concludes, 'that the prisoner accept, to some degree, that they are wretched and contemptible – this is an aspect of the system designed particularly for them.'

In Auschwitz, Améry writes, survival in the face of systemic dehumanisation necessitates a kind of rat cunning, a set of skills most intellectuals lacked. 'Camp life demanded', he explains, 'above all bodily agility and physical courage that necessarily bordered on brutality. The intelligentsia were only seldom blessed with both, and the moral courage that they often tried to employ in place of the physical was not worth a trifle.' He presents, by way of example, an encounter with a professional pickpocket stealing other inmates' shoelaces, a confrontation that could best be resolved by a physical violence of which intellectuals were mostly incapable:

> Superfluous to say that only very rarely did the lawyer or gymnasium teacher know how to execute an uppercut properly; rather, he was far more often the receiver, and in taking it hardly more able than in giving it.

Working-class prisoners fared better not only because of their physical tenacity but because they could integrate the experience into their existing knowledge of social brutality. Poor people already understood that the powerful mercilessly persecuted the weak and were accustomed to mounting small resistances. For them, 'the camp logic was merely the step-by-step intensification of economic logic, and one opposed this intensification with a useful mixture of resignation and the readiness to defend oneself'.

Literary intellectuals lacked such resources. Typically, they refused at first to believe that something as senseless as Auschwitz might be real. Then, when the materiality of the camp asserted itself, they collapsed into embracing Nazism as inevitable, with 'the power structure of the SS state tower[ing] up before the prisoner monstrously and indomitably, a reality that could not be escaped and therefore finally seemed *reasonable*'.

Like Améry in Auschwitz, Boochani becomes in Manus a number. 'Slowly but surely I must get used to that number', he says. 'From their perspective, we are nothing more than numbers. I will have to forget about my name.' He, too, encounters a system that, to the inmates, appears entirely arbitrary. For instance, the authorities distribute food according to a method devoid of equity or even consistency, allowing the most determined and selfish refugees to eat far better than everyone else. As a result, 'the prisoner who behaves in a more despicable and brutish manner has a more comfortable lifestyle'. Boochani acknowledges his own desire to beat up the queue-jumpers but also recognises that his physical frailty makes violence untenable. Like the intellectuals Améry describes, he's incapable of 'execut[ing] an uppercut properly' and must therefore survive on less food.

Yet where Améry concludes that culture provides no solution, Boochani insists that the key to surviving 'all the suffering inflicted by the prison' lies in the exercise of creativity. How do we explain that? Obviously, part of the answer pertains to real differences between Auschwitz and Manus. The first is a death camp; the second is not. Améry notes that even within Nazi facilities the varying degrees of violence endured by prisoners altered their relationship to art. His friend Nico Rost could take refuge in high culture when incarcerated in Dachau, even to the extent of identifying 'classical literature as a substitute for Red Cross packages'. But Améry insists that Rost's experience only made sense because the Dachau regime was markedly less brutal than the regime in Auschwitz.

In Manus, Boochani describes a man he calls 'Maysam the Whore' who mounts a cultural rebellion that would have been impossible in a Nazi camp. Maysam performs a kind of satirical cabaret, both to annoy the Australian guards (no noun in the book conveys as much contempt as the word 'Australian') and to entertain the inmates. His act, Boochani writes, is a form of resistance, intended to 'spite those people who exiled them to the prison'. With the guards posting notices declaring 'games prohibited', the pretence of happiness allows refugees to preserve their humanity.

> [Maysam the Whore] employs a beautiful form of rebellion that has enormous appeal for the prisoners. … He stands in direct opposition to a system that wants to fatten up lambs for slaughter. With just one word spoken by him, we experience the essence of life.

Maysam's resistance eventually falters and fails, with his dances ultimately unable to counter the brutalisation of the camp. 'As days go by in Manus Prison, even Maysam the Whore becomes more secluded and starts to deteriorate.'

Boochani's strategy for survival is different. It rests precisely on the high literary culture that Améry declares ineffective in Auschwitz. As translator Omid Tofighian explains, the manuscript of *No Friend but the Mountains* emerged from the surreptitious transmission of short passages in Farsi, sent from the camp via WhatsApp and similar platforms. Translated and compiled by Tofighian, the messages make a text that is deliberately and defiantly literary – 'rich with cultural, historical and political frames of reference and allusion.'

In an interview with author Arnold Zable, Boochani describes how literature facilitated precisely the transcendence that Améry sought but couldn't find in poetry. '[W]hen I was writing', he says, 'I was completely free ... those moments were the most exciting ... because I found myself out of the prison as a free man.'

Améry suggests that literature – or, more specifically, German literature – failed in Auschwitz partly because of its complicity with fascism. This is an argument compatible with the verdict famously delivered by George Steiner in *Language and Silence* (1967):

> In a disturbing number of cases [during the Nazi era] the literary imagination gave servile or ecstatic welcome to political bestiality. That bestiality was at times enforced and refined by individuals educated in the culture of traditional humanism. Knowledge of Goethe, a delight

> in the poetry of Rilke, seemed no bar to personal and institutionalised sadism. Literary values and the most utmost of hideous inhumanity could coexist in the same community, in the same individual sensibility ...

The Jewish intellectual of German background was confronted with real evidence that, as Améry put it, culture 'did not belong to him, but to the enemy'. By contrast, in *No Friend but the Mountains*, Boochani draws on a cultural tradition explicitly understood in opposition to his gaolers. The book's very title, an invocation of an old proverb, proclaims the Kurdish necessity for self-reliance, while Tofighian emphasises the text's relationship to classical and contemporary traditions from Iran and (in particular) Kurdistan:

> Boochani's book is a contribution to the Kurdish literary tradition and Kurdish resistance. Interpretations need to be situated within the styles and structures that have characterised Kurdish creativity for centuries, collective memories of historical injustice and Kurdish political history, and their relational concepts of being and becoming that are connected to the land.

In *At the Mind's Limits*, Améry distinguishes the literary intelligentsia in Auschwitz from the political activists or religious believers who, he says, coped much better with their incarceration:

> One way or the other, in the decisive moments their political or religious belief was an inestimable help to them, while we skeptical and humanistic intellectuals took recourse, in vain, to our literary, philosophical, and artistic household gods.

For Boochani, however, it's literature that, quite concretely, enables solidarity.

*

From the first adoption of the mandatory detention policy in 1994, people imprisoned by Australia have fought back. The story of the camps is a tale of suffering; it's also a tale of demonstrations, hunger strikes, breakouts, petitions, legal challenges and other manifestations of defiance.

The struggle within Australia to change refugee policy has been determined. A wide range of groups have deployed a huge array of strategies in opposition to mandatory detention. Activist Richard Bailey describes the pro-refugee campaign as 'the most sustained and powerful social movement Australia has seen in 20 years.' The campaign has had some successes. Contrary to what's often assumed, the majority of Australians do not see punitive border policies as a priority. Indeed, in 2007, the widespread resistance to Howard's refugee policy led to Kevin Rudd campaigning on a platform that included opposition to 'temporary protection visas', the closure of Nauru and Manus, and the release of 90 per cent of those in mainland detention centres. Yet the terms of the debate have not fundamentally changed. Once in power, Labor responded to refugee flows from Sri Lanka,

Afghanistan and elsewhere with an intensification of 'border protection' rhetoric, culminating in the so-called 'Pacific Solution' announced in the dying days of the second Rudd administration. Since then, the commitment of successive governments to Nauru and Manus has shown the inability of activists to mobilise a mass constituency for change.

Instead, pro-refugee sentiment within Australia has tended to find institutional expression in particular pockets of liberal sentiment – one of which has been the infrastructure of Australian literature. That's the context for Boochani's book, a text that emerges from a scaffolding of literary activism that it itself helped facilitate. In his interview with Zable, Boochani explains:

> When I was first exiled to Manus ... I did not know anyone in Australia. I smuggled a phone in to work on as a writer and took a few months to find some contacts outside of Manus. I became friends with Janet Galbraith and then later she introduced me to you. Now my network of people who I am working with is getting bigger.

That network now includes Kirrily Jordan at the Australian National University, the Iranian intellectuals Najmedeen Weysi, Farhad Boochani and Toomas Askari; the translators Moones Mansoubi and Sajad Kabgani; and others. Before Boochani secured a contract with Picador, sections of what would become *No Friend but the Mountains* appeared in *Mascara Literary Review* and *Island* magazine. He thus credits literature with saving his life:

> Previously, at any time I expected a guard would attack my room. That's one of the reasons why I did not publish anything under my real name for more than two years. I did not feel safe and for a while I even thought that the system might kill me. At that time, when I was unknown, the system could have killed me in the way that it killed Reza Barati ... Being known, perhaps, and my work being recognised and supported by organisations and other thinkers and artists perhaps gives me an element of protection.

Yet if Boochani's relationship with an external literary network makes his book possible, it also presents certain difficulties with its reception. Politically, prison literature typically relies on either of two rhetorical claims. The first stresses the difference between life inside and life outside, to urge reform (in the liberal version) or to reveal the depravity of the underworld (the conservative version). The second proceeds in precisely the opposite direction. It uses the experience of prison to draw parallels between incarceration and freedom, with the inmate's suffering presented as embodying, in concentrated form, a more universal oppression. For instance, in his introduction to *Men in Prison,* Marxist scholar Richard Greeman describes Victor Serge's work not so much as a condemnation of penal conditions but as an analysis of 'a world organised for the purpose of repression and finding its ultimate expression (and the source of its own negation) in the brutality of prison.'

The diffusion of a liberal pro-refugee sentiment throughout the Australian literary community predisposes booksellers, reviewers, festival organisers and readers to appreciate a book from Manus. But the liberalism of the intelligentsia also encourages a reading of *No Friend but the Mountains* as making the first kind of rhetorical claim, even though it's quite clearly making the second.

Take, for instance, Richard Flanagan's introduction: 'Reading this book is difficult for any Australian', he writes. 'We pride ourselves on decency, kindness, generosity and a fair go. None of these qualities are evident in Boochani's account of hunger, squalor, beatings, suicide and murder.' On that presentation, Manus represents an anomaly, a crime that demands a reckoning before similar injustices are 'repeated on a larger, grander, and infinitely more tragic scale in Australia.' That's a legitimate and respectable argument – but it's not the one made by Boochani.

Throughout *No Friend but the Mountains*, Boochani employs the concept of 'kyriarchy', a term taken from feminist theology to refer to a complex intersection of oppressions. The Kyriarchical System in Manus, he argues, pits the inmates against each other, ensuring their isolation and loneliness 'until the prison's Kyriarchal Logic triumphs with their collapse and demise.'

But at several points Boochani also implies that the logic extends beyond the camp, with Manus merely one aspect of a 'border-industrial complex' that functions to atomise and control subaltern classes across the globe. In that sense, for Boochani, the Kyriarchical System already applies within Australia itself, where the existence of facilities like Manus fosters an anti-refugee sentiment that pits ordinary citizens against each other. Because those within Manus encounter border-policing through its most extreme manifestation, they are in a privileged position to understand the system as a whole.

Flanagan concludes his foreword to *No Friend but the Mountains* by hailing Boochani as a 'great Australian writer'. But the book's 'introductory reflections' by Omid Tofighian (which, somewhat confusingly, appear at the end) implicitly problematise that claim, by inviting the reader to consider two islands, which it identifies as 'polar opposites':

> One island kills vision, creativity and knowledge – it imprisons thought. The other island fosters vision, creativity and knowledge – it is a land where the mind is free. The first island is the settler-colonial state called Australia, and the prisoners are the settlers. The second island contains Manus Prison, and knowledge resides there with the incarcerated refugees.

In that passage, rather than being 'a great Australian writer', Boochani is presented as possessing distinctive insights precisely because he's not Australian and thus not part of a settler-colonial society in which the border-industrial complex is normalised. In this way, the form of his book fundamentally challenges the framework in which the so-called refugee debate plays out in Australia.

*

Prison literature generally doesn't dwell on the conventional judicial assessments. Instead of assessing the guilt or innocence of people behind bars, the genre focuses on the opposition between those imprisoned (whatever their crime) and those guarding them. In *No Friend but the Mountains* Boochani does not ask why inmates ended up on Manus: rather, he takes for granted their shared interest in freedom.

As journalist Sarah Lazare has recently argued, the distinction between refugees and migrants, so central to Australian discussions, was:

> ideological from the outset, formally emerging in the early 1950s as an anti-communist tool wielded by U.S. and Western European governments. Under U.S. law, the concept of a 'refugee' first emerged to describe individuals seeking sanctuary in non-communist countries. On the international level, the United States played a key role in developing norms that emphasise the liberties of political dissidents, while denying the right to live free from poverty.

From the perspective of a displaced person, the distinction between (good) refugees and (bad) economic migrants has never made much sense. If you're starving, you're in just as much danger as if you're menaced by armed men. Should we classify the Irish who fled to Australia during the Great Famine in the 19th century as refugees or migrants? More importantly, what about the millions who, scientists tell us, will be soon displaced by climate change? How will the current framework handle them?

Such examples illustrate the growing incompatibility between a globalised economy and the borders dividing nation-states, an incompatibility that, in the long term, makes internationalism, whether we like it or not, a precondition for successful social movements. Of course, we're a long way from that now, with the refugee struggle very much on the defensive. Yet there's definitely a sense in which *No Friend but the Mountains* can be read as a book for the future – an effort to create the readership through whom it will eventually become more intelligible.

What days are for

After he suffered a heart attack in Darlinghurst, doctors thought Robert Dessaix would die. Instead, he emerged from hospital with a book, *What Days Are For*, a bittersweet rumination about how one assesses a life as it draws to a close.

Always a writerly writer, Dessaix contemplates his mortality via his wide and eclectic reading: the great religious traditions (which he mostly assesses aesthetically), Gogol, Larkin, Turgenev and Dr Johnson. And then comes this:

'Enid Blyton ... shaped me in a way no other writer or book ever did.'

Sorry? Blyton? *That* Enid Blyton? The Famous Five? The Magic Faraway Tree? Noddy?

Enid Mary Blyton sold perhaps 600 million copies of her stories for children, mostly in the days before blockbuster movie tie-ins. Plenty of people have read her. But few would announce, as Dessaix does, that *that* 'Enid Blyton ... moulded my day-to-day imagination in a more profound way than either Shakespeare or Gogol.'

As it happened, Dessaix's reflection on Blyton resonated with me because, just before reading *What Days Are For*, I'd been browsing a junk shop and seen a job lot of books by Captain WE Johns, whose Biggles series I'd devoured as a child.

An almost exact contemporary of Blyton, Johns has suffered much the same fate. Like Blyton, he was remarkably prolific, pumping out some 160 books; like her, he sold by the trailer-load. Yet despite that popularity, in recent years he's become reduced – perhaps even more than Blyton – to little more than a punchline, with Biggles remembered merely as an aggregation of preposterous verbal tics ('By Jove, Bertie!').

Dessaix acknowledges the obvious black marks against the Famous Five: the repetition, the clunky writing, the undertones of racial and class prejudice. But he continues:

> I forgive them their peccadilloes. I refuse to watch the cruel spoofs on their adventures, too – what are they called? *Five Go Mad in Dorset, Five Go Mad on Mescalin* and so on. The Famous Five were my friends.

I think I bought the (surprisingly expensive) Johns titles for the same reason. When I saw the books in the shop, the lurid dust jackets were instantly familiar. I recalled how much time I'd spent with Biggles as a kid; I wanted to meet him again.

Suffice to say that some acquaintances are best not renewed. Johns – how to say this kindly? – is not a great writer.

He can't do dialogue (and let's move quickly past Biggles's tendency to the terse ejaculation). Nor can he do character. The gaggle of chums who support Biggles through his various exploits are allocated extravagant marks of differentiation – Bertie's a toff; Ginger's a naive kid and so on – but these ostentatious distinctions only accentuate their essential interchangeability. The Biggles mysteries are never particularly mysterious; the later books, in particular, manifest all the racism you'd expect from an Empire loyalist writing in the sour era of British decline.

Moreover, reading as an adult, I realised that as a kid I'd entirely missed the most impressive aspects of the books: the genuinely frightening accounts of Great War aerial combat. Johns himself had been a fighter pilot in an era in which the average life expectancy of a new aviator was a matter of weeks. The recruits were usually in their teens. Many had never driven a car before and were in the air with only the briefest training; often they died without even seeing the plane that shot them down.

In the early stories, we're told of Biggles's high-strung nervous laugh: he doesn't, he says, expect to live long. At one point, his commanding officer notes Biggles has begun drinking heavily and comments that he'll probably be killed soon.

Of course, as a kid, I didn't register that Biggles had been traumatised. No, what I liked was the adventures: precisely the aspects of the books that now seem unreadably formulaic.

In his study *Blyton and the Mystery of Children's Literature*, David Rudd identifies a similar phenomenon in respect of Blyton. It is, he says, common for children to lose themselves in Blyton's books – and then just as suddenly abandon them. If they re-read the stories later, the experience is not only disappointing but positively mystifying.

Of his own return to the Famous Five books he'd once loved, Rudd writes:

> I found the magic lacking, while the simple vocabulary and the old-fashioned and often embarrassing attitudes obtruded woefully ... We adults are left with empty words, whereas our children, like millions of others, are transported.

Rudd makes a simple but persuasive argument – namely, that as children, we read in a quite different way to adults.

Blyton's power comes from her ability to create a world foreign to our own, a place in which different rules apply. The anachronisms that jump out at adults – especially Blyton's peculiar and much parodied vocabulary ('lashings of ginger beer') – help create that estrangement, inducting readers into a realm in which they can safely explore identities and experiences that would otherwise be threatening. The condemnations of Blyton for not providing a realistic representation of English life entirely miss the point.

'Those that read and enjoy the fantasy', says Rudd, '... are doing so in a way that is, by definition, not realistic: the enjoyment depends on readers engaging in the play of the text, thus making it their own.'

Johns's stories operate in the same way. Like most protagonists in books for children, Biggles and his pals are neither quite adults nor quite children. They're boy-men, who adventure like grown-ups while lacking all the usual signifiers (homes, families, interior lives, etc.) of adulthood. Biggles books often come with a glossary of terms, a list of aviation lingo that the reader must learn, much like a traveller preparing to venture into strange lands.

No child reads Biggles as realism: on the contrary, the dated language, the peculiar settings and attitude are accepted as a necessary estrangement, like the magic in Harry Potter.

'Much children's reading ...' argues Rudd, 'falls outside the way that many adults conceive it; neither slavish identification, passive consumption nor ideological servitude. Basically, children are out to maximise their pleasure, by personalising it, revisiting favourite moments'.

That's precisely what Dessaix says, too. He came, he says, to the Famous Five at the right age; he seems never to have gone back. What did he learn from them?

> [I]t was more a question of the subtext: the idea of loyalty to your close friends no matter what, the sharing of secrets with them (an important part of growing up) and also the unusual gendering (although I wouldn't have known as a child what to call it): I was always rather taken with Julian, such a willowy yet manly youth, fair-haired and tall (like Peter, who is still quite willowy), good natured and firm (as Peter is), with marvelously determined eyes and a strong chin ... and his cousin George such a bossy girl, the real boy of the group ('a son to be proud of', somebody says of her).

He notes their neighbour on Kirrin Island, 'the sulky loner Martin, who has no parents, is artistic and apt to sob, just like me, really, which is, we're told, a feeble thing for a man to do. Men, as we know, are meant to enjoy doing things, not appreciating things of beauty for their own sake. [...] Martin's a boy, but isn't like that at all. Martin made quite an impression on me'.

That's scarcely the canonical reading of Blyton, generally upheld (by supporters and detractors alike) as the zenith of a twee Englishness. But it neatly illustrates Rudd's point about the freedom children can find in their reading.

None of this concedes anything to the tedious Little Englanders (or their even more ghastly antipodean equivalents) who hail Blyton's gollywogs as emblematic of Britain's vanished greatness. Of course teachers and parents and librarians should use passages about 'gypsies' for discussions about prejudice and bigotry. Of course they should! What's the point of a book if you don't talk about it?

Nor should we fret particularly about editions rewritten to remove the more offensive passages. Rudd notes that Blyton herself, a writer who banged out 10 000 words daily, regularly recycled her stories, reshaping them to suit changing mores. Johns did the same – Sopwith Camels became Spitfires, while later versions of the Great War stories replaced the whisky with which Biggles and his friends sedated themselves with more wholesome lemonade.

Yet Dessaix's example might serve to assuage the perennial anxiety about what kids read or watch or (increasingly) play. He attributes his love of travel to 'The Famous Five, the first explorers I ever knew'.

Blyton's Kirrin Island is, he says, the prototype of the places and tongues he has subsequently investigated, both in life and in fiction. 'In the end, what we're all doing, we inventors of lands and languages, is refusing to accept the world as we've found it. We are utopians.'

The Famous Five as a gateway to Utopia? Why not? People have got there from stranger places.

Len Lawson: Australia's most infamous comic artist

> I have received quite a number of letters asking if *Action Comic* has been banned. Let me say definitely that *Action Comic*, which features the Lone Avenger, is acceptable to the censorship authorities and I do not anticipate any trouble whatever with this magazine.

That was Len Lawson, perhaps the most successful comic book artist in Australia at the time, addressing the 'Junior Lone Avengers' of his fan club in an undated editorial (almost certainly from 1953). With a furore raging over the propensity of violent comics to corrupt children, Lawson reassured readers that his work 'always featured stories of the Crime-does-not-pay kind.' Yet, within a year, *Action Comic* (sometimes *Action Comics*, also the title of the American series that featured Superman) had indeed been censored, less because of its contents than as a response to Lawson's own extraordinary depravity.

I first came across the Len Lawson story when researching the communist role in the great comic book panic of the 1950s. Today, with superheroes so dominant in popular culture, those who remember the campaign against comics in the years after the war often attribute the hostility to McCarthyist paranoia. But while the 1954 United States Senate's Subcommittee to Investigate Juvenile Delinquency did, in some ways, resemble the more famous red-baiting House Committee on Un-American Activities, the impetus for the anti-comic hysteria came as much from the Left as the Right.

Crusaders drew, in particular, on the work of psychiatrist Dr Fredric Wertham, whose book *Seduction of the Innocent* presented a purportedly scholarly account of the effects of comic books on juvenile readers. His discussion of the 'subtle atmosphere of homoerotism which pervades the adventures of the mature "Batman" and his young friend "Robin"' seems to modern readers both ridiculous and bigoted. Certainly, recent critics have exposed Wertham's research as relying on carefully curated 'evidence'. Yet while he shared the widespread homophobia of his day (Robin, we're told, 'often stands with his legs spread, the genital region discreetly evident'), he also voiced arguments of a more contemporary stripe.

Wertham worried about the violent misogyny of horror, true crime and war comics, and noted the propensity of artists to depict heroes as Aryans and villains as 'natives ... Negroes, Jews, Indians, Italians, Slavs, Chinese and Japanese [and] immigrants of every description'.

These themes were echoed in Australia too, but there was

a distinctive local element, reflecting the anxieties produced by the changing relationship with the United States.

In 1941, John Curtin had re-oriented foreign policy away from the declining British empire and towards the rising American one. With the Second World War over, Australians found themselves face to face with their new ally's unfamiliar mass culture, a culture epitomised by American comics.

'[M]ost of the comics bear not the slightest resemblance to those we knew in our childhood', complained the principal of Marsden Girls College, Eleanor Appel, in 1952. '[From] America, under the name of comics have come the most lurid strips which glorify violence, brutality, immodesty and disrespect.'

With the war in Korea raging, the comics often depicted American soldiers shooting down reds. The Communist Party of Australia's Rex Chiplin thus identified them with Robert Menzies's militarism. Comics, he said, were 'teach[ing] our youth to be brutal, to glorify in killing'.

Such arguments also reverberated throughout the trade unions. In Queensland, the Trades and Labour Council voted in 1952 to oppose 'the corruption of Australian children's and adolescent minds by mass distribution of murder, crime, horror and sex publications'. The following year, the council placed the issue on the Australian Council of Trade Unions agenda above 'full employment and national health insurance' and just below 'the nationalization of key industries'. The unions' concern was not merely ideological. In 1940, bans on importation of printed matter had spurred a local publishing boom. Peace had ended that, with American comics blamed for locals losing their jobs.

But, if other artists were struggling, Leonard Keith Lawson was not.

Lawson's family came from the New South Wales Riverina region, where his father once boxed as 'Wagga's Wonder Walloper'. They moved to Manly in the 1940s and Len, a skilled schoolboy artist, won a competition to publish with the legendary artist Syd Miller (best known for his 'Chesty Bond' character) when he was only 15. By 1946, he was writing and drawing all the material for *Action Comic*.

Lawson's talent lay in the skilful imitation of American adventure stories, offering readers the science-fiction explorer Spencer Steele, the racer Johnnie Star, the detective Michael Justus, and Diana, the 'Queen of the Apes'. But his biggest success came with the cowboy hero Paul Nicholls – better known as The Lone Avenger.

The title featured a masked lawman fighting outlaws and 'Indians' in an Old West town called Redrock. Though unabashedly modelled on Fran Striker's Lone Ranger, it became hugely popular, so much so that, by 1949, *Action Comic* was regularly publishing full-length Lone Avenger specials.

Lawson married when he was just 18. By the early 1950s, he had three young children and was earning a substantial salary from his work.

The novelist Robert Drewe was one of thousands of members of the Junior Lone Avenger Club, an organisation with branches in New Zealand and Fiji as well as Australia. He recalls winning a Lone Avenger gun belt and holster in the monthly 'find the bullet' competition, in which readers were invited to guess at exactly where their hero was firing. The prize came with an injunction to obey the Lone Avenger's Code, a 'strict and all-encompassing' doctrine that included pledges to worship God, venerate the Queen, be kind to animals, study hard and follow the law.

In 1953, a Catholic priest called Father Cornell read several hundred comics so as to advise parents on which were 'risky' and which were 'poison'. He duly classified Lone Avenger as 'safe' – a category that also included Donald Duck, Captain Marvel and Kokey Koala.

But if the Avenger was safe, his creator was not.

In May 1954, Lawson hired five female models (two of whom were only 15), telling them he was producing a calendar. He drove them into the bush in Terrey Hills, in northern Sydney, produced a rifle and explained he was suffering from cancer and wanted to die. He tied up the women, raped two, attempted to rape a third, and sexually assaulted the others. He then took them back to Sydney, paid them and let them go.

His arrest and subsequent trial transfixed the nation. 'No court case perhaps in Sydney's history', explained the local tabloid *Truth*, 'and certainly none since the war, has aroused such great public interest'.

Lawson's legal team used all the squalid methods common in rape cases at the time, including forcing the teenage victims to disclose their previous sexual histories for a defence that implied they invited the attack. 'You are entitled to have regard', his lawyer told the jury, 'for the fact that, gun or no gun, one would expect more than a mere token resistance from women'.

Nevertheless, Lawson was found guilty, and the judge

sentenced him to hang. In the wake of that sentence, unprecedented since the 19th century for a crime other than murder, *Truth* noted that Lawson's work 'frequently depicted bosomy heroines', and helpfully republished an image of one of them. The Queensland Literature Board of Review, formed in response to the Trades and Labour Council's anti-comic agitation, promptly banned *The Lone Avenger*, while authorities refused to allow Lawson to draw comics in prison.

He did, however, keep making art.

With his death sentence commuted to a 14-year term, Lawson embraced Catholicism and began painting religious iconography and portraits of Church officials. In his essay collection *Fortune*, Drewe suggests that Lawson's new devotion impressed the New South Wales justice minister, Jack Mannix, who released him after a mere seven years' incarceration.

Outside gaol, Lawson pledged to remain dedicated to art and to God, offering a portrait he'd painted of Melbourne's Archbishop Daniel Mannix (unrelated to the New South Wales minister) to the Catholic Church.

That presentation never took place. Within three months, Lawson had raped and murdered a young woman he'd asked to pose for him, writing 'God forgive me' on her torso in eyeliner. After the killing, he drove to the Sydney Church of England Girls' Grammar School with a rifle and took the students and staff hostage. He demanded to speak to a nun who'd visited him in prison, as well as to the reigning Miss Australia, Tricia Reschke, and the Olympic athlete Marlene Mathews. As the police arrived, some of the teachers rushed Lawson, who began shooting wildly. One of his bullets killed a 15-year-old student called Wendy Luscombe. Lawson went back to gaol, adjudged never to be released.

Again he turned to art. Again he seemed a model prisoner. In 1972, as president of the inmates' association, he helped organise a charity concert in Parramatta Gaol's chapel, which had been decorated with his paintings. After the performances, Lawson was invited to deliver a speech of thanks. He rose to the podium – and then grabbed one of the dancers, a woman called Sharon Hamilton, and put a knife to her throat.

'Everybody leave but her', he said.

Though Lawson was quickly overpowered by other prisoners, the assault traumatised Hamilton, who feared he'd find her again. She received extensive psychiatric treatment but later took her own life.

Lawson remained in gaol. He died in 2003, by then one of New South Wales's longest serving inmates.

*

It would be wrong to attribute the collapse of the local comics industry solely to the sociopathy of Len Lawson. Comic books were, after all, already under threat before his arrest.

In 1953, creators in both Australia and America were adopting a voluntary code of conduct. In his definitive history of Australian comics, John Ryan describes how censors began painting out the guns and knives from comics, so that frames depicted heroes reeling back ludicrously from the empty fists of villains. Then, in 1959, the removal of import restrictions wiped out many of the local publishers who were already struggling with increasing costs and competition from television.

Irrespective of Len Lawson, the industry in the 1960s would have looked very different from what had come before. Nevertheless, his conviction certainly helped the anti-comic cause – an extraordinary confirmation, some thought, of the real-world consequences of pernicious literature. It's difficult to look at Lawson's art today without thinking about his crimes.

The State Library of New South Wales's Mitchell Library holds a large collection of *Action Comic*, which displays Lawson's talent for striking, dynamic images. On the cover of No. 31, the Lone Avenger crash-tackles a pistol-wielding desperado; on No. 8, he glares out from the eyeholes of his red and black hood as Comanche warriors tie him to a pole.

Flicking through the yellowing paper on the reading room table, I wondered about the significance of the Lone Avenger's disguise, a strange outfit that occasionally leaves him looking less like a cowboy than a Klansman or a bank robber. I speculated that the character represented Lawson's own cloaked desires, but recalled how ubiquitous masked heroes were in the comics of the time.

The Lone Avenger's adventures aren't, in fact, particularly violent and rarely involve women. The Junior Lone Avengers page features relentless pictures of well-dressed children posing with their dogs or ponies, and a substantial section for 'Pen Friends Wanted' (with, for instance, Ian W Berry of Minnivale, Western Australia, describing himself to prospective pals as 'a boy ... interested in sport, comics and agriculture').

Perhaps to the modern reader the most disturbing elements of *Action Comic* express not Lawson's own pathologies but the sensibilities of the era, as with the casually racist depictions of Native Americans.

Lawson's Mannix painting (dated 'Goulburn, July 1958') now belongs to a John Stevens, who bought it at auction without knowing its history. It's tempting to think Lawson has deliberately portrayed the archbishop as a severe, almost foreboding, figure, but, again, that probably reflects a contemporary perception of Catholic authority more than anything else.

On YouTube, you can find an interview Len Lawson did with *60 Minutes* a few years before his death. In the footage, he's frail but articulate. Interestingly, he no longer claims to be religious, and he certainly doesn't blame comics for his crimes.

'Whatever happened to me mentally, I'm damned if I know', he says. 'I had a normal upbringing, a great family life. But something happened up here and I went haywire.'

It's not much of an explanation.

The perfect combination of art and science

'Some for one purpose and some for another liketh, loveth, getteth, and useth Mappes, Chartes, & Geographicall Globes.'

So explained John Dee, the occult philosopher of the Tudor era.

The mystical Dr Dee would, perhaps, have understood the passion stirred by Geosciences Australia's recent decision to stop producing or selling paper versions of its topographic maps, citing dwindling demand.

In the 21st century, digital files might be more practical, particularly for a cash-strapped federal government agency. But not everyone loveth and getteth their maps for purely practical reasons.

Just ask Brendan Whyte. He's a curator at the National Library of Australia (NLA), responsible for acquiring a copy of every map published in Australia, as well as managing a collection of perhaps a million or so charts and about the same number of aerial photographs.

A geographer by training, he knows that some people don't appreciate electronic cartography.

'One of the problems with the development of GIS [geographic information systems] and everyone making their own maps is that people just dump their data without thinking about the aesthetics or what the map is trying to tell a reader.'

A map, he says, needs beauty so that users want to look at it and absorb what it contains. But that's less about particular platforms, whether digital or otherwise, than the cartographer's skill.

Whyte gives, as an example of what can be done with data, Charles Joseph Minard's famous map of Napoleon's Russian campaign, on which a band represents both the progress and the extent of the Grande Armée juxtaposed against temperatures in 1812 and 1813, so that the viewer necessarily imagines the privations of a disintegrating army throughout a terrible Russian winter.

Whyte also admires the artistry of the Marshall Island stick charts from the NLA's own collection, believed to be from the early 1970s.

'They're thin pieces of coconut wood put together in a sort of lattice like a cat's cradle and wherever there was an atoll they'd lash on [a] little cowrie shell to represent that island. The bits of coconut wood represent the routes, the wave patterns, the winds, the currents. So they're not a geographical representation like a modern map, but more how a navigator might get from one island to another via the sea route in a canoe with a big sail.'

His favourite catalogued item might also be one of the

smallest, an atlas from Queen Mary's dollhouse. 'A lot of publishing companies and authors produced real books for her dollhouse. The famous map shop and publishers Stanfords made her the *Atlas of the British Empire*, reducing it to about two inches high.'

At the State Library of Victoria (SLV), the librarian Sarah Ryan also nominates an atlas – albeit a rather bigger one – as a particularly treasured item. 'It's known as the first modern day atlas, even though it was produced in 1572: Ortelius's *Mirror of the World*. The printing of that volume is beautiful and the maps are very colourful, and you've got lots of iconography like sea monsters and ships and compass roses.'

She agrees that, while digital maps can be more convenient, a lot of people still prefer paper, particularly for recreational uses. Ultimately, though, it's relationships that matter.

'What pulls you to maps', she says, 'is that connection with people and place and culture'. By way of example, she talks of looking at the SLV's Atlas of Paris from 1739, just after her own first trip to the city. 'I'd visited all those places, so that has a strong connection to me.'

Maps, of course, also document territorial claims. The catalogue describes the SLV's rarest map as coming 'from the survey of Mr Wedge and others'. The attribution sounds innocuous until you identify the surveyor as the John Wedge who accompanied John Batman on his expedition across Bass Strait. The yellowing paper thus signals the plans for a township in Port Phillip – and the beginning of Indigenous dispossession.

Yet, if maps represent power, they can also show change. It's a point made by Kay Dancey, the CartoGIS Services

Manager at the College of Asia and the Pacific at the Australian National University (ANU). A cartographer by training, Dancey provides data visualisation for ANU researchers, as well as managing a collection of hardcopy and digital maps. Her holdings feature items dating back to the 17th century, and include 18th-century works by the French hydrographer and philosopher Jacques-Nicolas Bellin.

'The sheer craft of how they produced these maps ... They're invariably copper engravings, and there's such skill required in this process. And then there's the beauty: the fabulous colours and cartouches that they employ.'

But, when asked to describe a favoured map, she nominates something very different. 'There's a lovely map here', she says, 'a wall map of Africa from the 1950s. It's one of my favourites because it has hand made corrections to the country name Zaire or the Democratic Republic of the Congo, as it is now. I particularly love that because it has been in this mapping unit for sixty years and these hand annotations have been made by cartographers over that time. So it's a gorgeous link back to the people who have worked as cartographers at the ANU, a reminder of changing sovereignties and what a map is: a snapshot of time and an abstraction of place.'

In that spirit, she notes the real innovations of digital technology making both data and mapping platforms more widely available, and thus facilitating what she calls 'a democratising phase of cartography'. The maps of Adam Mattinson provide an obvious example. By day, Mattinson works as a geospatial analyst for an engineering firm. In his own time, he uses his cartographic training to represent the local landscape in strange and fantastical forms. In one project, he depicts a Melbourne constructed on Port Phillip as it looked in the Ice Age; in another work in progress, he imagines the city after massive rises in sea levels.

In the book *How to Lie with Maps,* Mark Monmonier notes what he calls 'the cartographic paradox.' To present complex information from a three-dimensional world clearly in two-dimensional format, the surveyor must abstract and distort. In other words, as Monmonier says, 'to present a useful and truthful picture, an accurate map must tell white lies.'

Mattinson's work takes that idea to its logical conclusion. He's probably best known for his Tolkienesque depiction of the Yarra Ranges, in which The Patch looks almost like Hobbiton and the warning 'Puffing Billy Roams this Area' appears alongside a depiction of a dragon.

'It's covering an area in which I grew up', he says. 'To me, the landscape there really lends itself to a Middle Earth kind of quality.' As a child, Mattinson used to open the street directory at a random page and then trace his finger to find his way home. 'I think that's where the passion for maps springs for a lot of kids. They look at a map and they see that the world is bigger than they had thought.'

Though he works with digital platforms, he loves how physical maps encourage people to gather and discuss the landscape. 'It really is a perfect combination of art and science, cartography. To have something that's beautiful to look at but also an object you can look at and think, "Oh, I used to live near here" or "I want to go there" and so on. It's part of the beauty of mapping, the shared experience.'

A kind of magic, as John Dee understood.

U2, Apple and the strip-mining of punk rebellion

'Wasn't that the most incredible single you ever heard?' asked Apple CEO Tim Cook as the last note of The Edge's guitar died away. Cook was playing U2's new single 'The Miracle (of Joey Ramone)' to the audience at the end of a press conference this month for the new iPhone 6. 'We would love a whole album of that.'

As George Orwell knew, totalitarians have a thing for grammar. Cook's two-sentence shift from the second-person singular to the first-person plural neatly encapsulates the dystopian core of Apple's new alliance with Irish rock bores U2.

'The question is now', replied Bono, 'how do we get it to as many people as possible, because that's what our band is all about. I do believe you have over half a billion subscribers to iTunes, so – could you get this to them?'

Indeed they could, and indeed they did, with the whole *Songs of Innocence* album magically appearing, several seconds later, on the devices of Apple iPhone users the world over.

In retrospect, the alliance between U2 and Apple seems almost inevitable, not least because they're both grappling with a late career slump. Throughout the post-Jobs era, Apple has struggled to live up to the expectations of its fanboys. This year, CEO Tim Cook faced the unenviable task of generating the customary buzz around an iPhone not appreciably different from earlier iterations.

As for U2, its fortunes have been on the slide for decades. Remember the 2009 album *No Line on the Horizon*? No? Neither does anyone else. In the United States, it shifted, as they say, 1.1 million units, a significant decrease from the 3.3 million copies of *How to Dismantle an Atomic Bomb* and 4.4 million of *All That You Can't Leave Behind*. The band has seen 'a steady decline in sales even steeper than the overall industry trend', says the *Wall Street Journal*.

But the iTunes deal represents more than a convenient lash-up between two businesses on the fritz, because it also highlights the aesthetic compatibility between the band and the brand.

Famously, Apple badged itself as the computer company associated not with nerdy IT-types but with cutting-edge artists and rebellious freethinkers. 'I'm a Mac', explained Justin Long in the iconic commercial, inviting viewers to contrast his own laid-back demeanour with the dorky and uptight PC guy beside him. 'Here's to the crazy ones', toasted Steve Jobs, Apple's LSD-gobbling CEO, 'the misfits, the rebels, the troublemakers, the round pegs in the square holes.'

In reality, Jobs's shamanistic persona depended upon the mostly invisible labour carried out in Foxconn factories in Chinese free trade zones, where the manufacture of iPhones and iPads takes place according to a system so regimented that workers cannot move their stools away from a yellow and black striped line. As the (mostly) young women perform the same tedious tasks, over and over again, they're invited to contemplate quotations from the philosophy of Foxconn's CEO, Terry Gou. 'Growth, thy name is suffering', reads one. 'A harsh environment is a good thing', says another. 'Outside the lab, there is no high-tech, only execution of discipline', explains a third.

So much for the misfits and the rebels.

Similarly, U2 have built their career upon tropes of rock rebellion entirely divorced from any radical content whatsoever. The casual listener might mistake 'Sunday Bloody Sunday' as a response to the infamous civil rights massacre, but Bono famously assured crowds that 'this song is not a rebel song'. The iconic photo from that period shows him soulfully waving a white flag, in a kind of symbolic protest that's neither for nor against anything at all.

In the song 'Pride', Bono sings, in that prophet-on-the-mountain-top voice, about Martin Luther King, earnestly informing us that ... what? Love is good – and so are Jesus and MLK? The banality of the lyrics correlates inversely with the fervour with which Bono emotes them.

The new album – the one that turned up uninvited on millions of digital doorsteps – carries all of this a step further, as U2 strip-mines the punk acts of their youth. Hence the invocation of Joey Ramone in the tune that Tim Cook likes so much, a track about as distant from the bratty nihilism of The Ramones as it's possible to get.

With 'This Is Where You Can Reach Me Now', U2 even

channel Sandinista-era Clash. 'After we saw the Clash, it was a sort of blueprint for U2', Bono told *Rolling Stone*. 'We knew we couldn't possibly hope to be as cool, and that's proven to be true, but we did think we could get behind a sort of social justice agenda.'

A sort of social justice agenda? Could anyone imagine U2 titling a record after a Marxist insurgent group that the White House was actively seeking to crush?

U2's career has coincided with the steady retreat of the Left, something that's facilitated the deployment of empty protest signifiers. But Bono and Co. are also now confronting the demise of stadium rock, as popular culture fragments and diversifies in ways that make traditional pop stardom increasingly untenable.

So, with the iTunes deal, U2 attempts to appropriate rock and roll itself. That is, *Songs of Innocence* offers a simulacrum of the old-fashioned rock blockbuster, an album that (because it colonises millions of electronic devices) will be as ubiquitous as any record in musical history. At the same time, it renders traditional fandom entirely redundant, since the songs appear whether the device-owners like them or not.

It's form without content, a musical experience that seems like rock, except without everything that rendered rock important. Teenage lust, the vagaries of fashion, obscure subcultural identifications: all of those components of musical taste have entirely vanished, as Tim and Bono simply make your choices for you. 'Phony Beatlemania has bitten the dust', sang Joe Strummer. He didn't know the half of it.

The U2 tie-in might be seen as a high-tech version of those old-timey promotions where you get a free toy with your cornflakes – except that unwanted content appearing in your music collection inexorably prompts much more complicated considerations of the peculiarities of digital ownership than a plastic whistle. The Apple giveth – and the Apple can presumably taketh away, too. In what sense, then, is either the music or the machine that plays it actually yours? Furthermore, if Tim Cook can reach through your screen and rummage around in your record collection, what else can he do? What can other people or government institutions do? (Hello, NSA!)

Like rock itself, the digital revolution once promised unbridled freedom. As another old punk once said, 'Ever get the feeling you've been cheated?'

The Magic Pudding

'Eat away, chew away, munch and bolt and guzzle/ Never leave the table till you're full up to the muzzle.' This sage advice comes, of course, from Norman Lindsay's *The Magic Pudding*, a classic children's book which celebrated its centenary in 2015.

Famously, the book emerged from a dispute about what attracted children to reading. His friend Bertram Stevens claimed kids loved fairies; Lindsay insisted they craved food. Publisher Angus and Robertson glossed the volume that resulted as detailing the 'Walks, Talks, Travels, Exploits, Fights, Stratagems and Sing-songs of Bill Barnacle (a Sailor), Sam Sawnoff (a Penguin) and Bunyip Bluegum (a Native Bear), told in prose and verse ... and illustrated in 100 pictures'.

At its heart lies Albert, the Puddin' at whom, Bill tells the astonished Bunyip, 'me an' Sam has been eatin' away ... for years, and there's not a mark on him'.

The book's longevity suggests Lindsay correctly estimated the appeal of a 'cut-an-come again' pudding, particularly one that changed with a whistle from steak-and-kidney to plum duff. But *The Magic Pudding*'s success might also be taken as confirmation of Stevens's argument, given Albert manifests all the wilfulness traditionally associated with elves, sprites and similar creatures.

When Bill and Sam explain to Bunyip their possession of 'this remarkable Puddin'', they tell of their shipwreck on an iceberg. There, an obese cook named Curry and Ice concocts 'in a phantom pot/a big plum-duff an' a rump-steak hot' – but refuses to share with his starving shipmates.

Bill stops his song midway. 'There's a verse left out here', he says, 'owin' to the difficulty of explainin' exactly what happened when me and Sam discovered the deceitful nature of that cook.'

The Puddin' will have none of it. 'I had my eye on the whole affair', he replies, 'and it's my belief that if he hadn't been so round you'd have never rolled him off the iceberg, for you was both singing out, "Yo heave Ho" for half-an-hour, an' him trying to hold on to Bill's beard.'

Albert's spite ('He's that artful, lawyers couldn't manage him!') causes the Puddin' owners nearly as much trouble as their ostensible antagonists, Watkin Wombat and his friend, 'that snooting, snouting scoundrel, the Possum.'

Norman Lindsay might seem a rather unlikely author of a treasured book for children, given that, throughout the 20th century, the government censor repeatedly banned his work for obscenity.

When, for instance, the conservative *Argus* discussed his 1930 novel *Redheap*, the reviewer concluded: 'all the characters are warped and some of them are bestial. These creatures wallow in dirt until the book ends after a number of episodes possibly unrivalled in repulsiveness.'

The product of one of those extraordinary families blessed with multiple talented members (think of the Mitfords or Pankhursts), Norman joined, while only a teenager, his older brother Lionel in Melbourne's bohemia. They lived so impecuniously among the youthful painters of the 1890s that a member of the city's larrikin gangs once bailed them up demanding to know the lurk by which these 'artists' so successfully avoided work.

During the war years, Lindsay supplied the *Bulletin* with jingoistic cartoons lambasting wicked Huns, pacifists and socialistic shirkers.

In the book, when Bunyip sings the national anthem, Watkin Wombat must remove his belltopper for fear of being thought disloyal. The stratagem reveals the stolen Puddin' sitting on Watkin's head, but it also recalls the atmosphere of 1918, when Billy Hughes's government imprisoned scores of 'disloyalists' under the War Precautions Act.

Later, the judge presiding over a trial of Puddin' thieves in the town of Toolaroo calls another character 'an unmitigated Jew.' It's a reminder of Lindsay's attachment to some of the nastier prejudices of his era – as, for that matter, is his depiction of koalas, bandicoots and other native animals adventuring through a landscape entirely white and exclusively male.

Yet we should also acknowledge that Lindsay's otherwise unfortunate enthusiasm for Nietzsche, Wagner and similar thinkers gives *The Magic Pudding* its distinctive sensibility.

In 2000, Hollywood produced a film version, with

John Cleese providing the voice of the Puddin'. The online film database IMDb puts a glossy sheen on it, describing a narrative of 'an old man, a young anthropomorphic koala, a South Pole penguin and Albert, a magic sentient walking and talking bowl of pudding with an attitude ... searching for the koala's missing parents'.

Lindsay, however, depicts Bill not as a harmless old man but as a brawling sailor, with Sawnoff Sam as his violent sidekick. At one point, the Penguin warns Watkin Wombat (who is affecting a limp):

> I take no shame to fight the lame
> When they deserve to cop it.
> So do not try to pipe your eye,
> Or with my flip I'll flop it.

As for Bunyip, he's not searching for his parents but escaping his Uncle Wattleberry, offended by the older bear's flowing whiskers. The characters express, in other words, Lindsay's own disdain for wowserism and milksop Christianity. They enjoy instead the simple pleasures of eating, singing and fighting; they're eternally vigilant about those who would take their Puddin' by force or by guile.

They inhabit, we might say, the moral universe of every younger sibling who worries about a brother snatching the dessert. Indeed, the book exudes a child's unabashed joy in wordplay, rhyme and badinage. Bill, in particular, anticipates by several decades the beloved Captain Haddock of Tintin fame.

'Of all the swivel-eyed, up-jumped, cross-grained sons of a cock-eyed tinker', he says to a bad-tempered bird, 'if punching parrots on the beak wasn't too painful for pleasure, I'd land you a sockdolager on the muzzle that ud lay you out till Christmas.'

Lindsay's serious art hasn't aged well, by and large, with many of his once-scandalous paintings striking modern eyes as vaguely silly. But his superb illustrations for *The Magic Pudding* capture perfectly the delightful nastiness of his characters. We recognise the swag-carrying Parrot as a disreputable boozer, but he's somehow still an actual bird.

The book ends with the Judge repeatedly clouting the Puddin' thieves with a bottle of port, as he sings, 'As I find great satisfaction/Hitting anybody who/Can offer that distraction/Why, I'll have a go at you.' As for the Puddin' owners, they make a home in a tree belonging to a 'grave, elderly dog named Benjimen Brandysnap', with Albert corralled in 'a little Puddin' paddock' from which he can shout rude remarks at the people passing by, a habit, the narrator explains, to which he's particularly prone.

Happy birthday, Albert! May you enjoy 'throw[ing] bits of bark at the cabbages and pull[ing] faces at the little pickle onions in order to make them squeak with terror' for another hundred years or more!

Live in the moment

Over the last few days, the streets have filled with Situationists, as *Pokémon Go* sends its legions of players out on prolonged *dérives*.

OK, the comparison's slightly ridiculous. Yet consider Situationist pioneer Guy Debord's description of the *dérive*, the psychogeographic technique his coterie was trialling in Paris in the fifties:

> In a *dérive* one or more persons during a certain period drop their relations, their work and leisure activities, and all their other usual motives for movement and action, and let themselves be drawn by the attractions of the terrain and the encounters they find there. Chance is a less important factor in this activity than one might think: from a *dérive* point of view cities have psychogeographical contours, with constant currents, fixed points and vortexes that strongly discourage entry into or exit from certain zones.

Anyone who's downloaded *Pokémon Go* knows exactly what that's like.

The game's buggy. The app empties your battery and it eats your data and its servers are constantly overloaded. Yet for all its flaws, it manages – at least temporarily – to set you wandering a city landscape that's been re-enchanted, a place where monsters appear in everyday streets and where familiar landmarks serve new purposes according to the logic of a different universe.

Look at the photos *Pokémon* users are uploading.

An Avian Duodo poses outside a KFC restaurant; a Psyduck sits at the bottom of an aquarium. Two senior citizens wander unknowingly into the path of menacing creatures twice their size. A Bulbasor frolics in a university lecture theatre.

That's the beauty of *Pokémon Go*'s augmented reality – it defamiliarises and thus repurposes the places that we know.

'We are bored in the city', writes Situationist theorist and poet Ivan Chtcheglov in his 'Formulary for a New Urbanism', 'there is no longer any Temple of the Sun. Between the legs of the women walking by, the dadaists imagined a monkey wrench and the surrealists a crystal cup. That's lost ... We are bored in the city, we really have to strain to still discover mysteries on the sidewalk billboards ... A mental disease has swept the planet: banalization.'

The augmented reality of *Pokémon Go* offers, we might say, a downloadable alternative to that banalisation, presenting players with startling juxtapositions between the city as is and the city as dreamed. Hence the remarkable testimonies circulating about the game's effects, with, for instance, *The Mary Sue* collecting tweets from those afflicted with depression and other mental illnesses discussing how they've been inspired to leave the home and socialise.

Look, for instance, at the photo posted by reddit user Haloi, an image showing dozens of *Pokémon* players gathered at 11 pm on a Friday evening on the steps of the State Library of Victoria, drawn there by a number of active 'lures' – an in-game version of Debord's 'currents, fixed points and vortexes'.

The building's a beautiful piece of architecture, with a rich and fascinating history. But Melburnians take the library for granted, and young people don't, as a rule, hang out there on Friday nights. Suddenly, though, it's become the locus for a temporary community, invisible to all the non-players passing by.

Of course, that's only part of the story. 'If you visit the Triangle Shirtwaist Factory site while using *Pokémon Go*', tweeted @BenRegenspan a few days ago, 'you get three free Pokeballs.

The comment crystallised some of the unease I'd been feeling walking around Melbourne and observing the virtual city springing up alongside the real. The system incorporates prominent landmarks – buildings, sculptures, statues, etc. – into its gameplay, retooling them as PokéStops and gyms.

On the one hand, that's way cool – suddenly, the old pub near your house is inhabited by monsters.

On the other, there's something faintly distasteful about the recuperation of specific real histories into a billion-dollar corporate mythology. Nearly 150 people lost their lives when the Triangle Shirtwaist Factory burned to the ground, entirely needless deaths caused by the atrocious working conditions of the garment trade. The tragedy became a rallying point for the trade union movement; the name of the factory a shorthand reference to employers' greed.

Now, though, it's three free Pokéballs.

We might also say, then, that, even as the game leads players to embrace the *dérive*, it also offers a remarkable demonstration of the phenomenon that Debord critiqued. 'The whole life', he wrote, 'of those societies in which modern conditions of production prevail presents itself as an immense accumulation of spectacles. All that once was directly lived has become mere representation.'

In particular, Debord emphasises the remarkable ability of the modern city to destroy its own past. 'The "new towns" of the technological pseudo-peasantry', he argues, 'are the clearest indications, inscribed on the land, of the break with historical time on which they are founded; their motto might well be: "On this spot nothing will ever happen – and nothing ever has." Quite obviously, it is precisely because the liberation of history, which must take place in the cities, has not yet occurred, that the forces of historical absence have set about designing their own exclusive landscape there.'

Augmented reality might defamilarise urban banality, but it does so by colonising fantasy for multinational branding: nothing says 'forces of historical absence' like an elaborate mythos accreted by years of corporate marketing.

Then again, why should it be otherwise? Capitalist banalisation inevitably seizes every aesthetic critique of capitalist banalisation, while utopia and dystopia always shadow each other. And there's something still deeply attractive about a game that invokes, even for a minute, the new kind of urbanism about which Chtcheglov mused:

> The architecture of tomorrow will be a means of modifying present conceptions of time and space. It will be both a means of knowledge and a means of action. Architectural complexes will be modifiable. Their appearance will change totally or partially in accordance with the will of their inhabitants.

Isn't that the vision that makes *Pokémon Go* so addictive – the momentary glimpse of a world that might be?

Fangs for the memories

It is a truth universally acknowledged, that a publisher in possession of a million-dollar bestseller, must be in want of another million-dollar bestseller.

In 2009, Seth Grahame-Smith's *Pride and Prejudice and Zombies*, a book that revealed Elizabeth and Jane Bennet as fearless ninja warriors driving the undead from Regency England, sold an astonishing 850 000 copies.

Since then, mash-ups of the classics have multiplied like zombies at a mall. A quick Amazon search reveals *Sense and Sensibility and Sea Monsters* (the Dashwood sisters find romance at the bottom of the ocean), *Android Karenina* (a steampunk Tolstoy), *Little Women and Werewolves* (you can probably figure that one out), and many, many more.

Monsters traditionally embody the kind of social tensions that literary classics hide beneath their mannered pages. You would not know, for instance, that Darcy woos Elizabeth in an England in which the Luddite rebellion has recently been savagely crushed. That's why zombies, in particular, prove so compatible with Austen: the world of *Pride and Prejudice* can, with only the slightest tweaking, assimilate the undead, in much the same way as it treats the shuffling multitudes of the poor.

'Mr Darcy soon drew the attention of the room', writes Grahame-Smith, 'by his fine, tall person, handsome features, noble mien and the report which was in general circulation within five minutes after his entrance, of his having slaughtered more than a thousand unmentionables since the fall of Cambridge'.

Well, either you find that funny, or you don't.

If the latter, you almost certainly won't like *Dawn of the Dreadfuls*, the Quirk Books prequel that explains how the Bennet daughters acquired their proficiency in the deadly arts. When the corpses start rising from the grave, Mr Bennet hastily ushers the girls into his backyard dojo.

'What if we don't want to be warriors?' Kitty asks.

'Then I will disown you, and you will, most likely, be torn apart and eaten by a pack of festering corpses', he replies.

So far, so pleasingly silly.

Pride and Prejudice and Zombies works because it not only follows the original narrative but it also cannibalises great chunks of Austen's prose – to often hilarious effect. Thus: '[N]o sooner had [Darcy] made it clear to himself and his friends that [Elizabeth] hardly had a good feature in her face, than he began to find it was rendered uncommonly intelligent by the beautiful expression of her dark eyes, and her uncommon skill with a blade'.

With *Dawn of the Dreadfuls*, however, Steve Hockensmith retains the Austenite characters but not the Austenite style. Indeed, in places, the novel seems to have been written by the undead, for the undead, and so, despite a gratifying abundance of disembowellings, palls very quickly.

Perhaps wisely, Seth Grahame-Smith eschews Austen (and Quirk) to follow *Pride and Prejudice and Zombies* with a pastiche of a different kind. His *Abraham Lincoln: Vampire Hunter* rests on a half-decent conceit: the vampires of Europe have fled to the New World, attracted by the southern plantations where slaves offer such easy pickings. A young Abe Lincoln discovers this awful secret ('So long as this country is cursed with slavery, so too will it be cursed with vampires') and accordingly puts his woodchopping skills to a different use.

It is, however, much easier to retool a novel than a life. Like a bad biography, *Abraham Lincoln* struggles with pacing. It dutifully (and sometimes cleverly) inserts vampires into the main episodes of Lincoln's career, but never really becomes more than a bare sequence of events, and, by the time John Wilkes Booth arrives, fangs extended, at the theatre, the reader is almost tempted to cheer.

In *Murder at Mansfield Park*, the only monster is Fanny Price, Austen's least-loved heroine. While Lynn Shepherd preserves *Mansfield Park*'s setting and character names, she changes most everything else. Rather than an impoverished moralist, Fanny's a rich heiress who makes everyone miserable until she's eventually murdered with a hammer. Mary Crawford, in this version poor but smart, becomes the heroine, in a book that's less Quirk-style schlock than an Agatha Christie whodunit in a Regency setting.

What are we to make of all this: a literary canon suddenly infested by vampires, werewolves and bugaboos of all kinds?

Traditionalists might wince at a Jane Austen reanimated with bolts protruding from her neck. But it's worth asking: has she not been, in reality, a zombie for years now? Austen's remarkable contemporary popularity stems less from her books than from the film and TV adaptations that resurrect *Emma* and *Pride and Prejudice* and the rest, and send them shambling out into the world as Mills and Boon romances.

There's always been a symbiotic (or, perhaps, vampiric) relationship between pop culture and the canon, and, in many ways, all Quirk's done is capitalise on the distinctive sensibility of the Web 2.0 generation.

Has the monster meme now run its course? Yes, quite possibly, but, if so, it's already left its mark. Even highbrow publishers are now experimenting with the promotional techniques pioneered by the mash-ups, with the zombie novels spurring, for instance, a general enthusiasm for YouTube book trailers. The digital age means, we're often told, the death of traditional literature. And perhaps that's so. Yet the recent proliferation of literary mutations should remind us not to turn our backs on the traditional novel, for it has a disconcerting ability to come lurching back from the grave.

EVERYBODY TALKS ABOUT THE WEATHER

In the mid-1960s, the German national rail system Deutsche Bahn launched a new campaign to advertise its services. The poster showed a train travelling at high speed through heavy snow.

'Everybody talks about the weather', read the text. 'We don't.'

During the political tumult of the period, radicals of the Socialist German Student Union (*Sozialistische Deutsche Studentenbund* or SDS) co-opted the popular campaign. Their version featured the same slogan alongside images of Marx, Engels and Lenin, implying that SDS militants shrugged aside the trivialities of bourgeois politics with the insouciance of a Deutsche Bahn locomotive ploughing through a blizzard.

From our vantage point, the SDS poster epitomises a vanished era: not just with its confident proclamation of the Marxist tradition but also – and perhaps more importantly – with its curt dismissal of climatic conditions as the stuff of tedious chit-chat.

Today, everybody talks about the weather – and for good reason.

Amid an environmental emergency, even the slightest variation in natural conditions take on a terrifying significance. What does a change in the temperature mean? What about the unexpected migration of a flock of rare birds? Has their habitat been destroyed? Can we attribute the floods devastating farmlands to bad luck – an 'act of God', as the insurers say – or did something knock the natural cycles out of kilter?

A sunny day is no longer merely a sunny day but a

portent for which we desperately seek interpretation.

Looking back from our era of climate catastrophe, it's clear that the activists of the SDS shared key assumptions with the rail planners they lampooned. Just like captains of industry, the young socialists treated nature as external to the human realm, and significant primarily as a resource for exploitation.

Since then, leftists – like everyone else – have been forced to rethink the attitudes of the 20th century, rediscovering an older materialism centred on the relationship between human beings and the natural world.

I've been on that journey, too. Like so many others, I've been writing increasingly often and increasingly urgently about the environmental emergency, pushing past the grief and pain associated with the topic to argue that the way we treat nature cannot be separated from the way we treat each other. This chapter contains a selection of those pieces.

For this collection, I wrote about the thylacine (the so-called 'Tasmanian tiger'), an essay less focussed on the possibility that the iconic species might still be alive than on the related but slightly different question: what would its survival mean? If, by some magic, we recovered the thylacine, would the miracle encourage renewed efforts at conservation – or does our obsession with the most charismatic of animals obscure the less dramatic, everyday destruction?

In 2019, I visited the Melbourne Zoo to meet with Wilbur the 100-year-old tortoise, for a *Guardian* feature about the ancient creatures whose longevity encourages us to think differently about nature.

In a similar mood, I re-read Elizabeth Bishop's poem

'One Art' to consider what she calls 'the art of losing' in terms of the environmental emergency.

In another *Guardian* article, I investigated whether – as so many people had told me – Christmas beetles were vanishing. Are insects and other common species palpably rarer now than in our childhood? How would we even know?

Since 1991, peregrine falcons have been nesting on a skyscraper in Melbourne's Collins Street. I wrote about the joy that a live stream of the birds brought to so many people: a simple reminder that nature persists.

In June 2021, Britain's Clarion Cycling Club abandoned the commitment to socialism central to its foundation in 1894. In another piece written for this collection, I investigated the astonishing radicalism of bike culture in the 1890s. Given the desperate need for less destructive forms of transport, what we might learn from the fin de siècle fad for cycling?

That *Deutsche Bahn* advertising campaign drew, of course, on an earlier epigram, one that's also taken on a new meaning.

The American writer Charles Dudley Warner once said (in a passage often attributed to his friend Mark Twain) that everybody always talks about the weather but nobody does anything about it.

Today, it's well past time that they did.

What if we found a thylacine?

The deliberate extermination of the thylacine haunts the Australian imagination, a ghastly reminder of colonial ignorance and malice. But what if we got a second chance? If, by some miracle, we rediscovered the so-called Tasmanian Tiger, how, precisely, would we respond?

Environmental scientist Barry Brook from the University of Tasmania says much would depend on the circumstances: 'If the person just shows me an image of a thylacine but they won't tell me where it was, there's little that I or anyone else can do.'

A genuine identification would, he thinks, almost certainly come from professionals, such as the staff working for the Tasmanian Land Conservancy or the Save the Devil Program. 'The reason I say that is that scientific monitoring outperforms amateur efforts by an order of magnitude or more in terms of the number of cameras, quality, locations and so on.'

A scientific team would bring its data to the authorities, and then work with them to establish a recovery plan. That program would begin, Brook says, with saturation monitoring to establish the population size, a precursor to longer-term genetic sampling, captive breeding and the other measures necessary to reintroduce thylacines as the top carnivore in the Tasmanian ecosystem.

That's the best-case scenario. But Nick Mooney isn't quite so confident expertise would prevail. As a former Parks and Wildlife Service (PWS) officer, Mooney devoted much of his career to investigating the more credible thylacine sightings received by the Tasmanian service.

In 1982, for instance, he spent months in the bush near Smithton after an experienced parks officer called Hans Naarding reported a night-time encounter with an adult male thylacine.

Naarding delivered his account – described by the PWS director at the time as 'irrefutable and conclusive' – with calm confidence, explaining that he swept his spotlight across the animal from a distance of 6 or 7 metres and counted the twelve stripes on its sandy coat.[1]

'We thought we were on to something', says a laconic Mooney, 'and I operated up there for a year trying to confirm it. Because he was one of our employees, we were able to keep it pretty quiet'. Only after the exhaustive search proved inconclusive did Naarding speak publicly.

A similar incident would, Mooney thinks, be much harder to contain today. He fears a contemporary sighting would be perceived (not least by politicians) as a potential gold mine, with scientific protocols abandoned in the rush to cash in.

'The Naarding case was pre-social media – and social media, as we've seen many times with this issue, dominates it completely. It's quite possible – likely even – that someone would show us footage and never tell us where they took it.'

Tiger hunter Murray McAllister says pretty much the same. A physical education teacher by day, McAllister began looking for the thylacine back in 1998. The pursuit now dominates his life. 'I've found evidence', he declares. 'I know that Tasmanian tigers are there on some of these farm areas that I track on a regular basis.'

He describes seeing, behind a couple of tussocks, a golden-brown tail that he thought initially belonged to a kangaroo. 'I thought it was going to get up and – doink! doink! doink! – hop away but then it didn't. I ran to the tussocks and there was this Tasmanian tiger just heading into the bushland.'

McAllister is working on a book. Though he's drafted eight or nine chapters, he's waiting for definitive evidence before going to print. 'At the end of the day, I want some clear photos of the thylacine, so I can say, there he is in all his glory – there's his stripes, his tail, everything.'

Palaeontologists say thylacines became extinct on the Australian mainland thousands of years ago. In the Western Australian museum, you can see a mummified specimen that once hunted in today's Nullarbor Plains. Yet McAllister continues to search Victoria. He believes the creatures were reintroduced from Tasmania in the late 19th or early 20th century. He points to the activities of the Field Naturalists Club of Victoria, a group with a particular interest in Wilson's Promontory.

'They had half a dozen Tasmanian tigers in the zoo down there. And there were already a dozen up in the Melbourne

Zoo at the time. The theory is that they might've just let them go.'

At the time, the naturalists of the Acclimatisation Society of Victoria sought to introduce to the colony 'all innoxious animals, birds, fishes, insects and vegetables, whether useful or ornamental'.[2] For the most part, the society imported European species (one report proclaimed proudly that the rabbit had been 'so thoroughly acclimatised that it swarms in hundreds in some localities'). Yet the acclimatisers also took an interest in native animals, and thylacine enthusiasts have uncovered an *Argus* article from 1868 with a tantalising reference to breeding farms containing 'a tiger rat, a Tasmanian wolf and two Tasmanian devils'.[3]

Thylacine sightings in Wilson's Promontory reached their crescendo in 1996, when Peter Hall, the National Party environment spokesman, urged the government (unsuccessfully) to investigate one supposed encounter in the area.[4]

Other sites have a similar history. In the mid-1990s, former assistant police commissioner Fred Silvester claimed to have seen, standing by his garden fish pond in Loch Sport near the Gippsland Lakes, an animal 'about the size of a medium-sized dog, with a thick tail that came to a point, and dark stripes that went right to the butt of the tail'.[5]

In Wonthaggi, locals have wondered, ever since the 1950s, about the town 'monster': a cat-like creature said to haunt the nearby bush. One witness described it as 'a strange animal with a blood-curdling yell ... with large claws, large head, furry body striped like a zebra, and a long tail'.[6]

These and other stories circulate widely on the many online thylacine forums and Facebook groups. Most scientists don't give them much credence. Mind you, McAllister doesn't care.

He complains that university researchers receive lavish grants for their investigations but don't put in nearly the work that, for some twenty years, he's devoted to his self-funded expeditions.

That's why, if he captured a thylacine, he'd build a cage around it and then, before he released it, take hair and blood samples. He certainly wouldn't bring it to the Melbourne Zoo.

'They'd say, thank you very much, Murray, we will see you later', he scoffs. 'And then they'd do their own documentary, and my efforts would go unrewarded. I'd give them the general vicinity, but I wouldn't be disclosing everything. It's like playing a game of cards. You don't show your hand until you're ready to prove it to the whole world. Because if you can show that the thylacine is back out there, that's going to be enormous, with worldwide headlines.'

No doubt that's true. But it's curious to think about the publicity that a rediscovery would bring – given the last thylacine's death did not generate any headlines at all.

As the writer Nicholas Shakespeare notes, on 8 September 1936, the *Hobart Mercury* said nothing at all about how, on the previous day, the female thylacine known as Benjamin had perished after being inadvertently locked out of her cage in the old Beaumaris Zoo on a freezing Tasmanian night.[7]

Rather than recording what now seems an environmental calamity of almost epochal proportions, the paper concerned itself with the 'unseemly conduct' at the Bothwell

Hall during a recent concert, noting with disapproval the 'empty liquor bottles ... found in the dressing rooms'.

The *Mercury*'s response reflects, of course, a colonial indifference to antipodean ecology, one deeply enmeshed with the broader project of white settlement.

In December 1642, the Dutch navigator Abel Tasman became the first European on the island that would later bear his name. When his crew returned to their vessel, they were marvelling at 'certain footprints of animals, not unlike those of a tiger's claws'.[8]

That might well have been the first colonial encounter with the thylacine. Then again, it might not – quite possibly the men saw the clawed prints left by wombats.

But Tasman's sailors, exploring the fabled Terra Australis Incognita, were already inclined to find portents and wonders. Though they witnessed no people during their brief landfall, they talked of 'sounds resembling the music of a drum or a small gong' and gaped at trees marked for climbing. The wide cuts gouged into the trunks came, they concluded, from men of prodigious size.

In reality, the Indigenous inhabitants were not, of course, the giants that Tasman's crew imagined. They simply knew how utilise the island's natural resources, including hunting the possums sheltering high up in the trees. Over thousands of years, the First Peoples developed a profound understanding of the local flora and fauna, a wisdom that extended to the animal they called variously 'corinnah', 'lagunta', 'laoona' and 'ka-nunnah' (though precisely what role it played in traditional culture is not known to Western scholarship).[9]

Indigenous lore gave the Aboriginal Tasmanians a

demonstrably higher standard of living than most early modern Europeans. Yet, when the British established their military outpost on the Derwent River in 1803, they classed the natives as crude primitives, dismissing as worthless a culture they could not understand. As an 1820 visitor to Hobart remarked, '[t]he aborigines of this island are supposed [by white settlers] to be the most degraded of any known in the world.'[10]

Sporadic conflict intensified into the murderous Black War of 1824 to 1831. The white press became openly genocidal: the *Colonial Advocate* called for Indigenous people to be 'exterminated or removed', the *Colonial Times* urged the 'annihilation of the whole race' and the *Tasmanian* declared 'extermination [...] the only remedy.'[11]

Hundreds, perhaps thousands, of Aboriginal people were killed – and those that survived were forcibly transferred to a bleak reservation on Flinders Island. In many ways, the subsequent war against the thylacine mirrored that earlier campaign against Indigenous people. Just as Tasman's fascination with the unknown southern land's enigmatic people gave way to a British scorn for Aboriginal 'backwardness', curiosity about the mysterious tiger became overt contempt for an animal blamed for thinning the settlers' flocks.

The colonists spoke variously of 'a Tasmanian wolf, a Tasmanian hyena, a Tasmanian zebra, a Tasmanian dingo, a Tasmanian panther and a dog-faced dasyure.'[12] Whatever it was, they wanted it gone.

Towards the end of the Black Wars, the authorities proclaimed Government Order No 2, offering 'a reward of £5 [...] for every adult aboriginal native and £2 for every child, who shall be captured and delivered alive to any of the police stations.'[13] To destroy the thylacine, they used a similar expediency. By 1830, the Van Diemen's Land Company was offering a reward for the killing of 'noxious animals', a category under which it listed the 'hyena'.[14]

In 1882, a *Mercury* headline promised 'Tiger Extermination,' as landowners in Buckland discussed wiping out both thylacines and eagles, with 'a reward of £5 to be paid for each full-grown tiger caught in the district, and £2 10s, for all cubs equal in size to a full-grown domestic cat, the skins of all the animals caught to become the property of the association.'[15]

A few years later, the politician John Lyne – a representative of the Tasmanian rural lobby – proposed the government bounty that constituted an official death sentence. In the debate at the House of Assembly, Lyne claimed, quite preposterously, that '30 000 or 40 000 sheep' were taken each year by the animals he described as 'dingoes' and 'one of the greatest pests the colony had'.

As Lyne vowed the thylacine's complete destruction, the assembled MPs joked about also exterminating the Chinese, whom one described as 'another animal his constituents were suffering from'– an illustration of how the anti-tiger campaign rested on a deeper commitment to Tasmania as a domesticated and European land.[16]

Scientists estimate the total thylacine population pre-white settlement as perhaps 5000. Between 1888 and 1909, the authorities paid so-called 'tiger men' for some 2184 carcasses – a figure that doesn't include the separate rewards offered by local farmers.

In 1902, hunters claimed 119 skins. Four years later, the figure had fallen to fifty-nine. The next year, it was two – and, after that, thylacines had become so rare that no-one delivered hides at all.[17]

In 1914, the biologist Professor Thomas Flynn (father of the Hollywood swashbuckler Errol Flynn) warned that thylacines faced extinction. But nothing came of his call for a sanctuary's establishment. Legislation protecting the species only passed the Tasmanian parliament in 1936 – and, by then, just one animal remained.

Today, National Threatened Species Day falls on 7 September, the anniversary of Benjamin's lonely death outside her cold, concrete cage.

Nick Mooney thinks that a collective guilt about the thylacine ('such a great lesson in what not to let happen') spurred the relatively rapid response to devil facial tumour disease. Tasmanians knew just how suddenly a species could vanish – and no politician wanted another iconic animal's destruction on their conscience. Yet, in other ways, little has changed.

In 2005, a journalist from the *Mercury* took Hans Naarding back to the site of his thylacine encounter. A photograph from the visit shows the gaunt, white-haired ranger standing on a burnt-out stump, distraught as he surveys a ruined vista of mud, tree roots and charcoal.[18]

Loggers had been at work on the northwest coast since the 1980s. Even as Mooney desperately tried to confirm Naarding's sighting, chainsaws were reducing some 37 000 tonnes of native forest to woodchips and sawlogs. By the 2000s, no thylacines could survive in the wounded landscape that remained – and nor could much of anything else.

The philosopher William James wrote of travelling through North Carolina in the 1890s and staring, aghast, at the devastation inflicted by the settlers as they cleared the land. 'The forest had been destroyed', he wrote, 'and what had "improved" it out of existence was hideous, a sort of ulcer, without a single element of artificial grace to make up for the loss of Nature's beauty'.

But he recognised his revulsion as an outsider's perspective, divorced from the ideology of progress to which the American pioneers were committed. '[T]he clearing, which to me was a mere ugly picture on the retina, was to them', James concluded, 'a symbol redolent with moral memories and sang a very pæan of duty, struggle, and success'.[19]

The passage recalls the destruction of Tasmania's Lake Pedder in the early 1970s. Today, environmentalists decry as calamitous the hydroelectric project that flooded a serene valley of unparalleled beauty, obliterating precisely the kind of landscape in which a fugitive thylacine might, just maybe, have sheltered.

At the time, however, politicians lauded the project in terms James's settlers would have understood, with the dam embodying the state's progressive modernisation. 'Our engineers have changed contours with the aesthetic achievement of landscape gardeners', boasted the Labor Premier Eric Reece.[20]

The colonial imperative to transform a frightening wilderness into a reassuring garden wreaked havoc everywhere. In Australia, endemic birds, plants, animals and insects have disappeared at a dizzying rate, with many species vanishing before scientists can properly identify them. Given that great dying, isn't the fascination with a single species – even one as spectacular as the thylacine – something of a distraction?

Mooney hesitates. 'On Mondays, Wednesdays and Fridays, I think the interest in the thylacine is a positive and on the other days I think it's a distraction. I've had to make the decision as to whether, in my own small way, I keep servicing it. But there is a slim possibility the animal's still there – pretty slim but a possibility. And so you have to remind people that we all have to be sensible if it gets found.'

But, yes, he does worry that an obsessive focus on rare, endangered animals obscures more systemic problems. 'I've always been interested in birds of prey', he explains. 'When people ask me about my favourite, they always expect something incredibly rare and exotic like the harpy eagle. But my favourite bird is the common brown falcon because you see it every day and so you can get to know it really well. What's the point of having a favourite bird that's so rare that it's almost just an idea?'

On that basis, he proposes supplementing Threatened Species Day with Common Species Day. 'Exactly the polar opposite in the year, six months away – a day we look at all the common animals that actually drive the ecology. We tend to know the most about the rarest animals and the least about the most common, even though you can argue, from a simple ecological point of view, the most common animals are the most important.'

He nominates the green rosella: a bird endemic to

Tasmania, and as such barely noticed. Experts study each and every orange-bellied parrot – a bird teetering on the very edge of extinction – but creatures like the rosella don't receive anything like the same attention. 'We wouldn't know if there's two million of them or two hundred because there's no effort put into monitoring them.'

Scientists often can't access research funds unless an animal's already in trouble – and by then it can be too late to intervene. 'I think we're just on a hiding to nothing. Look at the number of species that are on the threatened list versus the numbers that come off. I think the only one that's ever come off in Australia is a saltwater crocodile, which dropped from endangered to vulnerable.'

The journalist Jon Mooallem describes humanity as now 'living in the eye of a great storm of extinction, on a planet hemorrhaging living things.'[21] Yet the prioritisation of the rare and the endangered allows specific environmental crises to be abstracted from the systemic devastation humanity continues to wreak.

'If we properly managed common species, we'd all have to change our behaviour, addressing issues like climate change. And I'd say the threatened species concept has been grabbed by governments and industry, because while it's slightly inconvenient, it's far better than having to change fundamental behaviours to look after all ecology.'

Yet Barry Brook could not disagree more. The popular attachment to certain animals cannot and should not be ignored, he says: not least because, when iconic species die, the public – quite understandably – despairs. 'It has a depressive effect. People think, well, you can't even be bothered to save these things we really care about, so why should we invest emotionally in anything else?'

Conversely, the allure of particularly exotic animals – and what could be more exotic than a thylacine? – serves, at least potentially, as a force multiplier, creating environmental opportunities that mightn't otherwise exist. For instance, a rejuvenated thylacine population would, almost by definition, require a rejuvenated habitat, which would assist all manner of other creatures.

'If you found a handful of thylacines, you'd want to restore them to being thousands of thylacines. You'd want to get them back to their former ecological position and that would involve investments in habitat protection and restoration and connectivity: all the issues that go along with restoring a wide-ranging predator. That brings benefits for other species, the other mammals and birds that need habitat protection, as well as the invertebrates and the fungi and the mosses and all the other things that are otherwise invisible.'

It would be foolish, Brook says, not to harness the undeniable pull of charismatic animals. He points out that prior to colonisation, Tasmania possessed its own distinctive emu, a smaller subspecies isolated from the rest of the population during the Late Pleisotocene. Within thirty years of white settlement, the emus were gone, wiped out so thoroughly that we lack even basic information about where and how they lived.

Some scientists think that, because collectors sought the more exotic variant, the Tasmanian bloodline might persist in overseas zoos and could, perhaps, be recovered through selective breeding. Whether that's true or not, the re-introduction of emus (even mainland ones) would benefit the environment, since the birds probably played an important ecological role in distributing seeds.

Yet the restoration of emus would require active community support – and, for the moment, no-one can guarantee that such support would be forthcoming, precisely because Tasmanians don't have any emotional attachment to the species.

Thylacines would be different. The worldwide interest in a recovered thylacine population would, almost certainly, inspire locals, with ordinary people volunteering to do whatever is necessary for the animals to flourish. That enthusiasm might set a precedent. One could imagine that farmers newly accustomed to living with the once-hated Tasmanian tigers might, perhaps, warm to the prospect of emus once again striding over a rewilded landscape.

Mind you, none of that implies that Brook expects a healthy thylacine to surface any time soon. In a recent academic paper, he and his colleagues pored over every thylacine sighting documented since poor Benjamin's demise. Their statistical analysis suggests that a remnant population most likely survived in remote areas for several decades – but then, heartbreakingly, faded away, probably some time between the late 1980s and the early 2000s.[22]

Brook describes the findings as consistent with what we already know: namely, that the government bounty reduced a previously widely distributed animal to scattered populations in fragmented pockets.

The disappearance of the last wild individual from any endangered species typically takes place well away from the humans responsible for the extinction. 'There's a concept known as the extinction vortex, a positive feedback between a species becoming small and then that smallness itself creating genetic problems through the reduction of natural variability, which, in turn, makes the population smaller. Species can persist for much longer than you might think but the inherent problems caused by their decline makes natural recovery very difficult.'

On that basis, he thinks it's now more likely that we will resurrect the thylacine than rediscover it. Certainly, the rapid advance of biotechnology makes previously fanciful interventions become suddenly more feasible. Almost as soon as scientists engineered Dolly the Sheep in 1996, environmentalists speculated about dragging lost species back from the void. If we could clone a lamb, why not a dodo or a mammoth – or, indeed, a thylacine?

Yet the process still poses formidable challenges. The cloning pioneered with Dolly depended on somatic cells – and they don't survive in long-dead animals. Scientists have managed, for instance, to successfully clone the now-extinct Pyrenean ibex. But that was only because they took tissue samples from Celia, the sole remaining animal, a year before her death. Using those cells, they could create an ibex clone ... and it survived for a few minutes before its lungs collapsed.

With Benjamin long dead, we lack a thylacine Celia, which makes any hypothetical resurrection almost certainly dependent on gene splicing, a fiendishly difficult method that melds an extinct creature's DNA with that of its living relatives.

Scientists intent on restoring the woolly mammoth

could, in theory, mix its genes with those of the Asian elephant so that the latter birthed a hybrid 'mammophant'. For the thylacine, the only comparable option would be a reliance on the Tasmanian devil – and it's by no means clear that an animal so much smaller could carry a baby with tiger DNA to term.

'I call it "clowning" rather than "cloning"', says Nick Mooney. 'If someone ever managed to do it for the thylacine, it would just be a freak show.'

A genetically engineered thylacine would, after all, be worth millions upon millions. Rather than reviving an emblem of wild Tasmania, the process would create a copyrighted genetic commodity requiring the tightest of security.

That's why, for Mooney, cloning merely serves to avoid a grim reality: thylacines once existed – and we killed them forever. 'There's also the implication that, if we can just get the economy working, we can fix the environment with technology. And, of course, it helps raise money to develop biotechnology. But it's nothing to do with thylacines.'

Again, Brook disagrees. Yes, he says, de-extinction attracts investors. But what's wrong with that?

'The argument often proffered is that whatever you spend to resurrect the thylacine, you could spend that more strategically to secure a hundred species that are not extinct yet, or maybe not even critically endangered. And my response is that typically the funds are not fungible. A Jeff Bezos might invest in the de-extinction of the thylacine but he's not going to put that same money towards securing habitat for a hundred snail species that are in trouble, but not extinct. By securing money for a flagship project, like thylacine recovery, you're injecting new money to conservation that would never have arrived there otherwise.'

Projects that look like the *Jurassic Park* fantasies of rich eccentrics might, in fact, have huge implications for broader conservation management and recovery.

'In a sense, it's an investment in a technology with spinoff benefits to many other species. For example, a major problem in conservation biology is that we're losing the genetic diversity that once existed. The technology that might resurrect a thylacine or a mammoth or a passenger pigeon could potentially reinvigorate many highly threatened species by reintroducing ancient genetic material that has been lost from the population and therefore increasing their fitness.'

He compares the de-extinction of the thylacine to the moon landing, an extravagant venture, certainly, but one that created all kinds of unexpected applications, from Teflon to integrated circuits. But perhaps that still leaves questions.

Sure, tycoons would, almost certainly, invest to bring back this particular animal rather than any other. But why? What makes a once-despised creature suddenly so attractive, not merely to the super-rich but to so many ordinary people?

Brook wonders if the answer lies in a perception of an avoidable tragedy. 'This is effectively a member of the Pleistocene megafauna that survived the extinction even 40 000 years ago – and then we lost it in the 20th century. We've still got the devil, we've still got other animals but not the thylacine ... and we were just so close.'

Mooney thinks the 'tiger' nomenclature makes the difference, invoking an animal whose fearful symmetry resonates in both Western and Eastern mythology. 'I'm convinced', he says, 'that if it was called by its Aboriginal name, we wouldn't be having this discussion because no-one would care less.'

Both men agree that a conspiratorial narrative has now developed so that, for thylacine obsessives, at least, the animals represent all the secret truths repressed by experts and governments and the media.

On a vacation on Lord Howe Island, Mooney found himself inadvertently eavesdropping in the coffee queue as another holidaymaker casually discussed all the thylacines he'd seen in Tasmania. 'It was amazing. The guy was just so matter of fact. You'd come away thinking that, oh, yeah you can just drive through Tassie and you'll see thylacines everywhere.'

Murray McAllister exudes a very similar confidence. Unlike either Brook or Mooney, he possesses no doubt as to the thylacine's continuing survival. 'You're always coming across footprints, you can see where they've been and hear their vocalisations.'

He attributes the lack of any definitive proof to the animal's preternatural awareness. 'They have super-sensitive hearing and super-sensitive smell. Their peripheral vision must be way out there somewhere. A camera trap takes one or two seconds to activate but by then they know it's there. And, as soon as the Tasmanian tiger feels threatened, it takes off. That's why you get blurry images.'

He shakes his head. 'Oh, mate – they are just so cunning!'

Finding thylacines might not be possible. But perhaps not finding them has its own compensations. Certainly, despite his frustrations, McAllister has no regrets about decades spent searching.

'It's been such a journey', he says. 'I've met some amazing people. And here we are twenty years later. It's been exciting! It's been, well, magnificent!'

Australia's oldest things

Wilbur the tortoise has, in all probability, lived more than a hundred years.

'From his size and weight and general health', says Adam Lee, a reptile keeper at Melbourne Zoo, 'we put him at about 110 but there's no real way of telling with giant tortoises unless you have them from birth or as a hatchling'.

Lee holds out a carrot and Wilbur snaps at it.

He seems, in certain respects, even older than that – ancient, even prehistoric. He scrabbles on the concrete floor with ungainly dinosaur feet. When I stroke his massive shell, I can feel the scratches on the keratin. He snuffles as he eats, his leathery jaw jutting irritably, as if he were an aggrieved pensioner discussing franking credits.

Yet the idea that this creature, happily munching his carrot, pre-dates the First World War astonishes me.

Lee explains that giant tortoises (or 'GTs', as he calls them) can live more than 200 years, perhaps reaching 250.

This sounds preposterous. But I already know of Jonathan, a giant tortoise estimated to have been born in

1832 but still alive and well on the island of St Helena in the South Atlantic.

The picture of him taken in the St Helena Government House grounds in the 1880s almost seems evidence for time travel. It shows four men ('good types of Saint Helenians', according to the original caption) clearly belonging to the colonial era: a portly police officer wearing a custodian helmet; a groundskeeper working in a bowler hat and a waistcoat.

And there, at the feet of those long-dead gentlemen, stands Jonathan, looking entirely the same as he does in photos from 2019.

On the day of my visit, Melbourne is blustery, so much so that Lee warns via email not to expect 'much GT action', since Wilbur and his slightly younger companion (perhaps ninety), Little John, both dislike the cold. I can't bring myself to complain, given the prolonged warmth of Victoria's autumn.

In our times, unseasonal temperatures – even when pleasant – fill me with a vague dread. The novelist Delia Falconer discusses climate change ushering in 'a new age of signs and wonders', in which the most commonplace occurrences (a warm evening, the absence of birdlife at a particular spot, an unexpected change in vegetation) feel fraught with ecological portent.

'As the world becomes more unstable in the grip of vast and all-pervasive change', Falconer writes, 'it's difficult to discern exact chronologies, relationships and meaning'.

More than anything, I think, climate change politicises time.

Lord Byron considered the sea 'the image of eternity'. For us, however, it means flux and uncertainty, with new research suggesting the oceans could rise as much as 2 metres by 2100.

'Time is money', warned Benjamin Franklin, and the extractive industries built fortunes taking him at his word. Fossil fuels depend on million-year-old geological processes so that, in a sense, industrial society runs by burning natural history.

The emergence of Greta Thunberg as a global leader highlights the temporal inequity of climate change, a burden shrugged off by the old on to the young.

'[Our] future was sold', she explained in a speech to the British parliament, 'so that a small number of people could make unimaginable amounts of money'.

According to the UN Intergovernmental Panel on Climate Change, we have, perhaps, twelve years to avoid catastrophe – and one of those years has nearly passed. Yet, though we must act immediately, we need to imagine the aeons to come, planning for outcomes well beyond the threescore years and ten that scripture allots to a man.

Hence my interest in Wilbur and the other creatures whose lives extend longer than our own.

In 2007 biologists identified a 50-tonne bowhead whale caught near Alaska as more than 115 years old by examining pieces of a particular harpoon stuck in its shoulder bone. Because whalers only used that patented variety of exploding lance for a brief window in the late 1880s, the fragments confirmed scientists' suspicion that bowheads could live several centuries – providing, of course, they weren't harpooned first.

Three years ago researchers from the University of Copenhagen dated a female Greenland shark as 392 years old.

As the *Guardian*'s Nicola Davis explained, that means the animal 'was born during the reign of James I, was a youngster when René Descartes set out his rules of thought and the great fire of London raged, saw out her adolescent years as George II ascended the throne, reached adulthood around the time that the American revolution kicked off, and lived through two world wars'. It's a mind-boggling chronology, an illustration of just how wondrous our planet remains.

Yet there's a less ennobling aspect to the story. Where the Alaskan whale was classified by a projectile scar, scientists established the shark's age because of an atomic bomb. The nuclear tests conducted in the 1950s sent spikes of carbon-14 into the food chain of the North Atlantic, which then provided a kind of date stamp, marking a particular layer of proteins as they grew on the poor fish's eye.

The oldest creatures carry marks from the people of the past and so remind us of the scars we're already leaving on lives in the future. That becomes even more obvious when we turn from the animal kingdom to the realm of plants, the demesne in which the true ancients reside.

When I ask the Australian National University's Dr Matthew Brookhouse, an academic and forester, about the longest living trees in Australia, he tells me that a great deal depends on what qualifies as life.

'What we need to define is the age of what we're interested in: is it the age of the organism or is it the age of the stem?'

If we focus on the stem – the bit that looks like our traditional notion of a tree – then certain Huon pines can be dated as 2000 years old, making them more or less contemporaneous with Jesus.

'But what we see as the tree', Brookhouse continues, 'is really just the current aerial projection of the organism, like a potato or like a daffodil bulb. What's lying below the ground is the longer term embodiment of that organism.'

On that basis, particular clumps of Huon pine could be said to have lived for perhaps 11 000 years, with vegetative cloning rendering the 'individual' trees genetically identical.

Other forms of clonal life stretch way back into deep time. A stand of King's holly in Tasmania has been alive for an unthinkable 43 000 years, while the Wollemi pine of the Blue Mountains west of Sydney seems to have been cloning itself for even longer.

There is, Shakespeare said, 'no clock in the forest', and the Wollemi pine proves his point.

Brookhouse specialises in dendrochronology, the science of tree rings. The field itself stretches way back in history, with the ancient Greeks aware that trees produced new rings each year and Leonardo da Vinci describing the correlation between ring thickness and climate.

'Except for those very long records from ice cores, the temperature reconstructions spanning thousands of years come from tree rings', Brookhouse says. 'Much of what we know about how unusual the current temperatures are comes from trees.'

Experts described this year's bushfires in Tasmania as 'unprecedented', with the blazes devastating some of the oldest forests in the state. King's holly will, in all likelihood, become extinct in the wild, partly because of fires and partly from an introduced pathogen called phytophthora, something that also menaces the Wollemi pine.

Does Brookhouse feel an emotional tug when studying such ancient trees?

'Absolutely. I have a sense of quiet respect for an organism that predates us all.' He hesitates. 'Actually, the emotional response to plants of that age is strongest when you see them deteriorating or when you see one die as a consequence of something we've done – really, in the blink of an eye, relative to the tree's experience.'

Adam Lee expresses something similar. The Melbourne keeper explains that the reptiles and amphibians with which he works have been hit hard by the environmental emergency, with frogs, in particular, in the midst of a mass extinction.

The giant tortoises once roamed in great herds (known, delightfully, as 'creeps') across the volcanic atolls around the Seychelles.

'I wish I could have been there', says Lee, giving Wilbur's long neck a rub. 'It is like a dream.'

But sailors on the long voyages necessitated by the spice trade seized the giant tortoises as living meat stores, and now conservationists classify all the species as endangered.

Wilbur came to the zoo from the Seychelles in 1965, back in an era when keepers could casually swap a koala for a tortoise.

Since then, much has changed but Wilbur retains a long memory for his friends and for his enemies.

'I spent a lot of time bonding with him,' says Lee. 'At the start he'd be trying to bite me and over time the aggression diminished to the point where, when I came in, he would walk over and rest his head on my arm and let me give him a little scratch. He's much better these days but there used to be two or three keepers that he was friendly with – and with all the rest he was aggressive.'

He laughs.

'Well, as aggressive as a giant tortoise can be.'

Without question, Wilbur's age lends him a certain gravitas. He could, after all, live for another century or more – and, because of that, he seems almost a proxy for nature as a whole, separate from humanity and yet now dependent upon us.

'We have pets and you generally know you are going to outlive your pet', Lee says. 'It is weird to think that here is another animal with which I have a bond and it's going to outlive me. It's humbling.'

A single reptile or an organism as massive as the Great Barrier Reef: the fates of those other lives is now entwined with our own.

Lee rubs the tortoise's head once more.

'I am here with Wilbur now; I will do what I can to make his life positive. And then it will be someone else's turn.'

The art of losing

'The art of losing isn't hard to master.'

Since the New South Wales bushfires of 2019–2020, the opening line from Elizabeth Bishop's great poem 'One Art' feels remarkably apposite.

Bishop writes of loss and its acceptance, themes with a new and awful currency in the time of environmental collapse.

For this is an era in which, to borrow her words, 'so many things seem filled with the intent/to be lost'.

We've just watched koalas, creatures already at risk from deforestation, incinerated in their hundreds (perhaps thousands). We lost millions of other animals at the same time, and the devastation of habitats will doom more in the months ahead, especially since ecosystems that never previously knew fire now burn for weeks.

The Australian catastrophe mirrors events elsewhere.

In the past forty years, more than half the world's wildlife has gone.

Rainforests are disappearing at the astonishing rate of

thirty football fields a minute. Some estimates place 75 per cent of coral reefs at risk from either local or global stress.

As the environmental writer David Wallace-Wells says, most of the carbon we've burned has been consumed since the premiere of *Seinfeld*. In the remarkably brief time bookended between now and a show about nothing, we've set in train the destruction of wonders that we barely comprehend.

Researchers recently proved that bees perform basic arithmetic, a gobsmacking discovery with profound implications about the nature of intelligence. Yet in Europe some 800 varieties of wild bee species appear on the critically endangered list, a subset of the 40 per cent of all insect species said to be in decline.

We know now that, like birds, reef fish sing a chorus to the sun each morning. We also know that, like birds, they're dying – fish populations throughout the oceans are decreasing precipitously.

Bishop describes personal calamities in a poem referencing her notoriously painful childhood. She barely knew her father; she was separated from her mentally ill mother at an early age.

After inheriting a private income, she travelled widely, on journeys not always happy.

'I lost two cities, lovely ones', she writes:

> ... And, vaster,
> some realms I owned, two rivers, a continent.
> I miss them, but it wasn't a disaster.

Today we cannot help but read those lines differently, with the devastation of cities, rivers and even continents an imminent prospect.

Venice is flooding; the whole Murray-Darling basin is running dry; the Arctic (warming twice as fast as the rest of the planet) has been burning for months on end.

Will we miss them? Will their destruction be a disaster?

In the face of inevitable bereavement, Bishop writes of the acceptance – even the cultivation – of loss:

> Lose something every day. Accept the fluster
> of lost door keys, the hour badly spent.

In that way, she says, grief might become manageable. It's a strategy that many of us adopt.

'We are on track', tweets the UN environment program, 'for a temperature rise of over 3°C. This would bring mass extinctions & large parts of the planet would be uninhabitable'.

Who can assimilate a warning like that? How do we go about our daily business knowing that unless something gives, much of the world will be ruined forever?

Like Bishop, we adjust to small losses, one day at a time. We accept the strange absence of once-common birds. We forget that, as children, we saw insects in great numbers and variety and now ... we just don't. We adjust our holidays to visit the forests that aren't burned, the reefs that haven't bleached.

Like Bishop, we tell ourselves: 'None of these will bring disaster'.

Bertolt Brecht, a more directly political writer, phrased the same thought somewhat differently in one of his anti-war poems:

> When evil-doing comes like falling rain, nobody calls
> out 'stop!'
> When crimes begin to pile up they become invisible.

Or, at least, they become invisible for a while.

In the shattering conclusion of 'One Art', Bishop addresses directly the loss that haunts the poem: the absence of her lover:

> Even losing you (the joking voice, a gesture
> I love) I shan't have lied. It's evident
> the art of losing's not too hard to master
> though it may look like (Write it!) like disaster.

In those lines the discipline of a very controlled poem collapses, precisely because, while some losses can be artfully mastered, others just cannot.

The catastrophe unfolding around us falls into the second category. Whatever coping mechanism we adopt, no ironic distance will normalise the ruination of a planet: a disaster that cannot – must not! – be borne.

Where have the Christmas beetles gone?

How many Christmas beetles have you seen this year? The insects – a genus containing some thirty-five separate species – traditionally appear in summer. Many settlers saw the scarabs, shimmering in festive red and green, as embodying the European holiday tradition.

'Some forgotten chord is strumming', explained the folk poet Clement RE Grainger back in 1932, 'when beetles start their humming/for they speak of joy and gladness/perfect love and deepest woe'.

Today that humming's become much more difficult to hear.

Those of us who remember the beetles from our childhood can't help but notice how rarely they appear now.

Entomologist Chris Reid, a research scientist at the Australian Museum, says beetle populations have almost certainly declined.

'From my own experience, I have not seen Christmas beetles in numbers in the southern suburbs, where I live on the edge of Royal National [park], since about eight or nine years ago.'

But we lack hard data on their situation, in a country short of both professional and amateur entomologists.

'If you contrast Australia with western Europe', Reid says, 'there's no comparison with the number of people observing insects'.

Earlier this month, David Yeates, from the Australian National Insect Collection at the CSIRO, spoke about the widespread perception among experts that insects were in trouble, as were the creatures that fed upon them.

'The worry is', Yeates said, 'if insect populations are in decline, so are the populations of larger animals such as birds and lizards who rely on them as food. We know in alpine New South Wales, there's been a collapse in Bogong moth populations – a staple food source for iconic Mountain Pygmy possums in spring, and this decline is resulting in the possums starving. But for most species these detailed interconnections are unknown'.

Assessing populations poses a particular problem in an era of ecological collapse.

In a recent article for *New Scientist*, Adam Vaughan notes the difficulty in keeping perspective on wildlife abundance.

He cites an anecdote from the butterfly collector SG Castle Russell who, in 1892, reported such a proliferation of insects in England's New Forest that he could barely see ahead, with two sweeps of his net securing more than a hundred specimens.

We don't see butterflies in swarms like that – and nor do we think we should.

Hence the phenomenon noted by oceanographer Loren McClenachan, in which historical photos taken in Key West since 1956 show generations of anglers posing proudly with ever-smaller catches.

We adapt our expectations to the current reality, forgetting that not so long ago the natural world looked startlingly different.

'[The] big fish that used to be abundant ... aren't any more', says McClenachan, 'and that's happened really, really quickly'.

Many Australians don't realise that the land near modern Melbourne once resembled, as Tim Flannery puts it, 'a temperate Kakadu', in which a shockingly blue lake teemed with swans, ducks, brolgas, magpie geese, Cape Barren geese and other migratory birds.

Arriving in Sydney with the First Fleet, the surgeon Arthur Bowes Smyth wrote in wonderment of how 'the singing of various birds among the trees, and the flight of the numerous parakeets, lorikeets, cockatoos and macaws, made all around appear like an enchantment'.

In Hobart in 1804 the clergyman Robert Knopwood complained about the whales that disturbed locals with their bellowing and so crowded the local rivers as to make navigation by boat difficult.

Today, when Christmas beetles often appear in ones or twos, it's difficult to grasp Grainger's enthusiasm for their 'humming'.

But in November 1936, a local paper in Maryborough reported that the scarabs had 'made their presence felt' in the town, swarming in such numbers that 'the noise of their whirring wings in confined spaces between buildings was like the sound of a far-off aeroplane'.

Nine years later, the *Sydney Morning Herald* explained that 'where these gregarious pests gather their whirring fills the air and branches are quickly denuded of leaves', before adding a sinister coda: 'poison sprays and DDT are effective'.

Today, Reid blames the city sprawl for the lack of beetles, with, for example, the spread of western Sydney covering traditional habitat in the Cumberland Plain woodland with roads and new housing.

Their larvae live in the soil, feeding on roots and rotten wood until they pupate and dig their way out with their strong forelegs. That means they're particularly susceptible to drought. 'We know that if the soil is too dry and hard, they just die in the pupal cells because they can't get out.'

But Reid also sees a general decline in other species. 'When I'm out walking, I take a net with me. I'm always looking at what's on vegetation and I'm not seeing very much. And then with the fires, you've got another layer on top of everything.'

But we simply don't know how much we're losing.

That's why the Australian Museum offers a Christmas Beetle ID app. There are also citizen science apps such as iNaturalist Australia, Wild Pollinator Count and Butterflies Australia, programs designed to gather more data on threatened species.

It's an emotional time to be working as an entomologist, as the ecological diversity that once existed slips away.

'I've been talking about this a lot with colleagues', Reid says. 'One of the classic plants for insects in Australia is tea tree. And about this time of year, tea trees are flowering in abundance and there's normally clouds of insects all over them. And we're not seeing that.'

On the Collins Street falcons

Peregrine falcons have been nesting in a box high on the roof of 367 Collins Street Melbourne since the early 1990s. For most of that time, a crude closed-circuit video has broadcast their comings and goings to a monitor in the foyer. In 2017, the management replaced the old equipment with a modern webcam – and thus gave rise to one of the country's most wholesome fandoms.

This year, the falcons screen via Facebook Live, which, perhaps unexpectedly, adds a new pleasure: you can now witness the birds, as well as the unadulterated joy they bring to their many viewers.

'It is absolutely the best thing', writes someone.

'I could just watch them all day', says someone else.

With the great extinction grinding on, birds as a whole fare about as well – or, if you prefer, about as poorly – as you might expect.

A recent North American study reported a 29 per cent decline in populations across the United States and Canada over the past fifty years – a disappearance of something like 3 billion birds. Across the Atlantic, the European Bird

Census Council says that populations of farmland birds in twenty-eight different countries have fallen 55 per cent in three decades.

Amidst so much death, there's something genuinely touching about the concern shown by falcon-watchers about every possible threat menacing the Collins Street nest.

'Is it a night vision camera or is there a light shining on them?' asks Angela, while watching the female peregrine of an evening. 'She looks annoyed!'

'Infrared', reassures Suzanne. 'She can't see it. She always looks annoyed (or angry). That's her look. She's fierce!'

Indeed she is. Most of the time, the camera records her (or her much smaller mate) sitting serenely on three little fluff balls – and then, every so often, one of the birds appears with a recently deceased pigeon, which then gets ripped apart in grisly fashion.

You can find these kind of animal cams all over the internet. Animal Planet L!VE, for instance, offers a veritable Noah's Ark of streaming talent, from 'leafcutter ant cam' to 'black eagle cam', 'puffin cam' and 'sea turtle cam'.

When I tuned in, the polar bear feed had gone temporarily extinct but I did catch some walruses putting on a spectacular show of grunting and snorting. Jelly cam was undeniably trippy and the stream broadcasting from underwater on an Australian reef presented a relaxing combination of tropical fish and seaweed.

Still, I found myself coming back to the peregrines.

Why look at animals? John Berger poses the question in his famous essay lamenting the decline of our intimate contact with the wild. Today, we view animals mostly from a position of control, as in the spectacular but staged shots of nature photography – or, in particular, a zoo or nature reserve. But, for Berger, we can't truly 'see' an animal under such circumstances because its extraction from nature changes it totally, replacing its wildness with a dependence on the humans around it.

'Everywhere animals disappear', he says. 'In zoos they constitute the living monument to their own disappearance.'

Unlike many of the Animal Planet streets, the Collins Street falcons don't live in zoo. But they don't inhabit a forest, either – and, in many ways, it's their reappropriation of the modern city that makes them so compelling.

Modernity, says Berger, means the reduction of the animal, as part of the same process by which humans have been 'reduced to isolated productive and consuming units.'

Surely that's why so many of us cubicle drones obsess over the falcons: revelling in the incongruity of their wildness in a street synonymous with Melbourne finance.

'They are so stunning.' That, and similar sentiments, appear again and again on the livestream.

For Berger, such moments of aesthetic pleasure represent hope, even in the midst of deep alienation from the natural world. 'That we find a crystal or a poppy beautiful', he says, 'means that we are less alone, that we are more deeply inserted into existence than the course of a single life would lead us to believe.'

There's something of that in a city falcon.

Revolving on wheels

In June 2021, Britain's Clarion Cycling Club – a group founded by readers of the *Clarion* newspaper in 1894 – voted, at a bitterly contested annual general meeting, to drop from its constitution a commitment to 'the principles of socialism.'[1]

The decision became international news, mostly, one suspects, because many found the association between socialism and cycling incongruous, even quaint.

Yet the *Clarion*'s pedal-powered militants reflect a deep and fascinating history of two-wheeled radicalism.

'Human ingenuity, in evolving the bicycle', declared the great American socialist Eugene V. Debs in 1895, 'has given a mighty boon. It is to play a great part in the world's affairs.'[2]

Debs made those remarks from the gaol in which he'd been incarcerated after leading a quarter of a million Pullman rail porters out on strike, something that spurred the *New York Times* to dub him 'a lawbreaker at large, an enemy of the human race.'

Yet, when a reporter from the *Cleveland Plain Dealer*

visited him in his cell, Debs enthused about that 'mighty leveller upward and downward', the humble bike.

'The limits of an interview', he said, 'will only admit the merest glimpse of the possibilities of the bicycle'.

His ebullience makes more sense in context. The *Plain Dealer* had also asked for his opinion on the so-called 'New Woman' – and Debs a gave full-throated endorsement of women's struggles to become 'at least the equal of man'.[3] Those struggles had, in the mid-1890s, become entwined with what was often called the 'bicycle craze', so much so that the feminist leader Susan B Anthony labelled cycling as contributing more to the emancipation of women than anything else in the world.

'I stand and rejoice every time I see a woman on a wheel', said Anthony. 'It gives a woman a feeling of freedom and self-reliance.'[4]

Cycling, she thought, facilitated independent travel over considerable distances and so possessed a practical and symbolic importance for those previously confined to the hearth.

'The bicycle', predicted Elizabeth Cady Stanton, in an 1895 piece for *American Wheelman*, 'will inspire women with more courage, self-respect and self-reliance and make the next generation more vigorous of mind and of body ...'[5]

As early as 1890, women made up a third of the membership of the Cyclists' Touring Club in Britain, escaping the stuffy mores of late Victorian convention, on what journalists dubbed their 'steeds of steel'.

When the short story writer Marguerite Merington discussed cycling for *Scribner's* magazine, she commented on how many women loathed the narrowness of their allocated sphere. Cycling, she suggested, offered an antidote to this 'disorder of the soul', allowing a woman 'to flatten her sphere to a circle, mount it, and take to the road.'[6]

The bicycle enabled travel at an unparalleled speed, so much so that enthusiasts were warned about getting 'bicycle face' by rushing too fast against the wind. The velocities possible on the machine particularly appealed to the young: as the American urban planner Sylvester Baxter said, cycling 'quickened the perceptive faculties of young people and made them more alert.'[7]

A new generation of independently minded young women enthused about the physicality of 'scorching' or high-speed riding. The cycle took its rider out of the home and into the world, requiring – and, indeed, conveying – a familiarity with the traditionally masculine business of mechanics, sufficient at least to keep tyres pumped and chains oiled.

Upon her bike, the cyclist asserted a right to interests and hobbies of her own, as the vaudevillian Frank Dumont lamented in 1897. His satire *The New Woman's Husband* opened with its pitiable protagonist Mr Sheep on his hands and knees.

'Here's a nice position for a man', he moaned. 'I've got to scrub the floor and do the housework, just because my wife wants to go out riding on her bike. Oh! That's what I get for marrying a new woman!'[8]

In 1895, the Pennsylvania *Columbian* declared the 'woman on the wheel' to be 'riding to greater freedom, to a nearer equality with man, to the habit of taking care of herself, and to new views on the subject of clothes philosophy.'[9]

That last issue became particularly contested. The guidebook *Bicycling for Ladies* celebrated the 'absolute freedom of the cyclist' but explained that it could not 'be properly enjoyed unless the clothing is suitable'. Male cyclists of the day possessed multiple outfits, with an enthusiast donning a formal club uniform for a bicycle parade, a casual outfit for regular riding, summer gear for hot days and a racing uniform for competitions.[10] By comparison, Ward's stipulations seemed modest: she advised the aspiring wheelwoman to equip herself with knickerbockers, stockings, gaiters, hat, gloves and 'no skirt, or skirt with length decided by individual preference'.[11]

But the suggestion that young ladies might exercise preferences as to the length of their skirts – or, indeed, whether to wear skirts at all – horrified conservatives on both sides of the Atlantic.

Because cyclists necessarily eschewed tight corsets, moralists associated them with other immodestly dressed 'loose women'. The supposed link between cycling and sexual immorality reflected archetypically 19th-century preoccupations. A female rider straddled her machine in a posture deeply troubling to the Victorian mind, and so an extensive medical literature developed about cycling and self-stimulation.

A bicycle saddle, one practitioner cautioned, could be tilted 'as desired', allowing its lascivious owner to fit it 'snugly over the entire vulva and reach up in front, [to] bring about constant friction over the clitoris and labia'. Such pressure would, he said, be accentuated were the cyclist to stoop forward to race, with 'the warmth generated from vigorous exercise ... further increase[ing] the feeling.'

In other words, the faster a young lady pedalled, the more pleasure she received. As another doctor put it, 'the moment speed is desired', the female rider bent forward, thus causing her 'clothing to press against the clitoris, thereby eliciting and arousing feelings hitherto unknown and unrealised by the young maiden.'[12]

To dispel the suggestion their products might engender such sensations, manufacturers advertised ladies' models with the seats free of the 'harmful pressure exerted by other saddles' or the handlebars placed higher to prevent 'scorching'. Rambler, for instance, promoted its women's bicycle as designed to maintain 'an erect and graceful position, the secret of the well-known fact that ladies when riding Ramblers present a more pleasing and attractive appearance than on any other machine.'[13]

Bicycling supporters mounted a separate counter-attack with their own medical experts attesting to cycling's health-giving properties. An array of writings – including 'The Hygiene of the Bicycle', 'The psychological and Hygienic influence of the Bicycle', and HC Clark's *Hygienic Bicycling* – sought to align the hobby with the late 19th-century preoccupation with hygiene.[14]

Nevertheless, the connotations of women's cycling still troubled the religiously minded, with, in 1896, the American anti–sex work Women's Rescue League passing a resolution denouncing 'the great curse ... inflicted on the people of this country because of the present bicycle craze.'[15]

The League considered the machine 'the devil's advocate agent morally and physically', arguing that it 'helped swell the ranks of reckless girls who finally drift into the standing army of outcast women of the United States more than any other medium.'[16]

Yet the moralists increasingly found themselves a minority as cyclists grew ever bolder. In 1898, for instance, a certain Martha Sprague, landlady of the Hautboy Hotel in Sussex, denied refreshments to a cyclist dressed in what the newspapers called a 'rational costume' – that is, bloomers and a short jacket.[17] Unfortunately for Mrs Sprague, the bloomer-clad bike-rider revealed herself as Florence Wallace Pomeroy, Viscountess Harberton and the founder of the Rational Dress Society, and a member of the Cyclist Touring Club.

The formidable Lady Harberton promptly sued the hotel and, though the court eventually found the establishment not guilty of 'wilfully and unlawfully neglecting and refusing to supply a traveller with victuals', the proceedings brought considerable publicity to the dress reform cause.[18]

The Harberton affair exemplified how cycling made public issues that had previously been considered personal. The League might bemoan the bicycle's 'imprudent associations', but the typical scorcher conveyed neither shame nor embarrassment as she raced past her critics with a contagious exhilaration.

'It really doesn't matter much', said the *San Francisco Call* in 1895, 'where this one individual young lady is going on her wheel. It may be that she's going to the park on pleasure bent, or to the store for a dozen hairpins, or to call on a sick friend at the other side of town, or to get a doily pattern of somebody, or a recipe for removing tan and freckles. Let that be as it may. What the interested public wishes to know is,

Where are all the women on wheels going? Is there a grand rendezvous somewhere toward which they are all headed and where they will some time hold a meet that will cause this wobbly old world to wake up and readjust itself?'[19]

The prominent suffragette Frances Willard asked herself the same question – and set out to cover the answer.

'As a temperance reformer', she explained, 'I always felt a strong attraction toward the bicycle, because it is the vehicle of so much harmless pleasure, and because the skill required in handling it obliges those who mount to keep clear heads and steady hands. Nor could I see a reason in the world why a woman should not ride the silent steed so swift and blithesome.'

At age 53, Willard documented her struggle to master cycling in her book *A Wheel Within a Wheel,* helpfully subtitled *How I Learned to Ride the Bicycle.* She acknowledged that she laboured under several disadvantages: what she called 'the impedimenta that result from the unnatural style of dress', as well as the 'sedentary habits of a lifetime.'

A photograph in her book shows the stout campaigner clinging grimly to a bike as three top-hatted gentlemen ('all strong-armed and accomplished bicyclers') hold its frame steady. The caption 'A lack of balance' explains her predicament.[20]

By the 1890s, the bicycle had evolved significantly since the contraption unveiled in 1817 by Karl von Drais of Karlsruhe in Badenia. The English name 'hobby horse' hinted at how that proto-bike functioned mostly as a briefly fashionable diversion. The later pedal velocipede of 1869 enjoyed slightly more success, though again the label 'boneshaker' suggested its limitations as a viable conveyance.[21]

The invention of the 'Ordinary' or 'penny farthing', a contraption relying on its huge front wheel to cushion shocks, transformed the cycle into something more than a novelty. Ordinaries proved themselves mechanically reliable over considerable distances, with, as early as 1872, John Keen (the 'King of the Bicycles' or 'Happy Jack') riding 10 miles in under 36 minutes at an impressive pace of three and a half minutes per mile.[22]

Yet the Ordinary positioned its rider distressingly far from the ground, something that made a machine lacking brakes hazardous for the casual enthusiast.

'The greatest wonder to me', noted one contemporary, was 'that not more cyclers who rode high wheelers were killed'.

To most people, riding resembled an extreme sport, with its risks 'commonly imagined to be about the same as those which beset the professional tightrope walker'.[23] Both expensive and dangerous, the Ordinary defined its rider, suggest bicycle historians Steven E Alford and Suzanne Ferriss, as 'upper class, athletic and masculine'.[24]

The development of the so-called 'safety' bicycle inaugurated a new era. On Safeties, aficionados balanced between two equal-sized wheels, feet reassuringly near *terra firma*. Gearing, pneumatic tyres, chain-driven rear wheels: these innovations changed the bicycle from a specialised piece of sporting equipment into something more like a practical means of transportation.

Nevertheless, 'Safety' remained a relative term.

In Banjo Paterson's poem 'Mulga Bill's Bicycle', for example, the titular bushman purchases the new contraption, assuring a sceptical assistant that he would 'ride this here two-wheeled concern right straight away at sight'. Predictably, the attempt goes terribly awry, with the machine careering off the mountain road and depositing Bill in a nearby river.

'I'll give that two-wheeled outlaw best', he concludes ruefully, 'it's shaken all my nerve …

> To feel it whistle through the air and plunge and buck
> and swerve.
> It's safe at rest in Dead Man's Creek, we'll leave it lying
> still;
> A horse's back is good enough henceforth for Mulga
> Bill.[25]

Willard, however, was made of sterner stuff than Bill. Trundling along the lawns of Lady Henry Somerset's estate, Willard imagined her machine – which she dubbed 'Gladys' – speaking to her. 'Behold, I do not fail you', the bicycle said. 'I am not a skittish beastie, but a sober, well-conducted roadster.'

A second, happier illustration in the book depicts the author astride Gladys as two ladies in long Victorian gowns gaze enviously at the newly minted wheelwoman.

'So easy – when you know how', reads the title.[26]

Many riders of the 1890s expressed a similar self-satisfaction, a reflection of the substantial prestige attached to the bicycle. Mulga Bill, for instance, abandons his faithful horse out of a desire to outdo the flashy city folk. In town, he garbs himself in 'resplendent' cycling clothes; he wheels his 'shining new machine' with an 'air of lordly pride'.

Bill's conceit (prior to his terrifying descent) recalls Trotsky's assessment of the Tsar's 'bicycle battalion', the conservatism of which he attributes to the glamour of their machines. '[L]et a man find himself', Trotsky quipped, 'in distinction from others, on top of two wheels with a chain … and his vanity begins to swell out like his tires'.[27]

In America in the early years of the 1890s, a new bike cost somewhere between $125 and $150, a hefty sum when the per capita income stood at about $1000 annually.[28] The price tag contributed to its status, and ensured the dominance of riders from the middle and upper classes.

An 1896 drawing by *Punch* cartoonist Phil May highlights the class divisions running through the cycling fad. He sketches a smartly dressed enthusiast sailing past a working-class woman and her daughter.

'Wouldn't yer like ter 'ave one o' them things, Liza Ann?' asks the mother.

'No', says the child. 'I wouldn't be seen on one. I don't think they're nice for lidies!'[29]

The gag depended on *Punch*'s readers considering cycling an affectation of the elite, a practice to which the masses remained indifferent or even hostile. But that was not entirely true – or, at least, not always.

Bikes only became an unexceptionable part of working-class life after the First World War, by which time sportier members of the elite had already embraced the automobile.

Yet, if obtaining a cycle in the 1890s wasn't easy for those of modest means, it was not entirely out of the question, particularly with the emergence of hire-purchase schemes and a burgeoning secondhand market. Unlike horses, bikes did not demand feed or pasture, and that made them easier to justify on a tight budget.

In his bicycling novel *The Wheels of Chance,* the Fabian novelist HG Wells describes the draper's assistant Hoopdriver, striving 'against all the conditions of his calling, against the counsels of prudence and the restrictions of his means' to obtain a machine of his own.

The young Hoopdriver takes the precious bicycle to the road for his brief annual holiday and, pedalling along, feels himself transformed into 'a gentleman, a man of pleasure'.[30] After a series of adventures – mostly centred on his encounter with a fast-riding New Woman – the youth resolves to expand his horizons and remake his life.

Wells' novel showed how a passion for cycling could, despite its expense, still enthuse the lower orders.

Another *Punch* cartoon from the time makes the same point. It depicts a vicar's daughter conversing with a servant.

'Oh, Withers', says the lady, 'your mistress tells me you are saving up to take a little shop and look after your mother. I think it is such a sweet idea'.

'Well, yes, miss', says Withers. 'I did think of it; but now I've got the money I've changed my mind, and I'm going to buy myself one of these 'ere bicycles instead'.[31] For Withers, as for Hoopdriver, cycling, despite its expense, allows the humble to encroach on the realm of their betters.

Such transformational possibilities explain the bike's association with socialism. In 1891, Robert Blatchford launched the *Clarion,* one of the most influential radical papers Britain has yet known. Blatchford advocated a homespun doctrine of ethical fellowship, expressed most forcefully in his *Merrie England*, a book said to have sold more than two million copies.

'English socialism is not Marxian', Blatchford explained. 'It is humanitarian. It does not depend upon any theory of "economic justice" but upon humanity and common sense.'

The *Clarion* propagated this 'common sense' with tremendous panache, eventually reaching some 40 000 readers each week.[32] Ecumenical to the point of eclecticism, it made room for all the different currents of the British Left, with Blatchford himself belonging simultaneously to the Independent Labour Party, the Social Democratic Federation and the Fabians.

'There was never a paper like it', wrote the socialist feminist Margaret Cole:

> It was not in the least the preconceived idea of a socialist journal. It was not solemn; it was not highbrow; it did not deal in theoretical discussion, or inculcate dreary-isms. It was full of stories, jokes and verses – sometimes pretty bad verses and pretty bad jokes – as well as articles. It was written in language that anyone could understand, 'with no middle class unction' ... it believed that anyone whatever his condition or education, who could read plain English could be made into a socialist, and that socialism was not a difficult dogma, but a way of living and thinking which could make all men behave like brothers in the ordinary pursuits of life.[33]

That last point was particularly important. The *Clarion* positioned itself as an advocate of 'the new life', presenting the socialist future as prefigured in the everyday doings of its supporters. On that basis, it sponsored a whole range of activities understood as contributing something to the shared goal. The *Clarion* ran what it called Cinderella Clubs, regular events at which impoverished children could receive entertainment and food, as well as instruction in basic socialist principles. It promoted glee clubs and camping trips and photography classes and Labour Churches and much else besides.

In 1894, Blatchford formed a Scouting Corps that organised young people to spread 'socialistic principles' and destroy 'anti-socialist prejudices'. The Scouts were instructed to take tracts and leaflets into working-class neighbourhoods, 'their duty being', as Blatchford put it, 'to permeate their companions with Socialism'.[34]

That duty became more fun on a bike. 'How about a cycling corps of *Clarion* scouts', suggested one comrade. 'A pocketful of leaflets and an extra copy or two of the *Clarion* carefully left at the different stopping places maybe have good results.'[35]

A National Clarion Cycling Club duly emerged, aiming to organise 'cyclists for Mutual Aid, Good Fellowship and the Propagation of the Principles of Socialism, along with the social pleasures of cycling'.

Before the year was out, some eighty clubs had affiliated. Riding together to spread their gospel, the scouts undertook an adventure quite different from the humdrum routine of everyday life, with their shared convictions only accentuating the liberty of the open road. Their official anthem celebrated that spirit:

> Oh! Who rides by day and night, round about
> Tinkling his bicycle bell?
> Hark how he nears us with laudate shout.
> Hurrah! Hurah! 'Tis the Clarion Scout!

But alongside the merry bell-tinkling, Scouting entailed serious class combat, as the song also explained.

> Down to the haunts of the parson and squire
> Putting opponents to rout;
> Bestriding his steed with a pneumatic tyre.
> Through village and hamlet thro' mud and thro' mire
> Rideth the Clarion Scout
> Nailing down lies and disposing of fables
> Improving the landscape by sticking up labels ...[36]

In *The Ragged Trousered Philanthropists*, Robert Tressell writes of the reception accorded by the fictional town of Mugsborough to a group of cycling socialists (clearly based on Clarion scouts).

He describes 'a band of about twenty-five men and women on bicycles' riding into town, two of them carrying on their handlebars flags of crimson silk reading 'International Brotherhood and Peace' and 'One for All and All for One' in gold letters.

Tressell then depicts the locals attacking the visitors with rocks.

'We'll give the b--rs Socialism!' shouts one.

'We'll teach 'em to come 'ere trying to undermined our bloody morality', howls another, throwing a lump of granite at a scout.[37]

Tressell's deeply pessimistic novel reflected his despair at the political backwardness of the house painters with whom he worked. Symptomatically, the only bicycle possessed by his characters belongs to the foreman, Misery, who rides silently around monitoring the men.

'Hope the b--r falls orf and breaks 'is bloody neck', a worker mutters as Misery pedals past.

Yet despite their bleak lives, Mugsburough's painters defend the established order. They want, says Tressell bitterly, 'nothing but to be allowed to work'. It is only the few socialists among them who yearn 'to be able to go for country walks or bicycle rides, to go out fishing or to go to the seaside and bathe and lie on the beach and so forth'. The *Clarion* movement recognised that yearning, yoking the immediate pleasures of cycling to a deeper need for social change.

Socialists were not alone in capitalising on the cycling craze. In America at the same time, the Salvation Army established its own unit of peddling proselytisers. 'If the devil goes awheel about the world', explained Major Hanson Caygill of the newly formed Bicycle Brigade, 'we feel justified to take the means to combat him and his works'.[38]

Yet the bicycle arguably suited freewheeling socialists more than it did buttoned-up evangelicals. 'Being able to depart for where we will', says philosopher Hannah Arendt, 'is the protypal gesture of being free, as limitation of freedom of movement has from time immemorial been the precondition for enslavement.'[39]

The readers of the *Clarion* would have understood exactly what she meant. If they could somehow obtain a bicycle, they could leave their cramped houses and experience something of the liberty their newspaper advocated. In a largely gender-segregated society, men and women could together enjoy the camaraderie of the wheel. Bikes allowed them to promulgate their creed, even while it conveyed something of the fellowship they sought to universalise.

In Germany, cyclists organised into the Worker's Cycling Federation: Solidarity (*Arbeiter-Radfahrerbund Solidarität*). At its peak, it boasted some 300 000 supporters, operated a bicycle factory, bicycle stores, restaurants and repair stations, and published as a biweekly paper called *The Worker-Cyclist*. Describing themselves as the 'Enlightenment Patrols of Social Democracy and the 'Red Hussars of the Class Struggle', its members prided themselves on speeding away from the police after dispersing their leaflets in city streets.[40]

In Italy, militant riders joined the *Ciclisti Rossi* or 'Red Cyclists', whose newspaper *Avanti* advocated the bike as a machine 'created for the benefit of the organised masses of workers'; in the United States, the Socialist Labor Party created a short-lived Socialist Wheelmen's Club; in Australia, the Victorian Socialist Party equipped its comrades through its own Co-op Cycle Factory.[41]

But nowhere were bicyclers more significant to socialism than in Britain's *Clarion* movement, with its Scouts, as their song explained, 'as bold as Lysander/to push propaganda.'

The paper lost much of its working-class influence when the erratic Blatchford threw his support behind jingoism during the First World War. When it folded in 1931, the Clarion Cycling Club, like many of the movement's other cultural associations, continued as an independent group. The club retained something of a political tinge, but, as the years passed, the pleasures of riding became increasingly removed from the advocacy of socialism.

In that sense, the amendment of 2021, in which support for 'fairness, equality, inclusion and diversity' replaced an explicit commitment to socialism, merely brought the constitution into line with existing reality.

Yet one can't help but feel the club's repositioning oddly ill-timed, given the manifold crises of the 21st century.

In the 1890s, the bicycle had heralded the triumph of modernity. The French science writer Louis Baudry de Saunier even hailed it for ushering in a new kind of human: a 'man made of half of flesh and half of steel that only our century of science and iron could have spawned'.[42]

But after the First World War, enthusiasts for the future shifted their allegiance to newer and more spectacular manifestations of the machine age. The dizzying advance of technology reshaped the Left as well as the Right, especially after the Soviet Union embraced massive industrialisation. When the Soviet dictator Joseph Stalin launched Russia's first Five-Year Plan, he urged cadre to fight a war against nature, in rhetoric that linked progress with environmental conquest. Leftists everywhere embraced a Promethean doctrine of industrial transformation, one that made bike-riding feel old-fashioned and twee. Bikes suited schoolkids and countercultures; the proletarian future would be atomic, not pedal-powered.

Today, as every bulletin brings fresh news of ecological collapse, the Stalinist campaign against the environment – like the Stalinist campaign against the people of Russia – belongs to the dustbin of history. Nature doesn't confront us as an enemy to be subdued. How could it? We belong to the natural world, something that has become alarmingly apparent as we change the planet almost beyond recognition.

That's why we might think again about cycling and socialism.

The *Clarion* movement cared deeply about what we call the environment, even though its members didn't use that term. The very title of Blatchford's *Merrie England* – an invocation of a pastoral idyll – conveys their hostility to the industrial landscape.

'Do you find', Blatchford asked his readers, with withering scorn, 'the champions of the factory system despising nature, and beauty, and art, and health – except in their speeches and lectures to you? No. You will find these living as far from the factories as they can get; and you will find them spending their long holidays in the most beautiful parts of England, Scotland, Ireland or the Continent. These pleasures they enjoy are denied to you.'[43]

The bicycle helped ordinary men and women to reclaim such joys, taking them, even if only for a few hours, out of the squalid districts to which they were confined so that they, too, could appreciate fields and hills and rivers and trees.

That was Debs' great point: that bikes allowed the denizens of the cities freedom from 'the fetid odors their overcrowding conditions generate' so that they might enjoy fresh air and exercise.

'Men and women and children will all ride the bicycle', he said, 'and the enrapturing panorama of nature will no longer be forbidden glories to most of the race'.

That might sound quaint to us, accustomed, as we are, to covering vast distances in our cars and planes. But, in the 1890s, the freedom the cycle promised was never exclusively physical.

When the socialists of Debs' time celebrated the health-giving qualities of outdoor exercise, they were not advocating heading back to nature but rather presenting a movement forward. Capitalism, they knew, produced an intense opposition between the city and the country, something that socialism must and would overcome.

In his memoirs, the great Marxist historian Eric Hobsbawm recalls, as a youth in the 1930s, purchasing a Rudge-Whitworth bike on instalment and riding it through south England.

'If physical mobility is an essential condition of freedom', he writes, 'the bicycle has probably been the greatest single device for achieving what Marx has called the full realisation of being human invented since Gutenberg, and the only one without obvious drawbacks'.[44]

As much as he enjoyed rural rides, Hobsbawm did not see his bike as a substitute for political change. It's not a bad thing to pedal to work, but we're not going to end climate change by each altering our daily commute: we're well past the moment at which personal choices make any appreciable difference to a dying planet. To prevent global heating, we need a fundamentally different order, one that mends the metabolic rift capital creates between humanity and nature.

In that context, the bicycle matters most insofar as it helps us to think about the different priorities on an ecosocialist planet. For instance, Hobsbawm points out that bikes travel 'at the speed of human reactions' and, unlike automobiles, do not separate their users from the sights, sounds and smells of the country. As riders move through nature, they're reminded, in the most visceral manner, that they're part of the natural world around them.

A 21st-century socialism would foster that relationship, destroying the ecocidal imperatives of profit and re-integrating human life harmoniously into the rhythms of the one planet we know.

In that prison interview, Debs concluded his paean to the bicycle by anticipating a society in which 'monopoly and special privilege' have been abolished, and the 'variety, design and capacity' of bikes has increased exponentially so that everyone can use them.

'The world', he promised, 'will yet revolve on wheels'.

That prospect now matters more than ever before.

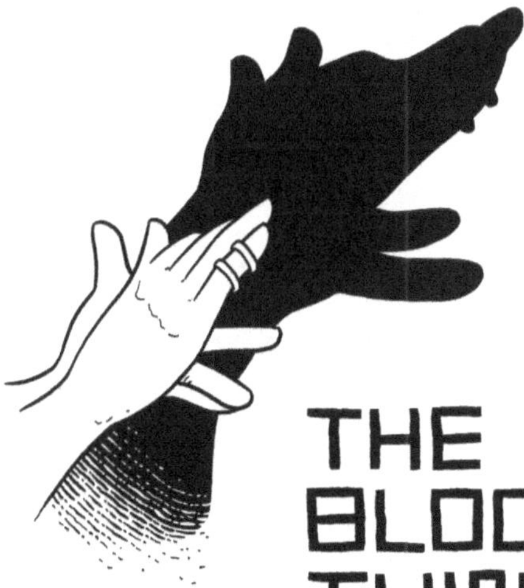

THE BLOODY THING

I grew up in a nation at peace, but almost everything I've published appeared during wartime.

Once upon a time, back when I was a child, it was just possible to believe that something had been learned from the atrocities of the First and Second World Wars; that, after the American defeat in Vietnam, the wealthiest nations had abandoned military adventurism; that war was becoming an anomaly in a world increasingly devoted to peace.

No-one believes that now.

On the contrary, war's been normalised to an almost astonishing degree. A prevailing austerity means that governments decry decarbonisation as ruinously expensive, yet the United States signed off on invasions of Iraq and Afghanistan that have now cost trillions. The generation of young men and women voting for the first time in Australia have lived with the 'War on Terror' the entirety of their lives, with military conflict a constant background hum that sporadically – as after the Russian invasion of Ukraine – becomes deafeningly loud.

I once wrote a book called *Killing: Misadventures in Violence* (on which some of these essays draw), which investigated the social and psychological consequences of deadly force. Researching it, I spoke to scores of men (all my interviewees were male) who'd taken human lives. Some were executioners; most were American army veterans who'd fought in Iraq and Afghanistan.

The soldiers talked about what they'd done and what had been done to them. They didn't all agree on the meaning of the wars in which they'd fought. But their stories left me in no doubt about combat as existentially toxic, not least because many said that they missed it more than they could express and that they dreamed of gunfights every night.

If war destroys people, it also corrupts nations, spreading its poison through the body politic like a carcinogen.

In 1918, the American writer Randolph Bourne described the pressure for social uniformity, describing it as a 'regression' to infantile attitudes. 'In your reaction to an imagined attack in your country or an insult to its government', he wrote, 'you draw closer to the herd for protection, you conform in word and deed, and you insist vehemently that everybody else shall think, speak and act together. And you fix your adoring gaze upon the State, with a truly filial look, as upon the Father of the flock, the quasi-personal symbol of your definite action and ideas'.

Anyone who lived through the early phases of the War on Terror will know what he means.

The pieces that follow cover a variety of different conflicts, in several different eras.

In 2012, I wrote a long essay for *Overland* about rage massacres, the mass gun killings that were once almost unknown but now take place with such frightening regularity that most readers won't even remember the specific atrocities that sparked my piece: the murder of twelve people in a movie theatre in Aurora, Colorado on 20 July and the shooting of six people in a Sikh temple in Oak Creek, Wisconsin, on 5 August. There were twelve mass shootings in the United States in 2012; there were eleven in 2021, despite the COVID-19 lockdown.

Depressingly, the argument as to why America's at war with itself remains just as relevant as a decade ago.

Meanwhile, in Australia, the service at Anzac Day – once barely marked – now possesses an almost religious character, treated with a reverence of which established churches could only dream. According to one calculation, the government spent a staggering $600 million on the anniversary of the First World War, a figure that becomes an even more remarkable $1.1 billion if it includes extensions to the National War Memorial.

In another *Overland* piece, written for Anzac Day in 2012, I argued that the slogan 'lest we forget' – central to all commemorations – prevents us from remembering anything significant at all. The white Australians who obsessively recall the First World War don't, as a rule, devote the same attention to the conflict fought against Indigenous people in the colonial era.

In 2014, I wrote about the so-called Black War in Tasmania, suggesting that remarkable parallels could be found between the white campaign against Indigenous people in Van Diemen's Land and the ongoing dispossession of Palestinians today.

While working on *Killing*, I became briefly obsessed with the fascinating subculture of military re-enactment. In a piece that didn't make it into the final book – but for which I retain a real fondness – I profiled a young Australian dedicated to recreating the minutiae of trench warfare.

I'd like to hope that these articles share a common attitude, one encapsulated in a story that emerged from the First World War.

In that conflict, the British authorities produced a now-famous recruiting poster, showing a cherubic little girl dandling on her father's knee, while on the floor a lad plays with toy soldiers.

'Daddy', she asks the abashed fellow, 'what did you do in the Great War?'

No doubt the campaign, with its carefully targeted appeal to ideas of masculine authority, did shame some men into enlisting.

The Scottish trade union leader Bob Smillie, however, offered a simple response to the girl in the poster. He'd answer her, he said, with these words: 'I tried to stop the bloody thing, my child'.

That, to my mind, remains a truly heroic reply.

‘When the burning moment breaks’: Gun control and rage massacres

On 23 January 1924, a man opened fire with a .44 repeating rifle on the families picnicking in Melbourne’s Botanic Gardens. He shot five people, seemingly targeted at random, before the gun failed. Three died. The murderer, later identified as Norman List, ran from the scene. On 2 February, his body was found in the bush in Pakenham, where he’d killed himself.

Today, in the wake of the Colorado killings and the new atrocity in Wisconsin, all the aspects of List’s deeds seem instantly familiar, recognisable components of what forensic psychiatrist Paul Mullen calls the ‘autogenic massacre’. Mullen defines the crime thus: ‘A heavily armed male, or just occasionally males, enter an area where people congregate and begins shooting victims indiscriminately, continuing with the killing until they turn their guns on themselves, or are shot and killed by police’.

In 1924, such massacres were largely unknown. List’s

killings were an outlier, an anticipation of a pattern that only became more general much later: as Mullen puts it, 'reports of autogenic massacres do not even begin to appear until the twentieth century and only emerge as a recurring theme in the last thirty years.'

It wasn't until 1966, when a young man opened fire on students and staff at the University of Texas, that what we might call the generic conventions of the 'autogenic massacre' established themselves. What was previously a vanishingly rare crime morphed into something increasingly understood as inevitable. In the past three decades, there have been more than thirty massacres in United States schools alone, with six mass killings already in 2012. As Mullen says: 'The autogenic massacre emerged in western society over the last fifty years and is becoming increasingly frequent.'

Why is this happening? What does it mean?

Considerable effort has gone into psychological profiles of would-be killers. But as Christopher Ferguson, Mark Coulson and Jane Barnett note in an academic study, 'Psychological Profiles of School Shooters: Positive Directions and One Big Wrong Turn,' 'Most scholars recognise that empirical evidence on school shooters is slim and that "profiles" of school shooters carry considerable risks of overidentification.'

Clearly, rage gunmen often have psychological problems, often profound ones. But it's necessary to tread carefully here since there's a certain circularity in diagnoses made after terrible crimes: normal people do not commit rage murders; by definition, anyone who does is not normal.

Interestingly, after analysing a number of killers, Mullen

concludes, 'they had personality problems and were, to put it mildly, deeply troubled people.' But he goes on to add: 'Most perpetrators of autogenic massacres do not, however, appear to have active psychotic symptoms at the time and very few even have histories of prior contact with mental health services.'

In any case, individual profiling cannot, by its nature, explain why 'deeply troubled' people today conduct massacres in a way that they did not fifty years earlier. What is required is a social and historical analysis.

Perhaps the most interesting attempt in that direction is developed by Mark Ames in his book *Going Postal*. 'The rage murder is new', he argues. 'It appeared under Reagan, during his cultural and economic revolution, and it expanded in his aftermath. Reaganomics has ruled America ever since.'

Ames's thesis is that the rage massacre entered public consciousness in the United States during the 1980s, after a series of killings by postal workers (hence his title). At the time, the postal service was under particular pressure from what we'd now call neoliberalism, as market reform fostered unbearable stress and unhappiness among the employees. When Ames interviewed massacre survivors, they sometimes expressed a surprising sympathy for the shooters. The experience of work – the activity that most people spend most of their lives performing – had become a waking nightmare, with any sense of job satisfaction destroyed and solidarity between employees collapsing into bullying and minor harassment.

Ames draws a provocative parallel between rage massacres and slavery revolts in the United States south:

both involved, he suggests, a blind rebellion against intolerable conditions, expressed via homicidal destruction. With unions and other forms of collective redress marginalised, employees, like slaves, lashed out at what surrounded them. The argument thus echoes philosopher Hannah Arendt's analysis of the roots of rage, an emotion that she saw as implicitly political.

'Rage', she writes, 'is by no means an automatic reaction to misery and suffering as such; no one reacts with rage to a disease beyond the powers of medicine or to an earthquake, or, for that matter, to social conditions which seem to be unchangeable. Only where there is reason to suspect that conditions could be changed and are not, does rage arise.'

Ames suggests workplace massacres migrated into the United States school system in the 1990s, precisely because the education system manifested the worst aspects of the Reaganite industrial culture. There was, he argues, the 'continuity of misery and entrapment from school to office ... Even physically, they look alike and act on the mind in a similar way: the overhead fluorescent lights, the economies-of-scale-purchased industrial carpeting and linoleum floors, the stench of cleaning chemicals in the restrooms, the same stalls with the same latches and the same metal toilet paper holders ...'

The values of the schoolyard represented, in concentrated form, the values of the society around it. School shooters, like workplace shooters, often complained in their suicide notes of bullying. 'One reason why our society has failed to curb bullying', Ames says, 'is that we like bullies. Hell, we are bullies. Research has shown that bullies are not the anti-social misfits that adults, in their forced amnesia, want them to be. Rather, bullies are usually the most popular boys, second only on the clique-ranking to those described as friendly, outgoing and self-confident. [...] Many kids (and adults) believe that the victims of bullying bring it upon themselves ...'

The power of Ames's case stems from its effort to periodise the phenomenon, in a way that most commentators don't even attempt. But one reason that such crimes resist analysis is that they often seem so undirected. The postal workers might have opened fire on the workplace that seemed the locus of their misery, but often rage killers gun down random strangers (as in Colorado). How to explain that?

Contextualising rage massacres shouldn't mean understanding them simply as goal driven. Or, at least, not exclusively. We need to also think about the act itself and the attractive power of deadly violence.

In his memoir of the Second World War, the philosopher J Glenn Gray remarks how combat constituted, for some of his comrades, 'the one great lyric passage in their lives.' It's a surprisingly common sentiment. One Vietnam veteran, a sniper, talked of a long-range shot as an aesthetic pleasure, almost like a poem or a great painting: 'A kill at two klicks, that is beautiful. It stays with you ... the bullet vaporises the guy, explodes into him. Satisfying ... hitting the target – beautiful.'

Much of the most overt writing about the pleasure of violence, about the attraction of war, emerged from the First World War. Indeed, the outbreak of the that war led to mass celebrations in almost all of the combatant nations. How to explain the enthusiasm?

As the historian Eric Leeds explains, 'It was commonly felt that with the declaration of war, the populations of European nations had left behind an industrial civilisation with its problems and conflicts and were entering a sphere of action ruled by authority, discipline, comradeship and common purpose'. The pleasure of war represented, in other words, an indictment of the peace that it shattered.

Peace meant that men and women were atomised, alienated and alone, impersonal cogs in the gears of industry; war offered an organic collectivity in which there would be a meaningful place for everyone. Again and again in the literature of 1914, you come up against a perception of modernity, with its factories and its technology and its bureaucracy, as soulless and anti-human: a world that was 'old and cold and weary', as poet and soldier Rupert Brooke says. Battle, by contrast, was thought to restore the values of an age that was passing, understood (in idealised terms) as honour and purpose and camaraderie. Modernity was emasculating, dominated by those Brooke called 'half-men'; combat restored a traditional virility.

Julian Grenfell, another soldier poet (and First World War casualty) expresses the sentiment neatly. Grenfell, who seems to have genuinely enjoyed combat, famously wrote, 'And he is dead who will not fight/And who dies fighting has increase', lines that replicate Brooke's sense of war as a kind of resurrection, an antidote to the bloodless half-life of industrial civilisation. The conclusion of that poem reads like a hymn to the berserker state of the rage murderer:

And when the burning moment breaks,
And all things else are out of mind,
And only joy of battle takes
Him by the throat, and makes him blind,
[...]
The thundering line of battle stands,
And in the air death moans and sings;
But Day shall clasp him with strong hands,
And Night shall fold him in soft wings.

Now, other 20th-century wars spurred outbreaks of patriotism. But not on a comparable scale – where the First World War began with delirious celebration, the Second World War commenced with a kind of weary resignation. Crucially, the world away from which men were turning in 1914 was one in which the industrial order was still new, a process that had only recently brought millions of people who had previously lived on the land under the sway of commodity relations. And the wrenching novelty of that experience, the sense of shock and dislocation generated by what was then a new phenomenon, helps explain the visceral enthusiasm for war.

There are, however, parallels in the 21st century. As I've argued elsewhere, the emotive response to the 9/11 attacks replicated, in many ways, the outbreak of the First World War. Broadcaster Glenn Beck named his Tea Party group the 9/12 Project, in recognition of what he called 'the feeling of togetherness' Americans enjoyed immediately after the terrorist strikes. By explicitly seeking to restore 9/12 rather than 9/10, Beck implies that the outbreak of war actually improved the country, in much the same way as Edwardian militarists thought the European conflict would save Western civilisation.

In 2001, modernity was not new in the way that it had been in 1914. Yet, since the 1980s, the United States, like most industrialised nations, had undergone decades of neoliberal reforms, a process that had extended market forces to every nook and cranny of human existence in a way that previous eras would not have believed possible.

The generation of 2001 could thus share with the generation of August 1914 a sensation of everything they held dear vanishing, a vague feeling of collective identities dissolving before the cold logic of the cash register. The experience of 9/11, the beginning of the war on terror, provided an overwhelming contrast to isolation, fragmentation, to the collapse of established authorities, an answer to the widespread yearning for meanings and belief.

The Prussian novelist Ernst Jünger described, in 1914, how 'the heroic feeling that a commercial age had slammed into the museums burst out, bright and living'. The same sentiment was expressed, over and over again, back in 2001. For instance, the influential columnist Peggy Noonan wrote of how 9/11 had restored John Wayne, banishing the domination of enfeebled sybarites. Prior to the attacks, America had been like Wayne's hapless sidekick Barry Fitzgerald – a 'small, nervous, gossiping neighborhood commentator ... who wanted to talk about everything and do nothing'. For Noonan, the Duke's return signalled the death of the neurotic and empty world of the 20th century, in the same way as Brooke turned from 'the sick hearts' and 'half-men' of his day.

This, it seems to me, provides a background to the proliferation of rage murder. On the one hand, ordinary Americans have been, as Ames says, experiencing a concerted assault from neoliberalism for some decades now, producing a profound *social* dislocation. The traditional bonds between people dissolve with the normalisation of an ideology of radical individualism. In Europe, the austerity agenda has provoked substantial resistance, and even where those struggles have failed the prospect of collective responses at least provide a framework in which the world can be understood. In the United States, however, the traditions of the Left are much weaker, with the result that individuals are more likely to perceive their misery as an existential personal failing.

What's more, more than any other industrialised nation, the United States remains deeply embroiled in ongoing imperial adventures, conflicts that foster a 21st-century version of the militaristic values expressed so forcefully in 1914. Throughout the early phases of the Iraq war, the army recruited under the slogans 'Be all you can be' and 'an army of one', catch-cries that replicate the Edwardian sense of battle as an experience that will restore the individuality crushed by capitalist modernity.

In that setting, is it really so surprising that Grenfell's 'joy of battle' takes a certain proportion of damaged men by the throat, that some of those who know themselves to be among the detritus of a neoliberal order seek the power and clarity that comes from aiming a rifle and pulling its trigger?

Ames recently discussed the rage murders conducted by One L Goh in Oakland California, who shot eight people, killing three, in Cleveland early this year: 'He failed at everything; he was one of those faceless, anonymous losers. But there was one thing he could still excel at, something that could get him attention, something that this country perversely celebrates: mass murder in a blaze of anti-glory. So long as you're ready to make that transformation-of-character into a death row inmate, that option is always available here.'

What conclusions can we draw?

Most obviously, the rise of rage massacres represents a profound social derangement. At the very least, it's positively perverse to talk about gun massacres without some discussion of America's permanent imperialist wars and the impact they've had on the culture. The First World War lasted four years; the United States has been occupying Afghanistan for eleven years and Iraq for nine. You cannot maintain combat operations for that length of time without fostering, both deliberately and otherwise, a militarism closely connected to a sense of personal liberation through violence. War is carcinogenic to the body politic, and the cancers it generates appear in all kinds of unexpected ways.

Yet that context – the unprecedented legitimation of violence provided by years of brutal war – almost never enters the debate. If, as novelist JG Ballard once said, the suburbs now dream of violence, shouldn't the first question be why? Consider: after the Colorado shootings, well-meaning journalists anguished about how the news might be reported without inspiring fresh crimes. Their worries were not unfounded – immediately after the massacre, tribute pages to the killer proliferated on Facebook; within a few days, a would-be copycat was arrested. But what does it say about a society if random acts of murder now exercise so great an attractive power that it becomes dangerous to even speak of them?

Instead of addressing such questions, the media discussion tends to move immediately to technical responses. The discussion of gun control provides a good example, since, wittingly or not, it channels the tremendously disturbing social implications of these acts in familiar and thus reassuring territory. Because all sensible liberals already know that gun control offers a solution to gun crime, this new willingness of ordinary people to commit unthinkable atrocities need not provoke any particularly uncomfortable social reflections.

But, of course, gun control in the United States is not nearly as simple as most Australian pundits suggest. As soon as you move from abstractions to real history, you discover a much more complicated narrative about guns in the United States than the 'Americans be crazy' caricature so beloved by the Australian Left.

In a fascinating article for the *Atlantic* in 2011, Adam Winkler makes a point almost entirely absent from discussions here. 'Indisputably, for much of American history', he writes, 'gun-control measures, like many other laws, were used to oppress African Americans':

> After losing the Civil War, Southern states quickly adopted the Black Codes, laws designed to reestablish white supremacy by dictating what the freedmen

> could and couldn't do. One common provision barred blacks from possessing firearms. To enforce the gun ban, white men riding in posses began terrorizing black communities. In January 1866, *Harper's Weekly* reported that in Mississippi, such groups had 'seized every gun and pistol found in the hands of the (so called) freedmen' in parts of the state. The most infamous of these disarmament posses, of course, was the Ku Klux Klan.

Nor is that simply a matter of the distant past. Winkler reminds us of the relationship between the right to carry arms and the black militancy of the 1960s:

> Before he was assassinated in 1965, Malcolm X had preached against Martin Luther King Jr.'s brand of nonviolent resistance. Because the government was 'either unable or unwilling to protect the lives and property' of blacks, he said, they had to defend themselves 'by whatever means necessary'. Malcolm X illustrated the idea for *Ebony* magazine by posing for photographs in suit and tie, peering out a window with an M-1 carbine semiautomatic in hand. Malcolm X and the [Black] Panthers described their right to use guns in self-defence in constitutional terms. 'Article number two of the constitutional amendments', Malcolm X argued, 'provides you and me the right to own a rifle or a shotgun.'

> Guns became central to the Panthers' identity, as they taught their early recruits that 'the gun is the only thing that will free us – gain us our liberation.'

Thus, contrary to what most commentators imply, the modern movement in support of 'gun rights' began not with the far Right but with the New Left. The key moment came in 1967 when the Black Panthers invaded the California legislature, rifles in hand. At that protest, Bobby Seale argued:

> Black people have begged, prayed, petitioned, demonstrated, and everything else to get the racist power structure of America to right the wrongs which have historically been perpetuated against black people. The time has come for black people to arm themselves against this terror before it is too late.

For blacks, the ownership of guns possessed an obvious symbolic importance. An armed black man or woman was someone who rejected the passivity of the slave or the servant, someone who not only asserted their constitutional rights but showed a willingness to defend them. Conservatives understood that message, too: that's why, in the 1960s, even the National Rifle Association (NRA) supported calls for gun control. The wave of laws passed in the late 1960s to limit gun ownership was a direct response to the new black militancy. As one critic said, the legislation was intended, 'not to control guns but to control blacks.'

It's easy, from the safety of history, to dismiss Seale's rhetoric but it should also be noted that, for those in the civil rights movement, guns weren't simply symbolic. In a context in which activists were regularly murdered by racists and police, the possession of guns was also seen as crucial for self-defence. This was not some peculiar fetish of the Panthers but was common throughout the movement. Winkler again:

> Civil-rights activists, even those committed to non-violent resistance, had long appreciated the value of guns for self-protection. Martin Luther King Jr. applied for a permit to carry a concealed firearm in 1956, after his house was bombed. His application was denied, but from then on, armed supporters guarded his home. One adviser, Glenn Smiley, described the King home as 'an arsenal.' William Worthy, a black reporter who covered the civil-rights movement, almost sat on a loaded gun in a living-room armchair during a visit to King's parsonage.

At the very least, this not-so-distant history illustrates that gun control is not as simple as many here would like to believe; that, in fact, there are real reasons why some Americans – and not just homicidal hillbillies – might be less than enthusiastic about legislation restricting their ability to arm themselves.

It's true that the political context today is entirely different. No-one is suggesting that James Holmes is an equivalent to Bobby Seale, much less Martin Luther King. It's also true that people of colour, particularly the poor, suffer disproportionately from gun violence in the United States. A recent piece from *Salon* noted that, while the

Colorado massacre was an exceptional event, 'mass shootings in Chicago are far from aberrations and any given weekend in the city can see reports of casualty figures that seem more appropriate to Kandahar than a Midwestern American city'.

Obviously, this is terrible; obviously, progressives need a response. There is no disputing that. But you cannot simply wave away the particular history attached to gun control in the United States setting. In any case, while much has changed since the 1960s, plenty has remained the same. The Panthers first agitated around the right to bear arms as part of what they called 'patrolling the police'. As a response to ongoing and systemic violence and brutality, they began following patrol cars as they came into the ghettoes, in order to make sure that local people weren't mistreated. Because the Panthers were (legally) armed, the police had to think twice about attacking them – and, because they were monitored, officers were much less able to harass or brutalise ordinary people.

Since that time, the relationship between the police and ghetto communities seems, if anything, to have deteriorated. The past few decades have seen an expansion of the United States prison system almost unparalleled in history. In America today there are some 1.8 million people in state custody of some sort. As the *Atlantic* says, 'the American inmate population has grown so large that it is difficult to comprehend: imagine the combined populations of Atlanta, St. Louis, Pittsburgh, Des Moines, and Miami behind bars'. Interestingly, the prison population remained stable throughout most of the 20th century: the real increase took place from the mid-1970s onwards, hypercharged by the boom in private prisons from the 1990s. Naturally, this mass incarceration is highly racialised: almost one in ten black men are behind bars; one in every fifteen black children has a parent in prison; one in three African-American boys born in 2001 stands a lifetime risk of going to gaol.

The growth of the prison-industrial complex has been accompanied by an enormous expansion of the police force. Journalist Stephan Salisbury notes that, with the money spent on armouring and arming law enforcement since 9/11, the federal government could have:

> rebuilt post-Katrina New Orleans five times over and had enough money left in the kitty to provide job training and housing for every one of the record 41,000-plus homeless people in New York City. It could have added in the growing population of 15,000 homeless in Philadelphia, my hometown, and still have had money to spare. Add disintegrating Detroit, Newark, and Camden to the list. Throw in some crumbling bridges and roads, too.

It's not just that budgets have increased. The police forces have been militarised to an extraordinary degree. Salisbury points out that Montgomery County, Texas, now has a weapons-capable drone, that the Tampa police have an eight-tonne armoured personnel carrier and two tanks; that the Fargo police have bomb detection robots; that Chicago operates some 15 000 interlinked surveillance cameras. New York's mayor Michael Bloomberg boasts: 'I have my own army in the NYPD, which is the seventh largest army in the world.'

Not surprisingly, lethal police violence in the United States has reached epidemic proportions. *Salon* notes:

> In the days bracketing the Aurora massacre, San Francisco police shot and killed mentally ill Pralith Pralourng; Tampa police shot and killed Javon Neal, 16; an off-duty cop shot Pierre Davis, 20, of Chicago; Miami-Dade police shot and killed an unidentified 'stalking suspect'; an off-duty FBI agent shot an unnamed man in Queens; Kansas City police shot and killed 58-year-old Danny L Walsh; Lynn police and a Massachusetts state trooper shot and killed Brandon Payne, 23, a father of three; Henderson police shot and killed Andy Puente Soto, 42, out in the desert wastes near Las Vegas. ...
>
> From January 2003 through December 2009, bureau statistics show 4,813 deaths occurred during 'an arrest or restraint process'.

What those figures show is that interactions with the police are already responsible for a substantial proportion of gun deaths. Entirely predictably, these deaths are racialised, with the young, the dark skinned and the poor far more likely than anyone else to become victims of police gunfire.

Once more, that's the context in which the calls for stricter gun laws are made. The very proliferation of weaponry means that guns can be found throughout poor communities in the inner cities. Passing new anti-firearm laws and then enforcing them means, almost by definition, unleashing militarised police forces upon inner-city populations, under circumstances where the police have a demonstrated track record of shooting suspects dead.

Yes, the tragedy of needless gun deaths constituted a genuine problem. But it's a complicated issue, and the knee-jerk invocation of gun control as a magical cure-all, especially when abstracted from the real circumstances of contemporary America, is simply not good enough.

None of this should suggest that the current proliferation of guns is in any way progressive. One doesn't have to be a pacifist to recognise that, actually, the Left succeeds, by and large, via collective social struggle rather than by mobilising individuals with weapons. The Arab Spring provides an obvious illustration: in the countries where the uprisings were most successful, the revolutions relied on mass mobilisations, with a turn to armed struggle tending to arise at the moment the movement begins to stall. The real threat posed for authorities by the Panthers lay not with the firearms they'd collected but with the widespread resonance of their defiant militancy within the black population. Indeed, in many respects, their military emphasis contributed to their downfall, by fostering direct individual confrontations with the state that the Panthers couldn't possibly win (a tremendous number of the most talented black leaders of the 1960s were shot dead by police).

Nonetheless, what the Panthers and similar organisations represented was a political alternative to the despair of the ghetto, a vision of responding to unemployment and crime and drugs and so on through collective social action. And in that you can see the embryo of what we might call 'gun control from below'.

That is, calls to 'get the guns off the street' fail to acknowledge that the process matters as much as the aim. There's a crucial difference between militarised police sending their tanks and drones into urban areas, and community groups within those areas organising themselves to drive out criminals, encouraging individuals not to carry weapons, picketing gun shops and gun fairs and other attempts to push firearms, and thus providing a collective security so that guns no longer seem necessary.

Grassroots activism of that type might also take up any number of other demands for palliatives to ease the violence, such as better mental health facilities or a stronger social security net for those under financial stress.

Most fundamentally, such efforts could begin to reknit the social connections severed by the neoliberal turn, and by so doing provide the sense of meaning and purpose missing in an intensely atomised society.

What becomes apparent when you hear veterans talking about war is that many of the pleasures of deadly violence are distorted reflections of the principles for which the Left has always campaigned. Combat appeals because, perversely, it makes life seem valuable, because it provides an immediate purpose and a common goal. War fosters camaraderie and connection; it promises to unite men in a way that's diametrically opposed to the ultra-individualism of late capitalism.

One marine, a veteran of Fallujah, I interviewed for my book *Killing* explained it to me like this:

> [N]othing I do from this point on in my life is ever going to compare. Ever. I do a lot of panel discussions and things, and I tell people, I could win the lottery today, have two hundred million dollars, have fast cars, mansions, you name it, and still, it's not going to compare to that feeling of leading marines, other human beings, into combat and doing what we did there. It's almost like I'm going through the motions now for the rest of my life.

That last line is of course the kicker, an extraordinary indictment of the world's richest country, where nothing that peacetime offers can provide an experience of comparable richness to house-to-house fighting in one of the bloodiest punitive missions in recent history.

That's why collective struggles for social change matter so much, and why they are what we should talk about, rather than calls for new state powers, for they contain within them the pleasures found in combat, albeit in a non-alienated fashion. Mass movements offer an alternative experience of solidarity, of collectivity, purpose, value and so on, an experience that can erode the appeal of violence.

'Perhaps the best kept political secret of our time', writes Barbara Ehrenreich, 'is that politics, as a democratic undertaking, can be not only "fun", in the entertaining sense, but profoundly uplifting, even ecstatic. My generation had a glimpse of this in May 1968 and at other points in that decade, when strangers embraced in the streets and the impossible briefly seemed within reach. Insurgencies again and again engender such moments of transcendence and hope.'

If you experience life as ecstatic, if you see the world full of transcendence and hope, rather than old and cold and weary, you don't have to turn away from it and you're less likely to see killing other humans as, in Brooke's words, 'into cleanness leaping'.

Of course, none of this is easy. There's no magical solution to deranged violence. But the creation of a Left that makes life seem more attractive than death would be a good place to start.

In any case, if that all seems utopian, consider the alternatives. Is the top-down gun control that John Howard and others advocate going to happen in the United States? No, of course it's not. There's no serious prospect of any American politician introducing gun laws that are anything other than token. Why? Partly because campaigns for laws lack a popular constituency, since, in the context I've just outlined, many ordinary Americans are understandably concerned about a diminution of their rights and an expansion of those enjoyed by the state.

The same point can be expressed in a different way: any attempt to bring in real gun laws so would generate a ferocious campaign by the populist Right, which the liberal Left would be largely incapable of challenging.

Think of how, during the presidential election, Obama's passing reference to rural communities becoming bitter and clinging to guns and religion became a rallying cry for the Tea Party types who now dominate the Republican Party. Any anti-gun legislation – certainly any anti-gun legislation serious enough to make any difference – would produce similar consequences.

Again, to understand the role of groups like the Tea Party in the gun debate, you have to look at history. As Winkler notes, by and large, in the 1960s, conservatives – including the NRA – mostly supported gun restrictions, precisely because they saw such restrictions as aimed at the New Left. It was only later, with the collapse of groups like the Panthers, that bearing arms became a totemic cause for the Right. The obvious example is the militia movement that emerged during the Clinton years: a version of right-wing populism absolutely centred on the same constitutional right to bear arms that the Panthers once invoked.

This was a new mode of conservatism, a paranoid defence of 'liberty' ostensibly mounted against the encroachments of Clintonian 'socialism'. In other words, during a period in which liberals were embracing neoliberalism, the far Right was able to appropriate radical postures that had once belonged to the New Left. As the Left fell in behind Clinton's corporate liberalism, the radical Right became the force most noisily hostile to United States foreign policy (via suspicion of the 'New World Order' and its black helicopters), positioning itself in opposition to state power and as the representative of 'freedom' against the government and its agents. Guns were part of that – once more functioning as symbols of resistance, albeit in a deranged, distorted fashion.

That's why, though the political prospect of extensive regulation can be assessed at approximately zero, the Left's call for state control of guns is a serious error, since it allows the far Right to claim the mantle of opposition to state power, at precisely a time in which that state power is increasingly discredited and distrusted. We've already seen what this might mean in the way that the politician Ron Paul – a sinister, racist libertarian – was able to appeal to many young people by articulating anti-state positions now completely outside the liberal consensus.

If the Left identifies with the idea that police should have more power to intervene in the communities of the poor at a time when there's growing opposition to the prison-industrial complex (remember those 1.8 million people in state custody!), it's an open invitation for the bigots of the far Right to project themselves as the only consistent defenders of liberty.

By contrast, if the Left instead begins on the long and arduous business of establishing a bottom-up solution to the proliferation of guns, we stand a chance not only of isolating the Right and of dissipating the reactionary gun culture, but of rebuilding a sense of solidarity, so that living becomes more attractive than killing.

Grey discussed combat as the single lyric passage in an entire life. But let's also remember what poet Octavio Paz wrote about the experience of struggle in Spain in the 1930s: 'Anyone who has looked Hope in the face will never forget it. He will search for it everywhere he goes.'

Memory and the anti-politics of ANZAC

Anzac Day celebrates forgetting.

Its revival, the transformation of a ceremony nearly extinct in the 1980s into today's turbocharged festival, coincides with the excision from national consciousness of the most important aspects of the Great War.

In their book *What's wrong with Anzac?*, Marilyn Lake and Henry Reynolds document the funding that the Department of Veterans' Affairs pours into resources promoting Anzac Day. Yet despite such educational campaigns, how many Australians can answer the simple question: what was the war about?

Conservatives, and most liberals, tell us that Anzac Day stands above politics. That's true, in a fashion. But the event's not apolitical so much as anti-political.

Where military theorist Carl von Clausewitz defined war as the continuation of politics by other means, Anzac celebrates the battlefield as a realm entirely removed from political life. The Great War spurred an unprecedented degree of social polarisation in Australia, and yet the obsessive retelling of the Gallipoli landing never corresponds to any equivalent interest in, say, the populace's remarkable rejection of conscription in two ballots in 1916 and 1917. The Bush/Blair/Howard War on Terror rendered that period more relevant than ever, since obvious parallels can be drawn between the hysterical patriotism of the 'Freedom Fries' days and the jingoism during which most Australian cities renamed their streets (if you live in Victoria Street, there's a pretty good chance it was once called Wilhelm Road), while the state-sanctioned suspicion of Arabs and Muslims after 9/11 corresponds to the widespread persecution of Irish and Catholics in the wake of the Easter Uprising, and the unparalleled freedom granted to security agencies echoes former prime minister Billy Hughes's promulgation of the open-ended War Precautions Act.

Yet Anzac Day functions not to celebrate but to prevent that kind of history. It lauds bravery yet allows no room for what the Prussian leader Otto von Bismarck called 'civil courage', a trait that many non-combatants showed in abundance when, against all the newspapers, politicians and mainstream political parties, they opposed the slaughter in Europe.

Again, in these endless discussions about the young men of that time, how often does anyone point out that Australians saw one of the very first anti-war protests anywhere in the world, when the Industrial Workers of the World (IWW) called a rally on the Domain the weekend the conflict broke out? Everything that the IWW predicted about the war came to pass, just as everything that the official jingoes said proved entirely wrong. But amidst all the Anzac headshaking about the horrors of Gallipoli, there's no room to mention those who tried to stop the killing taking place.

The anti-politics of Anzac Day not only diminishes the experiences of the millions of Australians who did not fight, it renders entirely monochromatic the experiences of the soldiers themselves. We can tell, for instance, the story of the Christmas truce of 1914, but only because a certain version of the story supports Anzac's presentation of war as a time out of time, an experience in a realm where normal rules did not apply. The perversity of men shaking hands and wishing each other luck before obediently ducking back into the trenches to commence hostilities supports Anzac's general depiction of combat as a social anomaly, a mysterious business entirely disconnected from what Archbishop Mannix called 'a sordid trade war'. That's why there's much less emphasis on the context of those unofficial armistices, which were, initially, made possible because so many ordinary Germans had been working in Britain and felt no particular animosity to the men in the opposite trenches, and which were systematically broken up by authorities terrified that if the soldiers fraternised it would be impossible to make them fight. Indeed, even if you only focus on combat (rather than the widespread mutinies that later took place), it's possible to tell the story of the Great War in terms of measures by officers to force their men to kill. In his fascinating book *Trench Warfare*, Tony Ashworth documents the regularity in which ordinary soldiers on both sides adopted what he calls the 'live and let live' policy, allowing unofficial truces punctuated by ritualistic exchanges of gunfire at certain times and certain places, exchanges specifically designed not to kill anyone and thus avoid retribution. In Ashworth's argument, the official tactics adopted by commanders were attempts to break down these proto-political refusals, to force the men into contact with each other and thus ensure that they would fight.

In other words, even in the most extreme circumstances, the Great War was a social conflict, shaped by internal contradictions. That's why, if the origins of the war are now never discussed, there's an equally determined silence about how the slaughter ended, with revolution in Russia and Germany, and near-insurrections in many other countries.

At the same time, one of the curious consequences of the anti-politics of Anzac is that the celebrations embrace the literature of disenchantment that emerged from the war, albeit with a distinctive twist. The war is now told, not in the bloodless narratives of contemporary Empire propagandists, but as a compendium of tropes taken from writers like Sassoon and Owen and Remarque and Barbusse. Every schoolkid knows about shellshock and bodies hanging on barbed wire and rats feasting on corpses and the rest of it, yet these details, which in the original texts contrasted what had been promised with what war delivered, are now used to bolster the presentation of combat as an experience entirely divorced from normal social relations.

As psychologist and philosopher William James noted, the 'possibility of violent death [is] the soul of all romance', which is why showing war's horrors does not, in itself, foster anti-war sentiment, since 'the horrors make the fascination. War is the *strong* life; it is life in *extremis*'.

It's a central part of Anzac's anti-politics: the hellishness of war separates it from ordinary life, transforming Clausewitz's 'politics by other means' into a transcendental experience at which civilians can only marvel. Whereas for the writers of the 1920s and 1930s, the Great War disappointed by representing, in concentrated form, the violent banality of industrial society, today the very bloodiness of the conflict is used to highlight the contrast with our own day-to-day life. The narrative therefore shifts from social critique (why did we allow these atrocities to happen?) to a veneration of sacrifice, the nature of which is largely irrelevant.

The Gallipoli pilgrimage provides the obvious example. The attendees at the dawn service do not ask themselves why Australians died invading a country thousands of miles away. No, that particular issue's rendered inherently irrelevant, since the backpackers go there not to think about history but to marvel at the height of the cliffs and the sharpness of the rocks, and to feel an awe at people their own age experiencing horrors that they couldn't imagine. The question arising from the pilgrimage is thus not 'why did it happen?' (a query that leads not only into history but into politics) but rather 'what did it feel like?', an aestheticisation of the past that's explicitly anti-political.

Or, rather, it's anti-political in one sense. In another, it's entirely compatible with the trend toward militarisation in the wake of 9/11, not simply because it fits entirely with the new consensus that there's something inherently underhand in debating the politics of war (recall how long the Afghan conflict had been running before Parliament convened a formal discussion), but because the question 'what did it feel like?' always implies a follow-up: 'I wonder what it would be like.'

Former Greens senator Scott Ludlam's fascinating diary from his visit to Afghanistan illustrates how this plays out in recruits. Speaking of the soldiers he meets, he writes:

> All the same, there's an eagerness to prove themselves. The further forward you get, the happier crew are to be there and the less interested in being pulled back into safety. Having spent years training, most of them really, really want to be in theatre.
>
> 'This is a great battle lab for us.'
> [...]
> 'I'd do this whether you paid me or not.'

If its horrors make war a transcendental experience, the contrast with the banality of late capitalist life make combat a perpetual source of fascination, in precisely the way James describes.

What are the consequences of this recognition of Anzac as an anti-politics? Most obviously, it implies a certain futility about debating its meaning, even through articles like this. Because Anzac's not an argument so much as an aesthetic event, it's largely impervious to critique. Everyone knows the newspaper formula: you devote most of your space to praising the diggers and republishing various 21st-century versions of the 'old lie' – and then you give half a column to someone to ponder what it all means. The ritualistic debates about the nature of Anzac are, to a large extent, part of Anzac, a means for keeping the commemoration in the centre of Australian life.

Which is not to suggest that critiques should not be mounted, nor that it's not important to foster genuine historical debate about the Great War, but simply to suggest that the terrain will not shift substantially without the re-emergence of an anti-war movement that offers a different way of thinking about conflicts.

If you look back at the shifting attitudes to Anzac, that's the real correlation. Alan Seymour's *One Day of the Year*, usually cited as evidence of post-war disenchantment, obviously emerged from the anti-Vietnam movement, just as the near-collapse of the celebrations in the 1980s stemmed from the rise of the anti-nuclear movement.

Contrary to conservative revisionism, peace activism has never involved an indifference to the plight of soldiers themselves. We're often told that anti-war activists spat at conscripts returning from Vietnam. What we don't hear is that huge numbers of the soldiers themselves supported the movement, both once they returned and, sometimes, while they were actually in theatre. In terms of the memory of the Great War, many of the most interesting studies of what was done to the troops have come from writers influenced by the peace movement, precisely because they're more likely to eschew the top-down approach of reactionary historians.

Some 35 million people died in the First World War. It is an extraordinary statistic. In the face of such overwhelming suffering, such tremendous devastation, the only decent commemoration entails ensuring that nothing comparable ever happens again.

When settlers dream

Some weeks ago, the academic Greg Shupak noted how the extremity of the violence unleashed during Operation Protective Edge had led some to describe Israel's actions as 'irrational'.

They were wrong. A settler-colonial state, Israel's existence depended first on the forced exodus of Palestinians and then the repeated destruction of their attempts at self-organisation.

Israel isn't unique in this respect. The so-called Black War between colonists and Indigenous people in Eastern Tasmania offers another example, one that makes a productive (though obviously not exact) comparison with Gaza, both because it's less well known to those in the Global North, but also because a raft of recent historiography has thrown fresh light on what settler colonisation meant for the island the British originally called Van Diemen's Land.

Nicholas Clements's book *The Black War* provides a definitive yet accessible account of the conflict. Clements chronicles the war in chapters that alternate between the perspective of the settlers and their Indigenous opponents, a conceit, as he explains in the introduction, borrowed from *The Palestine–Israeli Conflict: A Beginner's Guide*. It's a particularly effective mode of exposition for settlement narratives because, rather than attempting to adjudicate between the differing claims of the combatants, it shows how both perspectives arise from the process of colonisation itself.

When the Tasmanian landowner George Hobler organised a party of men to fire on a local Indigenous group, he saw himself as responding to the unprovoked spearing of one of his servants. Likewise, when two Aboriginal people attacked sawyers at a farm near Ben Lomond in March 1831, they seem to have intended to rescue an Indigenous girl living on the property. But the Black War cannot be understood as simply an accretion of these individual exchanges. Rather, we need to situate episodic clashes in their historical context: the establishment and maintenance of a settler colony that, by its nature, renders the lives of Indigenous people unbearable.

Think of the usual presentation of the recent Gaza incursion. The crisis began, we are told, with the kidnapping and killing of three Israeli teenagers. Of course, that's an entirely arbitrary starting point. Why not say that it started the day before that, when an Israeli airstrike killed a Palestinian man and a ten-year-old? But that too would be inadequate. As trauma specialist Gabor Maté says, 'There is no understanding Gaza out of context – Hamas rockets or unjustifiable terrorist attacks on civilians – and that context is the longest ongoing ethnic cleansing operation in the recent and present centuries, the ongoing attempt to destroy Palestinian nationhood'.

The conflict in Tasmania, like the conflict in Gaza, only makes sense as a totality. With the condescension of posterity, it's easy to dismiss the British colonists in Van Diemen's Land as monsters, genocidal racists carrying out atrocities for reasons unfathomable to liberal-minded folk of the 21st century. Yet, precisely as Israeli officials explained the assault on Gaza as a defensive reaction to Hamas's rockets, the Tasmanian settlers saw themselves as victims, driven to violence by the terror inflicted by the natives.

In December 1827, the land commissioner Roderic O'Connor wrote a personal letter to the government: 'Can we live in a wilderness surrounded by wretches who watch every opportunity and who take delight in shedding our blood?' The next year, settlers near Swanport sent 'a statement of the danger . . . of being ultimately exterminated by the black natives.'

To an outsider, the notion that the whites were in danger of extermination seems as perverse as the Western media's portrayal of the Gaza conflict in terms of the supposed threat to Israel. But, rather like Israelis today, the colonists explicitly condemned the assessments of such outsiders, who, they said, could not grasp the reality of their situation. In 1830, a Clyde Valley settler explained:

> We in the interior are in the most imminent daily danger of our lives and property — of having our houses and barns burnt about our ears in all directions, and our families butchered by these savages and are we to be smoothly informed how we are to act, and that, on the defensive, by a few comfortably seated

> Gentlemen in their well-furnished and well-protected houses?

The Marxist writer Isaac Deutscher famously described Zionism through a parable about a man who jumped from a burning house only to injure the person he landed on below. The analogy accepts Israel's self-presentation as a refuge from Nazism, a claim that historically simply isn't true. But it's less often recognised that Deutscher's fable applies with equal force to other settler colonies. Many of those arriving in Van Diemen's Land – the convicts, but also the soldiers – had no choice of their destination. Of course, from the perspective of the original inhabitants, the intentions of the settler-colonisers scarcely matter.

In Tasmania, convicts and ex-convicts were responsible for much of the bloodletting, so that many of the respectable colonists were able to disavow any direct involvement in killing Aboriginal people. But the convicts, James Boyce concludes in his magisterial *Van Diemen's Land*, 'can never be charged with the same level of responsibility as those whose interests they served, and their scapegoating by both the government and the free settlers is too obviously self-serving to be taken as seriously as it often has been'.

After all, as the historian of genocide Patrick Wolfe puts it, settler states 'typically seek to distance themselves from the activities of the ostensibly unofficial frontier mavericks on whose depredations they depend'. Think, for instance, of the Israeli government's relationship to the right-wing settlers in the Occupied Territories, whose activities they both disavow and encourage.

The mainstream consensus about Israel–Palestine holds that peace must begin with the Palestinians accepting Israel's right to exist as a Jewish state. But the Tasmanian example shows how, in fact, that very demand renders peace – or, at least, any kind of just peace – impossible.

Settler colonisation, by definition, must deny the legitimacy of the native population. The settlement of Australia rested on the doctrine of *terra nullius*, which held the land to be legally empty – and Zionism, of course, depends on the same concept.

The Zionist slogan of 'a land without a people for a people without a land' did not literally mean that Palestine lacked people, any more than the British settlers believed Van Diemen's Land was empty. In both cases, the absence was not of people but rather 'civilised people', for, as Land Commissioner Roderic O'Connor explained in 1827, it would be 'a disgrace ... to the human race to call [Indigenous people] men.'

The Australian founders saw the settlement of the colony as an established fact, with Indigenous people relegated to the margins of society. But the Australian constitution still signalled (albeit in passing) the fundamental identity of the new nation with the discriminatory Section 127, which stipulated that 'aboriginal natives' be excluded from official censuses. (In 1967, a referendum deleting that section passed with overwhelming public support, an event rightly considered a milestone in the struggle for Indigenous rights.)

What would it mean, today, to insist that Indigenous people accept Australia as a white or a Christian state? The very question sounds both absurd and offensive, precisely because explicitly chauvinist definitions of nationality are so discredited. That's why Judah Magnes, the first Chancellor of Israel's Hebrew University, opposed in 1942 the idea of a Jewish state because 'the slogan "Jewish state" (or commonwealth) is equivalent, in effect, to a declaration of war by the Jews on the Arabs.'

Likewise, when apologists claim that a state defined by the settler identity remains necessary to prevent a native massacre, they merely reveal how deep-seated the colonial mentality remains.

In the dying years of apartheid, some liberals opposed the attempts to break down the structures of the South African colonial regime, arguing the end of a racially defined state would mean the destruction of the white minority. The American writer William Safire, for instance, complained that 'real political equality' entailed:

> ... majority rule, and nonwhites are the overwhelming majority in South Africa. That means an end to white government as the Afrikaners have known it for three centuries; that means the same kind of black rule that exists elsewhere in Africa, and most white South Africans would rather remain the oppressors than become the oppressed.

Today, in the context of a multiracial South Africa, that position seems grotesque.

Let's recall that, in Tasmania, though some of the colonists favored military action, the head of the settlement,

Lieutenant Governor Arthur, was an early advocate of what today might be called a two-state solution.

In January 1828, Arthur explained, 'The measure which I rather incline to attempt, is to settle the Aborigines in some remote quarter of the island, which should be strictly reserved for them, and to supply them with food and clothing, and afford them protection ... on condition of their confining themselves peaceably to certain limits.'

He gave this plan official status in a notice published a few months later entitled 'Proclamation Separating the Aborigines from the White Inhabitants.' In other words, as Boyce says, 'the goal of colonial government policy from April 1828 was thus to reach an agreement with the Aborigines on the division of Van Diemen's Land.'

What were the results of Arthur's efforts? The most immediate effect of the supposed partition of Van Diemen's Land was the intensification of violence against those Indigenous people unfortunate enough to be on the wrong part of the island. As Boyce writes, the proclamation 'provided the first official sanction for the use of force against Aborigines for no other reason than that they were Aboriginal.'

In other words, it enabled settlers to ethnically cleanse the rest of the land, since, as Chief Justice Pedder put it at the time, 'the object of this proclamation is their expulsion wherever they may appear in the settled districts and however harmlessly they may be conducting themselves.'

Moreover, official hopes in a negotiated settlement were largely abandoned by October 1828, with the colony's executive council claiming that Aboriginal people's 'treachery' and 'lack of government' made them doubt 'if any reliance could be placed upon any negotiations which might be entered into.' Had Mark Regev, the telegenic Israeli spokesman, been present, he might have declared that, of course, the council wanted peace but it lacked a suitable partner.

Yet the war did, in fact, end with a two-state settlement, a result that was disastrous for the Indigenous people.

George Augustus Robinson arrived in Hobart in 1826, where, as the *Australian Dictionary of Biography* explains, he became 'secretary of the Seamen's Friend and Bethel Union Society, joined the committee of the Auxiliary Bible Society, visited prisoners and the condemned in the gaol, and helped to found the Mechanics Institute.' When the government advertised for a 'steady man of good character' to attempt a negotiation with Aboriginal people, Robinson stepped forward.

Over the next years, Robinson, known as 'the Conciliator,' embarked on a series of 'Friendly Missions' to induce Aboriginal people to cease fighting.

At first, most of the colonists reacted to him in the way that Israeli right-wingers respond to peaceniks today. The *Launceston Advertiser* wrote: 'Can it be that we are to thus suffer these people to destroy our Fellow Colonists, and is the Government to sit down supinely and view this destruction calmly and preach conciliation? No! rather let the sentence be extermination.'

The killing of Captain Bartholomew Thomas and James Parker by the Aboriginal people with whom they were seeking to negotiate fostered a hysterical clamour for reprisals. The *Advertiser* claimed the men were 'victims of a mistaken faith in the sincerity of these blood-thirsty savages' and denounced the 'barbarity of a race which no kindness can soften, and which nothing short of utter annihilation can subdue'. The *Launceston Independent* called for 'retribution, deep and lasting, not only upon the perpetrators of the deeds, should they come within our power, but upon the whole race'.

Again, all very familiar. But Robinson did, much to the surprise of most of the colony, eventually convince the majority of Indigenous people to accept resettlement on Flinders Island.

By 1830, Indigenous society had been shattered. The population had been decimated while the number of whites grew by a thousand or more each year. The historian John West, writing within a few decades of the Black War, explained that the constant harassment by armed parties meant that 'parents and children had been divided and families had been broken up in melancholy confusion: indeed, they had ceased to be tribes, and became what they were called – mobs of natives, composed often of hereditary enemies. Infanticide and distress, rapid flight, and all the casualties of a protracted conflict, threatened them with weedy destruction'.

Years later, Robinson himself noted in his diary that there was 'not an aborigine on [the Flinders Island] settlement nor an aborigine that has been at the settlement but what bears marks of violence perpetrated upon by them by the depraved whites. Some have musket balls lodged in them . . . Some of the natives have slugs in their bodies and others contusions, all inflicted by whites'.

When he approached the surviving Indigenous people, Robinson promised that if they accepted resettlement, their customs and culture would be respected; they would receive food, houses and blankets; and, most significantly, they would be able to return to their traditional lands once the violence had subsided.

It must have seemed like a decent offer – or at least the best one they would get. Of course, none of the promises were kept. Whatever Robinson's intentions, conciliation engendered less a homeland than a prison: as Charles Darwin noted during a visit in 1836, 'the Aboriginal blacks are all removed & kept (in reality as prisoners) in a Promontory, the neck of which is guarded'.

The parallels with Palestine are not exact: partly because Israel confronts a demographic challenge not faced by colonists in Tasmania – where, from very early on, white settlers constituted a majority – and partly because, while the settlement in Tasmania was (at the time) relatively unimportant to the British, Israel plays a crucial role for the American empire.

Nonetheless, the similarities are instructive. When, in 1847, forty-seven sick and elderly Indigenous people petitioned to be allowed to leave Flinders Island, the settlers organised a petition to prevent them, explaining that those who hadn't lived through the war could not appreciate what might happen when 'uncivilised creatures with all their savage and bloodthirsty propensities are admitted [sic] to escape into the bush to perpetrate all sorts of depredations and atrocities'. The whites might have been paranoid, but they were not prepared to risk any manifestation of Indigenous independence, which might have sparked further resistance.

Likewise, as Shupak says, Israel cannot allow an independent Palestinian state, because a successful expression of Palestinian nationalism represents a continuing threat to the project of an ethnically defined settler colony. Netanyahu has made that explicit, saying 'that there cannot be a situation, under any agreement, in which we relinquish security control of the territory west of the River Jordan' – something that effectively rules out a sovereign Palestine.

Which is not to say that a two-state solution is entirely impossible. But if it takes place, it will be akin to Robinson's 'Conciliation': the creation of a kind of guarded reserve, a Bantustan or blockaded open-air prison like Gaza rather than a nation exercising real sovereignty.

Or, put another way, the kind of state acceptable to Israel (and, for that matter, to the United States) will be one to which Palestinians will only agree if, like the Indigenous Tasmanians in 1831, they're convinced no other choice remains.

Hence the increasingly violent rhetoric coming out of Israel. Unlike the Tasmanian settlers, the Israeli authorities do not think they can get away with physically annihilating their enemies. They do, however, believe sustained violence can sufficiently cow the Palestinians so that they can be 'conciliated', induced to accept the 21st-century equivalent of a Flinders Island reserve.

For Israel, this is both necessary and urgent, a response to the so-called demographic time bomb that will bring a Palestinian majority in 'Greater Israel'. That's Shupak's point: the current crop of atrocities is neither an accident nor the result of ill-advised policies but a logical response by the Israeli regime to the situation in which it finds itself.

In the course of the Gaza incursion, Henry Siegman, former executive director of the American Jewish Congress, was moved to comment:

> When one thinks that this is what is necessary for Israel to survive, that the Zionist dream is based on the repeated slaughter of innocents on a scale that we're watching these days on television, that is really a profound, profound crisis – and should be a profound crisis in the thinking of all of us who were committed to the establishment of the state and to its success.

That crisis is necessary and long overdue. The Black War provides a chilling illustration of how settler colonialist dreams end.

Theatre of war

I rang the bell at a pleasant house in Greensborough, in Melbourne's northern suburbs, and a soldier from the Great War answered.

During our email exchanges I'd imagined Andrew Nolte as hefty, gruff and middle-aged, an impression that even survived a couple of phone calls. I didn't anticipate that someone boasting the accoutrements of a trench fighter – from sharpened bayonet to hard-tack biscuits – would live happily in his parents' home.

On the other hand, if I'd expected less youth, I'd also expected more ... well, eccentricity. Throughout the train ride to Greensborough, I'd agonised about how exactly to interview the mumbling gun-nut or bug-eyed fantasist awaiting me. Yet Nolte presented as eminently normal, an amiable, polite young man, who ushered me into a comfortable lounge and offered tea and coffee. Tall and thin as a knife, he spoke with a slow, careful seriousness that, when he settled into an armchair to talk, recalled an earnest lieutenant delivering a complicated tactical briefing – though that might have been because of the authentic Great War uniform he wore and the battle kit he'd spread out across the carpet.

I'd wanted to speak to someone about military re-enactment ever since I'd learned that, in the United States today, so many people dress in the colours of long-disbanded armies and skirmish with blank cartridges and blunted swords that re-enacting has become the fastest growing hobby in the country. A quick Google search summoned up an electronic army of these aficionados, posing uniformed on their websites with drooping moustaches, fierce stares and spindly antique firearms.

Before tracking down Nolte, I'd been exchanging emails with Jon Kulaga, a 47-year-old spice buyer who, on weekends, donned the uniform of a Seaforth Highlander Lewis gunner in the trenches of Pennsylvania. The Great War Association (GWA), in which he was an official, owned a full-scale First World War battlefield, with shell-holes and barbed wire and the lunar landscape of No Man's Land rendered exactly as in the old sepia photographs.

'We can', he'd told me, 'replicate a "quiet" portion of the Western front in 1918, at an infantry-sized company level on both sides: "quiet" since we really can't replicate heavy artillery'.

Shellfire or not, Kulaga and his friends made a pretty good fist of total war's total devastation. At the GWA's most recent event, two First World War–era aircraft buzzed overhead as 21st-century Americans fired combat rifles, threw grenades and launched trench mortars at each other.

That, however, was Pennsylvania. In outer suburban Melbourne, the full-scale battles Kulaga described seemed sufficiently distant to dismiss re-enacting with an 'only in America' shrug, had Nolte not so perfectly resembled a Great War soldier, even, I suddenly noticed, down to a distinctly Edwardian haircut.

How did a well-adjusted Melbourne boy end up in the khaki of a bygone century? It began, he explained, with the army cadets: the normal, 21st-century ones. At a cadet event at the Victoria Barracks, he came across some re-enactors at work.

'Here are all these guys dressed up in interesting, accurate uniforms, collecting stuff and showing it off, doing the drill, eating the food, and it looked like they were having a great time', he said. 'They were all great guys and knew a lot of stuff and sharing lots of knowledge, and it just seemed like a great thing to be part of it.'

That enthusiasm was not, at first, mutual. The key re-enactors were in their mid-30s and, at only 15, Nolte did not make a promising recruit for a hobby so prohibitively expensive. (Later, I priced a single authentic Mills bomb – 'complete, nice clean condition, w/nice patina' – at nearly $500.) But he persisted, taking a job as shift manager at McDonald's to fund a growing collection of Great War equipment.

Did local re-enactors manage anything as impressive as the mayhem Kulaga's men inflicted upon Pennsylvania? Nolte shook his head, a little enviously.

'Nothing like that. It's mostly static displays and ceremonials. Like at Anzac Day or if, say, the Whittlesea show wants a heritage event. We bring along most of our interesting stuff, on some trestle tables, and do a bit of static drill, fire our rifles, raise the flag, play bugles – that sort of thing. That's the only way you can get a gig.'

In part, his difficulties stemmed from the post-Port Arthur gun laws. For his Seaforth Highlander impression, Jon Kulaga wielded a fully operational Lewis gun, capable of firing 550 rounds in a minute. In Victoria, Lewis guns were seriously illegal. You couldn't even tote a pretend one – the legislation outlawed replica machine guns as ruthlessly as the real thing.

But that wasn't the worst problem. Like the generals of the era they mimicked, Australian re-enactors suffered from a perpetual shortage of men. Nolte's group comprised only five or six members with uniforms, occasionally bolstered by a few supporters in civvies.

'Going out in a trench with only two or three people because the others are unavailable that weekend defeats the purpose', he said. 'You're staring at the same two or three faces and you can't do anything. It just feels a bit silly after a while.'

Why was such a mainstream hobby in the United States so marginal in this country? Nolte blamed geography. American re-enacting centred around the Civil War, the popularity of which legitimised the recreation of other conflicts. Enthusiasts for the War Between the States could visit, in season, the actual battlefields where their ancestors contended, rather than worrying about recreating Somme winters in an antipodean climate.

But was there more to it than that?

Trawling through 'living history' websites, I came across an advertisement for a re-enactment of the Civil War's Battle of Resaca, originally an inconclusive but bloody engagement fought by the Confederate Army of Tennessee against General Sherman during the Atlanta campaign. The 2007 organisers had dedicated their event to 'fellow re-enactor LCPL Cody Warren who was killed in Iraq on November 10, 2006 while serving with the US Marines, and to all of the men and women of our US Armed Forces' – which seemed reasonable enough, until you considered that many of those attending would be modelling themselves on soldiers who, in 1864, had been assiduously shooting the United States armed forces.

The Civil War remained, as a psychoanalyst might say, over-determined, simultaneously sustaining any number of contradictory meanings. Marching with a Confederate musket could symbolise, at one and the same time, secessionist rebellion and patriotic enthusiasm, just as the rebel emblem expressed a particular (and not very pleasant) attitude to race while representing a class identification with Southern poverty against Northern prosperity.

Yet what of the Great War? Wasn't it, in some respects at least, an Australian equivalent? The acres of newsprint produced each Anzac Day display a remarkable hermeneutic pliability, with Gallipoli affirming both militarism and pacifism, duty and larrikinism, loyalty to empire and national independence, often within the confines of a single article. Yet, despite the huge ideological investment in the First World War within Australia, there were, astonishingly, more people recreating Australian Imperial Force (AIF) units in America than here.

The Civil War, in particular, seemed to provide a

blank canvas on to which any proclivity or talent might be projected. At the larger events, not only did the battles themselves offer scope for musicians in the bugle corps, nurses in the medical units and horsemen in the cavalry, but the organisers often also staged exhibitions of period crafts, so that those less given to marching and shooting and other martial skills could bake some Civil War bread, stitch a Civil War quilt or dance a Civil War jig.

At such events the barriers between fantasy and reality seemed disconcertingly permeable. Take, for instance, 'Christian Re-enacting', a niche within the living history community filled by organisations such as the Re-enactors Mission for Jesus Christ (RMJC), where believers participated in Civil War events authentically costumed as chaplains and itinerant tract distributors rather than artillerymen or musketeers. The RMJC director, one Reverend Alan Farley, took great pains to assert that his members were not, as he put it, 'sham play-actors bent on pretentious historical interpretation.' No, they were 'men and women of God, solidly committed to preaching and teaching the gospel and winning souls among the ranks of Civil War re-enactors across the United States.' So when Farley put on his frock coat to harangue attendees at historical commemorations, he simultaneously performed as an evangelist from the 1860s *and* actually preached the revivalist gospel, with sufficient fervour that 900 re-enactors had, he claimed, accepted Jesus Christ as their personal Lord and saviour.

In his extraordinary book *Confederates in the Attic*, Tony Horwitz writes of men so devoted to the Civil War that they starve themselves to achieve the emaciation of the malnourished rebels. They wax their beards with bacon fat; they practise 'the bloat', lying on the ground with stomachs protruding so as to resemble Confederate corpses decomposing in the southern sun; they welcome the hacking cough obtained by sleeping rough on a freezing battle site as an accurate reproduction of the phlegm rolling around the permanently infected throats of the 1860s.

The importance of the Civil War to the United States – and the importance of the United States to the world – meant that Confederate and Unionist re-enactors could be found scattered across the globe, including in Australia. Yet Nolte looked on such local Yanks and Rebs with a distinct disdain.

'I've done Civil War', he told me. 'But it has absolutely nothing to do with the history of this country.'

Likewise, Nolte didn't care overly for the fanaticism Horwitz documented. He gestured at his supplies of Great War–era Ideal condensed milk and Fray Bentos corned beef.

'I'll eat this kind of stuff', he said, 'if I'm going on an encampment but some blokes you'll go over to their place and they've got all this food in their pantry and that's all they'll eat. Then it gets weird ...'

Yet, even as he distanced himself from those sacrificing their health to their hobby, Nolte still campaigned for better standards within the Australian Great War Association.

'I've been pushing people to get a more realistic uniform', he said, 'so nothing with any polyester, trying to get accurate webbing, correct accoutrements for your weapon, eating utensils – trying to shy away from the Aussie Disposals, Camping City stuff'.

Which raised the obvious question. What did realism actually mean when the defining element of the event you sought to recreate – the deadly violence that soldiers inflicted upon each other – was necessarily always absent?

When I put this to Jon Kulaga, he made a point of distinguishing between the real suffering of real soldiers and the relatively minor discomforts experienced by hobbyists, but he also suggested that the battles in the faux trenches could become so intense that participants forgot that the bullets weren't live. As a younger man, he'd served in the real army; he found his first mock Great War battle disconcertingly real.

'German stick grenades were being thrown at us (me!) and they and the Germans that were throwing them seemed very real. My real military training kicked in and I knew when to fire, take cover and so on ... We have had accidents where re-enactors have shot each other at close range [a practice that's dangerous, even with blanks] or re-enactors getting hit on the head with mortar bombs flying through the air – all results of identifying too far with the combat situation and reacting on the personal preservation side.'

Accordingly, Kulaga's squad prepared for a big re-enactment with the authentic exercises used by real trench fighters, and he could speak with some authority about the relative virtues of various Great War weapons.

'I tend to favour my Webley pistol in the trenches', he explained, 'since it's a quicker response than a bolt action rifle and is much better in tight confines.'

When I asked Nolte about combat, he answered quite differently. His hobby simulated the more mundane aspects of Great War soldiering. He was adept, for instance, at the AIF's

1915 parade ground drills, subtly different, he assured me, from the equivalent today. In his lounge, he demonstrated the techniques necessary to achieve the maximum rate of fire – a series of motions sufficiently complex that, when he handed the gun to me, I became confused almost immediately after pulling the trigger.

Yet the real pleasures of the hobby were not, for Nolte, performative at all.

Two of his great-uncles were repatriated home in 1917 with lungs damaged by gas. With their experiences part of family lore, he'd done what he could to research their wartime service. In the process, he stumbled across some wartime ephemera.

'That's the start of any collection for anyone', he said. 'You see something, you buy it, even just out of impulse, and then you have to add to that collection.'

Collecting spurred his re-enacting, rather than vice versa. 'When you collect, you acquire a whole lot of expensive gear but no way of showing it off, no way to use it. Re-enacting means you can actually wear your gear. You do some work out in a trench, and eat the bully beef and biscuit and smoke the tobacco and drink the water and the rum from the same containers and it gives you a feeling of what it was like.' He smiled, almost embarrassed. 'In a vague way, at least.'

When we switched off the tape recorder and turned to the objects on his floor, I understood something of what he meant. His collection replicated the basic kit of an average soldier – a drinking flask, a packet of thin cigarettes, an ammunition belt and so on. They were objects for use, rather than pieces of craftsmanship, and they demanded to be handled. The belt wanted to be buckled; the pack worn; the combat rifle hoisted to the shoulder. Yet you could not touch any part of the collection without registering its authenticity, its historical weight, as if the past still clung to it like loam to a tree root.

Nolte showed me a Light Horseman's shoulder bag and explained how to carry it. Then he pointed out the bloodstain.

'They used to salvage whatever usable equipment they could find after a battle', he said. We both looked at the mark and fell silent, calculating where the wound must have been and the likelihood of its owner's survival.

I thought, then, about the German culture critic Walter Benjamin and his famous essay on book collecting. Benjamin made the same distinction as Nolte did between the genuine collector and the dealer only concerned with monetary value.

'One only has to watch a collector handle the objects in his glass case', wrote Benjamin. 'As he holds them in his hands, he seems to be seeing through them into their distant past as though inspired.'

In another context you wouldn't glance twice at that chipped enamel mug, but, when you know its wartime history, you experience an entire sensory world. You can't help but imagine a small tot of spirits in the early dawn, and feel a sympathetic stab of the pre-battle terror that the rum helped to suppress.

Kneeling amidst Nolte's collection, I understood, for the first time, the appeal of re-enactment. He'd acquired a metal trunk used to store medical equipment and he'd tracked down, item by item, its original contents, from the bulky pads used to staunch bleeding to the forceps with which bullets were removed. I looked down at the assembled display of Great War medical technology and, for an instant, historical distance evaporated. The war became, not an ancient abstraction, but an event palpable and solid, where real people writhed with agony at a makeshift dressing station and the staff treated the damage from machine guns with this primitive array of bone saws and placebos.

'For a collector', wrote Benjamin, 'and I mean a real collector, a collector as he ought to be – ownership is the most intimate relationship that one can have to objects. Not that they come alive in him; it is he who lives in them.'

If simply handling such objects brought these feelings of historical presence, was it really so hard to understand the sensations that might be stirred amongst even a small group of people authentically kitted out?

But why war, and only war? History happened during peace time, too, and the Great Depression changed the world as much as the Great War did. Why didn't thousands of Americans dress up as hoboes, jumping mock freight trains and lining up at fake soup kitchens? What made an industrial dispute or a flood or the discovery of penicillin innately less suitable for re-enactment than war?

Nolte told me that, to authentically recreate the soldiers' tinned supplies, he'd searched through the National Archives copyright section to find original labels. Okay, I understood the pleasures of historical detective work. Yet why did archival exploration need legitimisation from war? There were canned foods in the 1920s, too: what made them so much less fascinating than the tins served to soldiers a few years earlier?

When I put this to Nolte, his normal confidence faltered momentarily. 'I don't really know', he said. 'I suppose you could re-enact something else. I'd never thought of it before.'

I wondered, then, if the fascination wars exerted over re-enactors related to the emotions their outbreak usually generated. Think about the First World War – the real one, not the one in Pennsylvania. The population of the belligerent nations came to the most ghastly conflict in human history, not with a reluctant acquiescence to awful necessity, but with a hooting euphoria, a sentiment that looked very much like joy.

'All differences of class, rank and language were flooded over at that moment by the rushing feeling of fraternity', novelist Stefan Zweig famously wrote of that initial exultation. 'Strangers spoke to each other in the streets, people who had avoided each other for years shook hands ... Each individual experienced an exaltation of his ego; he was no longer the isolated person of former times, he had been incorporated into the mass, he was part of the people, and his person, his hitherto unnoticed person had been given meaning.'

Was this why the military experience seemed so much more attractive to re-enactors than any other – because war itself offered a unique alternative to, in Rupert Brooke's phrase, a modern world 'grown old and cold and weary'? If in peacetime men found themselves atomised and alone, was there an inherent attraction to events that bring them together, even if the encounters happened at bayonet point?

A few weeks after meeting Nolte, I read Jenny Thompson's book *War Games*, a major study of 20th-century war re-enactors in the United States. She had absorbed herself in the hobby for years, attending, in uniform, scores of re-enactments.

Thompson described how, when she began her long association with re-enacting, she initially found herself perplexed by the hobby's many contradictions. Everything suddenly made sense when she realised that its enthusiasts were doing something more complex than recreating war.

'Re-enactors try neither', she wrote, 'to relive history nor to transport themselves in time. Instead, they produce and simultaneously consume their own illusions – "watching it while acting in it". No longer are they passive viewers in a movie theatre or comfortable readers lounging on a sofa. Rather, they have assumed the powerful, dual roles of creator of and participant in a war experience ... In order to fully experience the phenomenon of an illusion, they must remain themselves. Like actors, they must have an ever-present consciousness that what they are experiencing is not historically real, but only looks as if it were'.

Re-enacting was not, then, about believing yourself to be in the past so much as creating the conditions in which your current identity could be inserted into an authentic-seeming representation of historical events. For Thompson, this understanding of re-enacting explained how the hobby opened up a special world for its participants, in which they could be and do quite different things than in reality.

Her first big event was a major Second World War re-enactment, a recreation of the Battle of the Bulge complete with genuine Sherman tanks. Waiting to move into position, alongside men kitted out in SS uniforms and carrying deadly automatic weapons, she was struck by an unexpected gender dynamic:

> As they talked about their clothing and accessories, the re-enactors almost exemplified, I hate to say it, the stereotype of women.
>
> 'Are those originals?' one asked another, pointing to his gloves. 'Yeah, cammo reversible to white. Minty, huh?' He extended his hand, and the other made clucking noises in admiration.

I'd noticed this, too, when I'd asked Nolte what his school friends had thought of his hobby. He laughed. 'They were like, cool: guns, bayonets! A real boys' thing.'

Of course, that was how it seemed: war, the quintessential masculine activity. Yet re-enacting actually involved pursuits that, in any other context, would seem classically feminine. Yes, Nolte possessed guns and a bayonet – but he knew as much about tailoring and groceries as any Edwardian housewife.

'The First World War was a useless war', Nolte said, just before I left him, 'a lot of useless deaths. Most re-enactors would agree with that: it was senseless killing.'

He was not, in other words, a militarist: violence, per se, didn't interest him. Yet a war that ended ninety years ago gave him something, allowed him to be someone, in a way that the everyday world simply didn't.

In Germany, in 1914, the young writer Franz

Schauwecker enthused about what was to come. 'The petty, aimless, lounging life of peacetime is done with,' he wrote. 'Life has suddenly been brought back to its simplest terms. Every movement is scrupulously precise, every touch is determined, every action is consciously directed towards its goal ... everything has its clear, palpable meaning ... '

The trenches actually delivered random and pointless deaths in place of clear and palpable meanings, but that doesn't diminish Schauwecker's critique of the everyday life around. One can imagine his reaction to the even less heroic world today.

For that reason, military re-enactment will, I think, grow in this country, as neoliberal Australia becomes as atomised and fractured as contemporary America. One of Thompson's interviewees explained, in a moment of agonised self-consciousness: 'The true secret of re-enacting is not that it offers a hobby for history buffs but that it addresses the failure of modern society to provide social interaction on a human scale.'

CONTROVERSIES

'Whenever people agree with me, I always feel I must be wrong.'

So declares Cecil Graham in Oscar Wilde's comedy *Lady Windermere's Fan*.

If you're committed to social change, you'll know how Graham feels. Almost by definition, you find yourself, on most subjects, in a minority, contending with those who argue that the way things are is the way things should always be.

But fighting for what you believe should not mean glorying in isolation. Later in the play, Cecil explains, in typical Wildean style, that he likes talking to a brick wall since 'it's the only thing in the world that never contradicts me.' Yet people, unlike walls, can change – and remarkably quickly.

For instance, sex between two men remained a criminal offence in Tasmania until 1997 – not very long ago at all. As recently as 2004, politicians still regarded same-sex marriage as sufficiently outlandish that, when John Howard introduced legislation to limit matrimony to heterosexuals, the Labor Party immediately backed him, signing off on the law without which the subsequent referendum would not have been necessary.

The American socialist Eugene Debs used to insist that it was much better to argue for something you want and not get it than speak in favour of something you don't want and see it delivered.

The overwhelming support for marriage reform in 2017 proves the point. Throughout the 2000s, so-called moderates (in the Australian Labor Party and elsewhere) offered 'civil contracts' as an alternative to full equality. In the wake of the referendum result, who remembers their proposals with anything other than contempt?

The shift in attitudes about sexuality constitutes one of the most remarkable social transformations in recent times. Not all debates are resolved so quickly. On many issues, progressives can feel more isolated today than they did a generation ago. This chapter contains interventions responding to various controversies.

The emergence of the so-called 'New Atheists' in the mid-2000s confounded many liberals. On the one hand, Christopher Hitchens, Richard Dawkins, Sam Harris and their many imitators aggressively challenged religious fundamentalists. On the other, their assault on believers often echoed the most bellicose rhetoric of the Islamophobic Right, just as the War on Terror reached a crescendo.

In 2009, I wrote about a Hitchens lecture in Sydney, trying to tease out the competing elements of his arguments. Today, the New Atheists don't hold nearly as much sway (partly because their rightward evolution became more apparent), but coming to terms with the nature of belief and non-belief is, I think, just as important as ever, not least because of the continuing political importance of evangelical groups like Hillsong.

Border policy in Australia constitutes one of the issues on which progressives have proved consistently unable to gain traction, even as the cruelty meted out to desperate people fleeing danger becomes ever more extreme. I've included here one of the many pieces I've written on the so-called refugee debate: a *Guardian* column that discussed a short story by the late Ursula le Guin in which a society enjoys prosperity and security – but only so long as it continues to torture a child.

Along similar lines, I wrote on the death of Sisto Malaspina, the much-loved Melbourne restaurateur whose murder by the deranged Hassan Khalif Shire Ali provided a pretext for some pundits to attack immigrants and immigration. In response, I outlined how Italian migrants like Malaspina's family had once been subjected to prejudices almost identical to those today directed at the Sudanese.

In a longer essay for *Counterpunch*, I discussed 'Soylent', a food substitute created by American entrepreneurs, arguing that the efforts by tech bros to make normal meals superfluous epitomised a profound social alienation.

In 2011, the conservative writer Andrew Bolt responded to riots in London by quoting at length from Enoch Powell, the race-baiting politician infamous for forecasting 'rivers of blood' unless Britain ceased immigration. In an article for the ABC, I used Bolt to illustrate the strange, mutually reinforcing relationship between social conservatism and the free market that destroys the traditions conservatives claim to uphold.

The devolution of Mark Latham from Gough Whitlam's protégé to Pauline Hanson's sidekick constitutes one of the more interesting (albeit depressing) stories in Australian politics. Back in 2015, Latham provided a perfect illustration of how identity politics now defines a conservatism that complains incessantly against identity politics.

In her poem 'The Veteran', Dorothy Parker describes youth as a time 'right was right, and wrong was wrong,' and then concludes:

> But I am old; and good and bad
> Are woven in a crazy plaid.

As her poem suggests, you're supposed to mellow naturally over time.

I've not found that to be the case. On the contrary, the longer I've been writing, the more I've been convinced that midway between two opposing opinions lies not the truth but the problem.

Unholy enthusiasm

When, in October 2009, Christopher Hitchens explained to a Sydney crowd how religion poisoned everything, he opened with a little joke. He'd been delighted, he said, to discover his hotel was situated in a locale where, if you took an evening constitutional, you could, without fear of embarrassment, ask a passerby, 'Am I heading for The Rocks?' The question had often previously occurred to him – but in Sydney, at least, the answer involved directions.

That was the first of several references to Hitchens's legendary thirst during a lecture advertised with its speaker, cigarette in mouth, glaring belligerently from posters like a drunk at closing time. Even with laughter still rippling around the hall, I found myself wondering why, in a talk about God, it should matter so very much that the audience knew that, yes, Hitchens really did like a drink.

But it was only later, after host Tony Jones insisted our lecturer recite – twice –Monty Python's drunken philosophers song, that I thought I understood. Hitchens was opening an event calling itself the Festival of Dangerous Ideas. At some level, the organisers sensed that, insofar as the evening featured only a middle-aged Oxbridge-educated intellectual – indeed, one who'd recently been profiled in *Vanity Fair*, boasting, like every other tiresome baby boomer, about quitting smoking and embracing exercise – we might struggle to believe that much risk lay in an utterly conventional denunciation of a deity in whom scarcely any of us believed. The arguments against God are, after all, sufficiently well established: as long ago as 1842, Marx was comparing atheists who brayed about their intellectual courage to 'children assuring everyone who is ready to listen to them that they are not afraid of the bogey man.' How, then, might a self-styled contrarian provide the frisson required for an evening of danger? The more, perhaps, he hinted at whisky-soaked debaucheries ('without God, all things are permitted'), the easier for us to persuade ourselves that we were all tremendously daring simply for listening.

These days, Hitchens specialises in slapping a veneer of militancy over arguments either entirely pedestrian or deeply conservative or both, spinning neocon talking points to *épater le bourgeois* in print or on television. With the New Atheism, however, he has found his metier, a cause in which posturing, parlour-room radicalism serves as both form and content.

If that seems unfair, consider a brief comparison. In 1884 an earlier unbeliever arrived in Australia. Like Hitchens, Joseph Symes came with a fearsome reputation as a polemicist; like Hitchens, he was a self-conscious provocateur, given to carrying bread in his pocket so that he could enrage believers by, as he putting it, having 'a chew on the body of Christ.' Symes, too, delighted in disputing with the pious (in 1892 he conducted a monster debate during which he buffeted the unfortunate Christian minister Isaac Selby over no fewer than six nights) – and, like Hitchens, he invariably crushed them.

Symes, however, did not receive an invitation to the main hall in the Opera House to address Sydney's good and great. In fact, when he sought to speak in the infinitely less grand Melbourne Opera House, the same class of people did everything to prevent him, eventually inducing Victoria's Chief Secretary Graham Berry to intervene and shut the event down. Nor did Symes attract the fawning media coverage enjoyed by Hitchens, with the respectable newspapers referring to him as 'that leprous-tongued reptile, Mr Joseph Symes' and his publication the *Liberator* as 'a cesspool of moral (or immoral) filth.' Symes's stay in Australia constituted, in fact, a narrative of more-or-less constant persecution: meetings cancelled, writs issued, newspapers burnt and so on. He was stoned in Woodend; he was charged for holding Sunday meetings; he was threatened with proceedings for blasphemy. A law was needed to 'consign such ruffians to the hangman's lash', opined the *Gippsland Mercury* – and most of establishment Australia agreed.

Symes's fate illustrates a fairly obvious point: that the political meaning of atheism has shifted in a way that few of its contemporary enthusiasts acknowledge. In the 1880s, anti-religious provocations required genuine moral courage. With a churchified establishment enforcing a compulsory Sabbath, Symes's denial of scriptural authority over Sunday opening didn't merely goad a few ridiculous fundamentalists, but rather offered an immediate challenge to governmental authority, in a campaign in which several of his associates were imprisoned (yes, Virginia: people really went to gaol for access to libraries in Australia!). Religion in Symes's day shaped policy on contraception, divorce, abortion, science, education and an array of issues: religion in Symes's day mattered.

In the 21st century, the traditional church in Australia simply doesn't possess such power. The Festival of Dangerous Ideas itself illustrates the point. It opened with Hitchens speaking against God; at a later session, Cardinal Pell spoke up on His behalf ('Without God we are nothing'). Which of the two events drew more pundits? Which lecturer confronted a more hostile crowd?

There are places today where atheists face persecution – but Australia is not among them. Religious rhetoric might, on occasion, impinge on the public sphere, but even social conservatives seek generally to express their prejudices in secular terms, recognising that appeals to Holy Writ no longer settle debates. The oily piety that Kevin Rudd, for instance, brings to hot-button issues (think, for instance, of the Bill Henson debate) seems, despite what he tells the *Monthly* crowd, less determined by theological imperatives than a deep conviction (shared equally with his secular colleagues) about the electoral appeal of social conservatism.

But the changing political meaning of atheism relates to more than simply the numerical decline of church attendance. With the *Liberator* so notorious that respectable butchers wouldn't wrap meat in it, Symes's subscribers were overwhelmingly working people, autodidacts trying to think their way to a better society. Their scepticism brought them into real and immediate conflict with the powers that be. Hitchens, by contrast, spoke at a $60 event at the Opera House to a crowd that, as you'd expect, was well educated, well heeled, overwhelmingly white and predominantly older – and nothing he said challenged his listeners in the slightest.

Today, when a celebrity non-believer fulminates in the broadsheets, at a writers week or on the ABC, they're staging, more often than not, a confrontation not with those listening but rather with those who aren't, a challenge issued not so much to our beliefs but to theirs; to doctrines, in other words, accepted by the kinds of Australians who don't go to the Opera House. Precisely because contemporary religion flourishes at the cultural margins (in the outer suburbs, for instance, or among immigrant communities) rather than amid the taste-setters and intellectuals, most New Atheist presentations contain more than a pinch of *bien-pensant* snobbery, so that the genteel crowd at a professorial demolition of some scriptural daftness or another leaves smugly satisfied with their superiority over those oiks for whom biblical fairytales still have meaning. That's why Daniel Dennett infamously suggested sceptics refer to each other as 'brights' and it's why Hitchens, in *God Is Not Great*, contrasts his childhood disbelief with the simplicities of his childhood teacher, a 'pious old trout'.

At the global rather than national level, the tendency becomes both more pronounced and more pernicious. If religion consists simply of a risible set of falsifiable and ethically wrong-headed propositions, then its adherents are, almost by definition, stupid and dangerous – and the more ardently they cling to their delusions, the more their stupidity and dangerousness grows. Furthermore, there are certain nations where, in these terms, the population seems very deluded indeed – and, wouldn't you know it, many of them can be found in the Middle East. So if the wild-eyed fanatics chanting *Allah akhbar* were to be confronted by the pointy end of Western rationality, well, would that be so very terrible?

Certainly, Sam Harris doesn't think so. In Australia, Harris might not be a name with which to conjure, but in the United States he's one of atheism's big three, part of an unholy trinity with Richard Dawkins and Hitchens. His breakthrough book *The End of Faith* begins as a general critique of God but morphs very quickly into a crass apologia for the war on terror and, precisely because Harris lacks Hitchens's political sophistication, his argument repays closer examination, since it illustrates quite openly some of the implications of the New Atheist methodology.

Harris, of course, excels at Symesian exposures of the contradictions and cruelties contained in the various sacred texts. He quotes, for instance, Deuteronomy on what believers should do if a family member proposes worshipping a different god:

> Show him no pity. Do not spare him or shield him. You must certainly put him to death. Your hand must be the first in putting him to death, and then the hands of all the people. Stone him to death, because he tried to turn you away from the Lord your God, who brought you out of Egypt, out of the land of slavery.

As Harris says, this – and the many similar passages in which the God of Love casually commends rapine and murder – goes a long way towards puncturing assertions that religion necessarily provides a basis for morality. But what follows from that?

In reply to objections that only a loopy fringe worries about the wilder reaches of the Old Testament, Harris argues that moderation in religion is scarcely less dangerous than fundamentalism, since the moderate retains, simply by accepting an unprovable God, the anti-rational methodology of the literalist:

> While moderation in religion may seem a reasonable position to stake out, in light of all that we have (and have not) learned about the universe, it offers no bulwark against religious extremism and religious violence ... The problem that religious moderation poses for all of us is that it does not permit anything very critical to be said about religious literalism. We cannot say that fundamentalists are crazy, because they are merely practicing their freedom of belief; we cannot even say that they are mistaken in religious terms, because their knowledge of scripture is generally unrivalled.

Yet for Harris, all religions might be bad but some are much worse than others – and there's no prize for guessing which particular faith falls into the latter category. 'We are', he explains, 'at war with Islam' since 'Islam, more than any other religion human beings have devised, has all the makings of a thoroughgoing cult of death.'

Do those of the Islamic faith have any genuine reasons for looking upon the United States in a less than favourable light? Apparently not: Harris, inevitably, quotes the political theorist Paul Berman to explain how 'in all of recent history, no country on earth has fought so hard and consistently as the United States on behalf of Muslim populations', while to explain Palestine, he defers to the equally loathsome Alan Dershowitz, the lawyer and right-wing pundit. 'No other nation in history faced with comparable challenges has ever adhered to a higher standard of human rights [than Israel]', Dershowitz tells us, 'been more sensitive to the safety of innocent civilians, tried harder to operate under the rule of law, or been willing to take more risks for peace'.

If the Iraqis don't show sufficient gratitude to the Great White Father in Washington, if the Palestinians complain of slaughter in Gaza, it can only be because of their oogety boogety religion of murder:

> In our dialogue with the Muslim world, we are confronted by people who hold beliefs for which there is no rational justification and which therefore cannot be discussed, and yet these are the very beliefs that underlie many of the demands they are likely to make upon us.

At this point, the careful reader might protest that Harris has already revealed the Bible and the Torah to be awash with rapine and slaughter. Do Christians and Jews also belong to death cults? No, not so much:

> Although we have seen that the Bible is a great reservoir of intolerance, for Christians and Jews alike—as everything from the writings of Augustine to the present actions of Israeli settlers demonstrates—it is not difficult to find great swaths of the Good Book, as well as Christian and Jewish exegesis, that offer counterarguments. The Christian who wants to live in the full presence of rationality and modernity can keep the Jesus of Matthew sermonising upon the mount and simply ignore the world-consuming rigmarole of Revelation.

You might think that Harris thus flatly contradicts his earlier argument about religious moderation – and you would be right. But, leaving aside the hypocrisy, a recognition that one can, after all, compartmentalise scriptural injunctions raises the obvious question of why particular verses take on especial significance in certain situations rather than others. In the wake of a homophobic beating in the United States, for instance, some newspapers carried photographs of a young tough tattooed with the biblical injunction 'Thou shall not lie with a male as one does with a woman. It is an abomination.' The remarkable image crystallised the problem: why do American evangelicals concern themselves so much with Leviticus 18:22 and not at all with the equally strident Leviticus 19:28 ('Ye shall not make any cuttings in your flesh for the dead, nor print any marks upon you: I am the LORD'), a verse generally take to mean that God hates tattoos just as much as he hates haircuts (Leviticus 19:27), people with flat noses (Leviticus 21:17–18) and different types of cattle grazing together (Leviticus 19:19).

Quite clearly, particular beliefs become activated in particular social and political settings: there's a historical context for the embrace of biblical homophobia, which is why the fundamentalist campaign against gay marriage does not extend to, say, demanding the death penalty for anyone who curses their parents (Leviticus 20:9). Harris, however, cannot acknowledge this most obvious of points, for his whole project depends upon understanding religion as a set of ideas divorced from history or culture or politics. He sees (in respect of Muslims, at least) the various sacred texts as divine instruction manuals, determinative of how believers interact with the world. That's why he takes fundamentalists as his paradigm – and that's why he explains away the conflicts in Palestine, the Balkans, Northern Ireland, Kashmir, Sudan, Nigeria, Ethiopia, Eritrea, Sri Lanka, Indonesia and the Caucasus as religious wars.

There were indeed religious sectarians in Northern Ireland who understood the Troubles in terms of theological dogma. But, by accepting their explanation of events (rather than, say, that put forward by secular anti-imperialists), Harris casually elides all the historical and social reasons why theological differences that, in other parts of the world, count for nothing whatsoever, became in Ireland a matter of life and death. One might, with equal validity, point to the role played by the colours green and orange during that struggle – and then blame the whole unfortunate business on the chromatic spectrum.

The inane insistence on religious doctrine as the explanation for all social behaviour runs throughout the New Atheist corpus, with even the much more genial Dawkins happy to wave away Ireland as a spat over God. That's why the movement really took off in the years following 9/11.

'Why do they hate us?' asked George Bush. If his answer ('They hate our freedoms') appealed viscerally to conservatives, the New Atheist reply ('They hate us because of their religion') provided an alternative rationale specially tailored for liberals. Thus, in the wake of 11 September, atheism opened the door to an understanding of the war on terror as – of all things – progressive. Here we were: sophisticated, democratic, secular; there they were: medieval, hierarchical, superstitious. Liberals who were too high-minded to invade Iraq for oil, and who found Bush's braying jingoism phoney and crass, knew that beardie weirdies reading from holy books represented only ignorance and repression – and, on that basis, regime change seemed long overdue.

Unfortunately for Harris, outside the United States, his career in the vanguard of imperial atheism laboured under a couple of unfortunate disadvantages. First, he proved himself something of a crackpot when, amid his polemic against faith, he off-handedly attested to the reality of psychic phenomena and then announced that 'there may even be some credible evidence for reincarnation'. (*The End of Faith* is a very strange book!) Second, and more importantly, Harris's American-style liberalism did not necessarily translate well abroad, particularly in countries with a stronger Left and thus a certain resistance to the transformative potential of preemptive war.

Hitchens, by contrast, learnt his politics as a Trotskyist, and so could more confidently access a rhetoric plundered from the progressive tradition. For Hitchens, the war on terror was, at a various times, about disarmament, about solidarity with the oppressed, about feminism, about liberation. Yet the struggle against religion remained fundamental, with the coinage of the meaningless portmanteau word 'Islamo-fascism' handily implying a battle waged simultaneously against Allah and Adolf.

Now, there's nothing inherently new about apologias for colonial adventures framed in terms of the backwardness of the natives and the foolishness of their religion. During the classical age of imperialism, it was a very familiar liberal argument: the East India Company would overcome the prejudices of the dusky Hindoo, the despoliation of Africa would liberate the dark continent from animism and superstition, and so on.

Back then, however, the beliefs of the subjugated were generally contrasted not with atheism but the God of the West: decent chaps agreed, for instance, that *sati*, the practice in which widows were forced to burn on the funeral pyre of their husbands, would be overcome only by shepherding Hindus into Christianity's kindly embrace.

But these days, as the Marxist literary scholar Terry Eagleton notes, God has shifted over from the side of civilisation to the side of barbarism. Precisely because, in the West, the enfeebled mainstream churches do not present a credible alternative to anything much at all, the old rhetoric works better if Christianity appears in the deficit column of the ledger, an example of backwardness rather than an instance of progress. By giving the traditional critique of native unreason an atheist twist (in which, rather than being foolish for refusing Jesus, the darkies are foolish for believing in God at all), Hitchens can free the old trope from colonial connotations and drape it, more or less credibly, in the vestments of radicalism.

But the liberals who nod along judiciously to his bluster about the Islamo-fascist threat (they're setting up a caliphate, don't you know!) rarely consider how an anti-religious conception of the war on terror leads Hitchens and the other imperial atheists to even more nakedly eliminationist positions than those adopted by the extreme Right. The most conservative elements in the Bush administration – the people who openly saw the conflict simply in terms of United States geopolitical hegemony – could, at least in theory, arrive at some accommodation with those locals willing to knuckle down under occupation. But if you interpret the wars in Afghanistan and Iraq as skirmishes in a broader struggle against an international death cult, any result short of extermination became tantamount to surrender: there is, as we have learned, no such thing as 'moderation' in religion. Hence Hitchens's rejoinder to those who quailed at the bloodiness of the siege of Fallujah, which, according to non-government organisations, killed between 4000 and 6000 people, and destroyed 36 000 houses, 9000 shops, fifty-six mosques and sixty schools. 'The death toll is not nearly high enough', he said. '[T]oo many [jihadists] have escaped.'

Wisely, his keynote presentation at the Opera House eschewed the 'exterminate the brutes' rhetoric in favour of more traditionally liberal jibes against creationists and cardinals and other stage villains. Elsewhere, however, he has been notably less restrained, on one occasion famously expressing a ghoulish enthusiasm for the atheistic effects of cluster bombs:

> If you're actually certain that you're hitting only a concentration of enemy troops ... then it's pretty good because those steel pellets will go straight through somebody and out the other side and through somebody else. And if they're bearing a Koran over their heart, it'll go straight through that, too. So they won't be able to say, 'Ah, I was bearing a Koran over my heart and guess what, the missile stopped halfway through.' No way, 'cause it'll go straight through that as well. They'll be dead, in other words.

A rhetorical flourish? No, a logical corollary. That's why Sam Harris, who understands religion in the same fashion, draws similar conclusions. As we've noted, for him, even religious moderation poses a 'threat to our survival' – and thus *The End of Faith* concludes its denunciation of the evils done by believers with a ringing defence of ... torture. 'Given what many of us believe about the exigencies of our war on terrorism', Harris intones, 'the practice of torture, in certain circumstances, would seem to be not only permissible but necessary'.

Back in the dungeons of the Inquisition, who would have imagined that, one day, men would be made to scream in the name not of God but of unbelief? Hurrah for the triumph of reason over backwardness! The irony in all this is that nothing in recent decades has fanned religion as successfully as Harris's War on Terror. In the years since 2001, all across the Middle East, secular movements and regimes have come under increasing pressure from various shades of Islamism. Is it really so hard to understand why?

In 2003, during the initial stages of the Iraq invasion, one of those pellets that Hitchens admires so much killed a 14-year-old Iraqi boy named Arkan Daif. Naturally, for the rest of the world, Arkan's demise didn't register amid all the other collateral damage in Iraq (perhaps as many as a million excess deaths to date); equally naturally, for his family, his death was all-consuming. In his book *Night Draws Near*, Anthony Shadid describes how Arkan's relatives turned, in their grief, to religion, with the traditional dictates of an Islamic funeral busying the family and providing a structure to cope with their anguish.

Since time immemorial, the loss of a child turns parents to the consolation of faith. But in Iraq in 2003 Arkan's death represented not a private tragedy but a particular manifestation of a generalised catastrophe. Shadid explains:

> During those days of war in Baghdad, there was often a sense of the apocalypse that the weather had seemed to foreshadow ...
>
> The Muslim funeral rite was sadly routine in Iraq, but equally dignified and unhurried whenever it was performed. During the bombing, in times so precarious, such traditions began to assume new meaning; they were constants, filling time, busying and distracting relatives when their grief was greatest.

> At once formal and intimate, like the Arabic language, the rituals brought consolation and solace as the world outside grew ever more threatening and unpredictable.

Under attack, with your house in ruins and your son casually slaughtered, it is not logic that you seek, for any rational assessment confirms that what's happened can't be undone. Now, as our New Atheists will bray, prayer really won't guarantee your family's safety. But with shock and awe raining down on the city, neither will anything much else – and, under such circumstances, miracles appeal precisely because they're impossible.

If we're worried by the growth of religion, if we see God as a delusion, how to respond to Shadid's description? Would anyone suggest that berating Iraqis about how, according to the Koran, Mohammed married a 9-year-old girl and was thus a pedophile would turn the Daif family and others like them away from Islam? Or is it not obvious that ending the random slaughter of Iraqi kids would do more to foster secularism in that country than any amount of undergraduate atheism, especially that churned out by the people who cheered on the attack that sent shrapnel into Arkan's young body?

Religion, says Marx, is the opium of the masses, a quotation that the New Atheists inevitably drag out, since it seems to confirm their approach. They, of course, see God as a kind of spiritual chloroform. For them, he's a magician's trick played on the weak-minded: that's why, if you reveal the hidden trapdoor behind the theological stage, believers will simply melt away like an audience walking out on a bumbling conjurer.

But Marx's argument was altogether different. Here's the notorious opium quote in context:

> Religious suffering is, at one and the same time, the *expression* of real suffering and a *protest* against real suffering. Religion is the sigh of the oppressed creature, the heart of a heartless world, and the soul of soulless circumstances. It is the opium of the people.

The passage expands and completes the metaphor. As anyone who's been to hospital knows, opiates aren't simply a source of befuddlement. Whatever their side effects, they provide genuine relief from pain. Accordingly, if you're unhappy about a sick friend's morphine habit, you begin by treating their underlying illness – you don't simply snatch away their prescription.

If God doesn't create us, then we create God – and we do so because something about how we live makes him seem indispensable. Religion isn't overcome simply by demonstrating the intellectual fallacies that underpin it. It's overcome by changing the conditions under which God seems necessary: as Marx puts it, 'the struggle against religion is, therefore, indirectly the struggle against that world whose spiritual aroma is religion.'

The New Atheists do, to a certain extent, link material reality to religion, but only in the crudest fashion. They generally identify faith as the legacy of a pre-scientific era, with the deity who sits in the clouds and sends down thunderbolts prefiguring a more accurate understanding of lightning. That's why they contrast religion with modernity: as if, with the rise of science, God became superfluous, and thus easily dispelled with a few zingers about the Pope or Muhammed.

Yet a moment's thought reveals that religion has always been protean, serving utterly different functions in different eras and different conditions. Christianity means something quite different to, on the one hand, the Anglican vicar who vaguely imagines Jesus as a kind of giant Englishman, pottering about among the roses of creation, and, on the other, the 16th-century Anabaptist rebel leading a peasant rebellion. If modernity sweeps away some religions, it fosters others in their place. In 21st-century Australia, most of the traditional churches have entered into a slow but steady decline, in part because their languorous rituals simply cannot cope with the frenetic pace of a hyperindividualised, neoliberal society. The dour Wesleyian divinity that Joseph Symes confronted in 19th-century Melbourne has, accordingly, been supplanted by what scholar Marion Maddox calls the Market God, that fearsome idol whose mysterious whims deliver prosperity or plunge us into destitution.

Yet, as Maddox argues, because the free market 'sabotages family and community life and tears away safety nets', the Market God has 'had to make Olympian room for another deity, one who brings ... a renewed sense of the security that the Market God took away'. The shriller evangelical sects grow, she suggests, as a complement to a marketised world where a significant proportion of the population feels isolated, unhappy and starved for any purpose or communion beyond cold cash transactions. Hillsong does not represent some quaint legacy of the past: it is, rather, a quintessentially 21st-century-phenomenon, as modern as derivatives trading or internet pornography.

Something similar might be said about Islamism. Since 2001, religion has grown in the Middle East not simply because, for families like the Daifs, it offered solace in the face of personal misery, but also because it provided a way of understanding what was taking place in the world – and, even, perhaps doing something to change it. With the secular Left across the region seen as impotent at best and, at worst, corrupt and complicit, Islamists could present themselves as a dedicated, ascetic and self-sacrificing alternative.

Given that the most obvious non-religious options were either Ba'athism or various forms of Stalinism, it's not so surprising that resistance to occupation in Iraq took on an Islamic colouration. The same story recurs again and again. What did the Taliban have going for them? Not a lot, except that unbelief, in the Afghan context, meant Soviet occupation, and the pious Talibs seemed less venal than other warlords. Western liberals might find the election of Hamas in the Occupied Territories utterly baffling, given the organisation's enthusiasm for sharia law. But the mystery of Hamas's popularity becomes less perplexing when we consider that, during the assault upon Gaza, Fatah – the voice of Palestinian secularism – was privately urging the Israelis to extend the incursion, hoping that prolonged war would settle their factional rivals.

Insofar as religion is, in certain contexts, on the rise, it reflects, more than anything else, the failure of secular alternatives in the face of intolerable conditions. That is what makes the self-satisfaction of the New Atheists so repulsive. If, in Australia, happy clapping evangelists are making inroads among the youth, it's not because the kids today are more stupid or gullible than their parents. In fact, the Hillsong-style congregations tend to be entirely at home with technology, and the young men and women drawn to them have, via the wonders of the internet, more information at their fingertips than any other generation in the history of the human race. Rather than glibly telling ourselves that the new religionists can't grasp our clever arguments, should we not consider another, less palatable, alternative: that they understand quite well what secular liberalism offers – and they don't find it very attractive?

To make the point another way, if, like Marx, we see religion as simultaneously an expression of alienation and a protest against it, where then does that leave the New Atheism? Do Hitchens and Harris and their ilk provide any kind of alternative to a lonely kid in the suburbs of Sydney? Or do they, with their Opera House lectures and their unholy enthusiasm for permanent war, counter the sigh of the oppressed only with the smug sneer of the oppressor?

The 19th-century freethinkers were not exactly secular saints. Symes, in particular, was a difficult and querulous figure, whose lectures often contained a degree of lordly patronage. Nonetheless, his atheism, whatever else might have been wrong with it, at least entailed a genuine crusade against some of the more obvious evils of his era. In that light, one of the slogans he formulated seems more relevant than ever. 'If you are going to offend', Symes suggested, 'do so thoroughly'.

Respectable Australia in the 21st century considers all manner of things sacred. But God, by and large, is not among them. If you want to cause thoroughgoing offence, you might, for instance, try speaking up against the Israeli apartheid state and its Australian partisans, on the basis that a modicum of justice for the Palestinians would do more to counter Islamism than the umpteenth plonking repetition of atheistic arguments already old a century ago. But that, of course, would be much less profitable than standing in the Opera House to tell the glitterati about how little you're scared by the bogey man.

What's the end game for Australia's border policy?

In her much-anthologised story 'The Ones Who Walk Away from Omelas', the great novelist Ursula Le Guin describes what seems at first to be an almost idyllic land.

The people of Omelas live by the sea, where they enjoy 'a boundless and generous contentment' in a wealthy and prosperous society. There's just one catch. Underneath a public building in Omelas sits a whimpering child, permanently imprisoned in a tiny room and deprived of all comfort and pleasure.

Everyone in Omelas knows that the child's there. But they also know that 'their happiness, the beauty of their city, the tenderness of their friendships, the health of their children, the wisdom of their scholars, the skill of their makers, even the abundance of their harvest and the kindly weathers of their skies, depend wholly on this child's abominable misery'.

Le Guin explains that, when young people in Omelas learn of the child, they're invariably sickened by what's been done to it. But the elders of the city explain the necessity:

> If the child were brought up into the sunlight out of that vile place, if it were cleaned and fed and comforted, that would be a good thing, indeed; but if it were done, in that day and hour all the prosperity and beauty and delight of Omelas would wither and be destroyed. Those are the terms. To exchange all the goodness and grace of every life in Omelas for that single, small improvement: to throw away the happiness of thousands for the chance of the happiness of one: that would be to let guilt within the walls indeed. The terms are strict and absolute; there may not even be a kind word spoken to the child.

And, by and large, the citizens of Omelas come to perceive 'the terrible justice of reality, and to accept it'.

Does that sound at all familiar?

In Australia, we don't have a room in which the innocent suffer. Rather, we have camps. One of them is in Nauru – and it's there that Omid Masoumali burned himself to death.

Omid had broken no law. It's perfectly legal to claim asylum. Besides, he'd already been assessed as a legitimate refugee – that is, the relevant officials had agreed that this young man faced a well-founded fear of persecution or death in his native Iran.

But the Australian government insists that no boat-borne asylum seekers will settle in Australia. As a result, Masoumali remained in limbo. If he returned to Iran, he faced the risk of being killed – and no other country would take him.

Masoumali had been in detention for three years. According to his wife, after his suicide attempt he received no morphine for ten hours – and it took twenty-four hours for him to be airlifted to Brisbane, where he died.

Why did he deserve such punishment? What fault had he committed, other than to flee a tyrannical regime that brutalised him and then seek assistance from a wealthy nation? No-one from the Liberal party or the Labor party can answer those questions. In fact they don't even try.

Instead, politicians and their apologists make the same argument as the rulers of Omelas. The borders must be secured, the people smugglers must be deterred – and that means no sympathy can be permitted for Masoumali or any of the other detainees engaged in self-harm in Nauru or Manus.

'Obviously nobody wants to see these scenes', said immigration minister Peter Dutton, 'nobody wants to see people harming themselves. But ...'

In that 'but', you can hear the code of Omelas, a land where not even a kind word can be spoken to the sacrificial child.

Le Guin intended her story as a cautionary tale. How did we end up with two political parties using it as an instruction manual?

Many in the liberal intelligentsia – particularly Labor supporters – blame the voters. Australians, we are told, demand the exclusion of refugees. As a result, the Labor party must embrace the harshest possible policies or risk electoral annihilation.

Even on face value, the argument doesn't make sense. We all know that there are lots of issues on which politicians ignore public opinion. Voters consistently hate privatisations, for instance – but that doesn't mean privatisations don't happen. The war in Afghanistan was unpopular for years, but both Labor prime ministers Julia Gillard and Kevin Rudd insisted they would stay the course. But let's leave that aside and look at the figures on asylum seekers.

It's certainly true that many voters lack any automatic sympathy for refugees. In November 2015, Essential Report surveyed people as to whether they thought the federal government was too tough or too soft on asylum seekers. About a quarter of respondents thought it was 'too tough', 31 per cent thought it was 'taking the right approach' and 29 per cent thought it was 'too soft'.

The result was in line with past surveys – except that the proportion opting for 'too soft' had increased from 18 per cent in July 2014 to 29 per cent in November 2015, during a period in which the Abbott government had substantially toughened Australia's border regime.

Yet the same report also included data on a more significant question. When investigators asked people to nominate the three most important issues determining vote allocations, 'treatment of asylum seekers' ranked only eleventh, selected as one of the three most important issues by 8 per cent of respondents. The highest ranked issues were: 'management of the economy' (47 per cent), 'Australia's health system' (46 per cent), and 'jobs and protection of local industries' (39 per cent).

These results, too, have been consistent for a long time. In other words, voters might not want to help refugees – but nor are they obsessed with punishing them. As researchers Peter Lewis and Jackie Woods write:

> Despite the heat and headlines generated by boat arrivals and asylum seeker policy, our research over many years has shown that Australians don't identify border protection as an issue that influences their vote, listing it well behind stalwarts like health and the economy. The issue, however, does feed into a general perception about government values, strength and competence.

That last sentence is key. Australians care most about good economic conditions and decent healthcare. But these are difficult outcomes for governments to deliver. It's much simpler to crack down on refugees than it is to, say, provide jobs for all those who want them or to cut hospital waiting times.

'Border protection was always a symbolic political issue', argue Lewis and Woods elsewhere, 'a proxy for immigration, terrorism and too much traffic in Western Sydney. It was about government taking a stand and protecting the nation from the outside world'.

The consensus on border security has, in other words, been driven by politicians, not because the issue's difficult, but precisely because it's easy. You might not be able to create work in the western suburbs. You can, however, rail against people-smugglers – and by so doing perhaps appeal to voters primarily concerned about the high unemployment for which you have no fix.

It's this toxic bipartisanship that has brought us to Le Guin's Omelas. After a decade or more of the major parties marching in lockstep, the most ludicrous policy decisions often escape scrutiny, simply because there's no real force capable of holding the government of the day to account over asylum seeker policy.

Take, for instance, Kevin Rudd's decision to open a detention centre on Manus Island. The initial announcement of the Papua New Guinea (PNG) solution contained within it all the seeds of the policy's eventual collapse. How would a desperately poor developing nation manage Australia's detention centre? More importantly, why would it want to, other than to reap the benefits of the hastily arranged payola? Where were the refugees ultimately going to be settled?

Note that the PNG high court's 2016 decision unanimously found that the centre had always been illegal – that is, the facility was a violation of the constitution from its very inception. How was this not apparent back in 2013?

The problem's not just the way that specific absurdities like Manus escape scrutiny. It's also the normalisation of the reactionary fantasy upon which the entire policy framework rests. The bipartisan commitment to offshore processing assumes that refugees arriving by boat constitute an almost existential threat, so much so that they must be deterred at all costs. Hence Manus Island. Hence Nauru.

But if that argument's true for wealthy Australia, it's surely equally true for other countries. If refugees arriving by boat are so toxic that none can be settled on the Australian mainland, why would any other nations put their hands up to resettle these people? How, exactly, are the unfortunates currently languishing in Nauru ever going to be released?

More generally, by definition, Australian deterrence only works if what's dished out to asylum seekers on our borders is significantly harsher than what they encounter elsewhere. How long's that going to be the case? If the boats are genuinely being turned back, why shouldn't we expect other countries to adopt the same approach, ratcheting up the deterrence they enforce? What's the end game – a world of walled city-states, each entirely impervious to outsiders? How is this possibly a long-term solution to international population flows?

In his endless self-justifications in *Quadrant* magazine, former prime minister Tony Abbott claims 'stopping the boats' as the great achievement of his administration. But counting that as a success is only possible if you ignore the consequences of an Australian policy fostering illiberalism and authoritarianism throughout the region. Australia's obsession with 'stopping the boats' meant deliberately undermining efforts to hold Sri Lanka to account for torture.

It's been the same everywhere. In Nauru, the detention centre has contributed to the diminishing rule of law on the island. In PNG, an Australian Federal Police officer last year argued that the Turnbull Government was turning a blind eye to extrajudicial killings in order to keep Manus Island operational, while the Human Rights Law Centre accused Australia of weakening criticism of Cambodia's human rights violations so as to facilitate the failed attempt to resettle refugees there.

In other words, the efforts to deter boats have led directly to an accommodation of the kinds of cruelties that spur people to flee in boats. What's being presented as a solution is, in fact, massively exacerbating the problem.

Surely it's time for a new perspective. We might start by

challenging the anti-humanist prejudice that declares people to be a problem. So much of the current debate simply assumes that Australia's permanently menaced by a heaving tide of humanity. This is nonsense. It's often forgotten that, until comparatively recently, immigration was something that most developed nations welcomed – think, for instance, of the Assisted Passage Migration Scheme by which the Chifley Government attracted British migrants in the years after the Second World War.

If we started talking about refugees as assets rather than liabilities, where might the discussion go then? Most economists agree that immigrants don't take jobs; that, on the contrary, they stimulate an economy by generating demand. If the anti-refugee sentiment is fuelled by anxieties about jobs and the health system, what would happen if we discussed immigration in the context of a massive works project, one that might provide work for new arrivals even as it created the infrastructure to help support them?

In the current climate, that might sound hopelessly idealistic. But it's much less utopian than the fantasy that the status quo depends upon. Displaced people are moving all over the planet – and they will continue to move, no matter how cruelly they're treated.

Le Guin's story concludes by noting that not everyone in Omelas accepts the suffering of the tortured child. Some people, she tells us, abandon the whole compact on which the city's based: 'They leave Omelas, they walk ahead into the darkness, and they do not come back.'

Surely it's time we did the same.

The death of Sisto Malaspina

> Melbourne will stop tomorrow and the nation will watch as the city pays its respects to an Italian-born cafe proprietor whose death at the hands of a deranged assailant has rubbed raw a debate about immigration numbers, refugee intake, ethnic crime and Islamist-inspired terrorism.

That's Fairfax columnist Tony Walker, arguing in 2018 that the murder of Sisto Malaspina, the co-owner of Pellegrini's, should prompt 'a root and branch conversation about the costs and benefits of Australia's immigration and refugee intake programs.'

Well, perhaps that's true – but not in the way he thinks. The history of Malaspina's beloved Pellegrini's illustrates the obvious similarities between the prejudices of the past and those that lurk at the edges of Walker's piece. In his book *Italians in Australia,* Francesco Ricatti explains the prism through which southern European immigrants were once viewed:

> In the late 19th century, and indeed well into the 20th century, the 'scientific' theories of Italian anthropologists such as Lombroso and Niceforo – who argued for the racial inferiority of southern Italians and their racial proximity to Africans – were very popular not just in Italy but also in the Americas. In countries of Italian migration like the United States, Brazil, Argentina, and Australia, these theories fostered the idea that southern Italian migrants were not really white, that they were racially ambiguous, that they had a drop of black blood in their veins, and that they were the 'Chinese of Europe'.

The use of southern Italians as replacement for the indentured labour of Pacific Islanders reinforced this identification of Italian immigrants as non-white.

In 1907, the *Bulletin* solemnly explained that, while northern Italians should be classified as degenerated Germans, southerners possessed distinctly African blood.

'By the 1920s', says Ricatti, 'Italians were often described as "black Mediterranean", and there is some anecdotal evidence that a variation of this expression, namely "black Italians", was still used in north Queensland in the 1960s.'

Furthermore, like many immigrants today, Italians were victims of religious bigotry. They might not have been Muslim but they were Catholic, which, at the time, was far, far worse. The respectable Protestant ruling class associated the Church of Rome with disloyalty (until 2013, Catholics were automatically disqualified from succession in the royal family), a prejudice reinforced by the involvement of

Catholics in the 1916 Easter Uprising against British rule in Ireland.

Thus, in 1920, *Smith's Weekly*, a publication oriented to returned soldiers, labelled the Italian migrant as a 'dirty dago pest' and campaigned against 'a greasy flood of Mediterranean scum that seeks to defile and debase Australia.'

That long history of anti-Italian racism makes the public embrace of Pellegrini's both remarkable and relevant.

In 1954, the year the brothers Leo and Vildo Pellegrini established their restaurant, a mass meeting brought some 2000 people to the Sydney Town Hall. They were there to protest, in very Walker-like terms, at 'the irreparable harm being done to our social structure and national culture by the immigration policy of the federal government.'

But they weren't upset about Muslims or Sudanese. Instead, they railed against 'further migration from southern Europe', with the main speaker, a Mr Aubrey Downer, denouncing 'a constant shuffle of Italian liners back and forth bringing some of the most undesirable residents.'

Today, Walker blames the political class for failing to address honestly and overtly concerns about immigration, except by surreptitiously imposing a ceiling on net overseas migration.

In 1954, Downer made a very similar claim:

'The number of Italians and other southern Europeans flooding this country', he said, 'are of vital statistical import if the object of the census is to collate fundamental facts. Is it that the Migration Department is desperately anxious that the number of foreign communities in this country be concealed?'

Walker tells us that in Melbourne, 'police are being run ragged in their efforts to combat ethnic crime', and singles out Sudanese youths for special mention.

That Town Hall meeting heard the same arguments about Italians. '[I]t is impossible', said Downer, 'to pick up a daily newspaper without some fresh crime by a new settler being reported, mostly of a serious nature.'

It was, in fact, an ubiquitous argument during that decade. A year earlier, *Truth* had denounced a 'terrorist racket on migration', in which the dreaded 'Black Hand' society was said to be smuggling Italians into Australia.

'New Australians should be photographed and finger-printed', it concluded, 'and rigorously checked to exclude undesirables.'

Along similar lines, the Sydney event passed a resolution linking immigration with criminality, in which the protesters demanded the deportation of 'all migrants convicted of serious offences in Australia.'

By 1958, Pellegrini's had grown large enough to extend from its original, tiny premises into a bigger space. That was the year that, during a parliamentary debate, an MP casually explained that southern Italians 'had no law but that of the tooth and the knife.' It's a passage the current rhetoric about Sudanese people grotesquely echoes.

Today, Australian expats claim the flat white coffee as almost a signature drink, a caffeinated emblem of antipodean culture. But in the 1950s the espresso machine deployed for the first time at Pellegrini's represented the heights of exoticism. When contemporary conservatives sneer at 'latte drinking' intellectuals, they're inadvertently channelling the prejudices of a half-century ago, back when only the effete intelligentsia would join Italians in enjoying a decent brew.

The centrality of Italians (and other southern Europeans) in industries like construction and manufacturing meant that they played a crucial role in the political and industrial struggles out of which contemporary multiculturalism emerged. But that's another story.

Suffice to say that the enormous affection for Pellegrini's exemplifies a tremendous social reform, with an identity once mocked and feared by respectable Australia moving to the very centre of the culture.

We might, if we so chose, see Malaspina's murder as the occasion for a renewed nativism, in which all the old fears about immigrants would be voiced.

Alternatively, we could understand the grief over his death as illustrating the potential to overcome prejudice, even in the most difficult of circumstances.

Soylent, neoliberalism and the politics of life hacking

Karl Marx famously argued that alienation of labour (our most basic activity) meant that we felt human only during 'animal functions' such as eating and drinking.

Of course, Marx had never met Rob Rhinehart, the entrepreneur featured in a 2014 Lizzie Widdicombe *New Yorker* piece for his efforts to replace food with a grey slurry he calls 'Soylent'.

Rhinehart's Eureka moment came while he was struggling to launch a tech start-up. Funds dwindling, he resented the expensive inefficiency of eating – and engineered a solution.

'You need amino acids and lipids, not milk itself', he explained. 'You need carbohydrates, not bread.'

Having calculated the various nutrients the entrepreneurial body might require, he ordered them online. Into a blender went his powders and potions – and, voilà, Soylent.

After three months on this food-free regime, Rhinehart realised he'd found the stuff from which fortunes were made.

With backing from Silicon Valley venture capitalists, he's now manufacturing commercial-grade Soylent throughout the United States.

Meal substitutes (Erasure, Slim Fast, etc) are nothing new. But Soylent's success, Widdicombe suggests, reflects the rise of 'life hacking', the conviction that one's daily routine can and should be optimised, much as savvy computer users download apps and tweak settings to optimise their machines. The always-zeitgesty *Gawker* empire features a site called *Lifehacker*, which helps you, it says, 'to work harder and save time' – pretty much the spiel with which Rhinehart touts his slush.

But save time for what?

Widdicome describes life hacking as 'freeing yourself up for whatever you'd rather be doing'. But Soylent actually exemplifies how, in most life hacks, leisure (the putative goal) remains an asymptotic horizon, while productivity becomes a good in and of itself. When Rhinehart describes non-Soylent meals as 'recreational food', he's implicitly acknowledging that his product doesn't foster recreation so much as displace the traditional pastime we call 'eating'.

Soylent's deliberately unflavoured because it's a utility rather than a snack, a system rather than a supplement. The terminology recalls the historic relationship writer Nikil Saval identifies between Silicon Valley-style life hacking and the 'scientific' management craze of the early industrial period. Where Frederick Winslow Taylor, the most famous industrial systemiser, specialised in harassing assembly line workers with his stopwatch, science-minded managers applied a similar methodology in white-collar workplaces, obsessing as to whether their clerks opened letters or filed papers quite as fast as they might.

In the 1920s 'scientific efficiency' was, by and large, imposed by employers upon an unwilling workforce. Taylor hacked other people's lives – and they hated him for it. As he wrote of his initial experiments, 'anyone who has been through such a fight knows and dreads the meanness of it and the bitterness of it'.

But, though today's life hackers might (like Rhinehart) have entrepreneurial aspirations, they are not, by and large, bosses themselves. Soylent's not purchased by the Mark Zuckerbergs or the Larry Pages or the other tech aristocrats (who, one imagines, prefer haute cuisine to Rhinehart's gloop). Rather, it's been taken up by white-collar workers and students destined for perpetual toil in the digital mills.

Their embrace of life hacking represents the internalisation of management practices by the managed themselves. 'The arc of scientific management is long,' says Saval, 'but it bends toward self-Taylorizing'.

In the mid-1990s, business gurus began urging cubicle jockeys to conceive of themselves as one-man corporations. In a characteristic 1997 piece, Tom Peters enthused about 'The Brand Called You', urging readers to foster their personal brand as carefully as Nike and Coca-Cola did, and to regularly check in with the market 'to have a reliable read on your brand's value'. And, as the writer Thomas Frank notes, Peters's essay concluded with an overt threat: 'Start today. Or else'.

The point's not that workers were bullied into embracing the practices of Peters's 'new brand world' (though, naturally, they were), but that, for many white-collar workers, restructuring the self around a corporate logic made sense as the tech world grew ever more competitive, and once-elite IT jobs became proletarianised and less secure.

Again, Soylent provides a handy illustration. Many of us do not fancy gulping down a yeasty slurry at our desks, for the simple reason that we enjoy breaking bread with friends or loved ones. But, of course, that's not an option for the people for whom the stuff's made.

Widdicombe describes a coterie of Soylent enthusiasts at a Caltech dorm called Ricketts House (yes, really!), which, according to the resident adviser, accomodates 'a lot of very busy engineering and physics students' who 'don't have time to do anything'. These kids don't worry about the health consequences of a Soylent-only diet since, for them, Rhinehart's brew represents a step up.

'I think about how shitty I eat when I'm not eating Soylent', one says. 'There've been weeks when I've eaten nothing but cheesy pasta.'

If you know your working life will involve crushing deadlines and an ongoing insecurity that leaves you always a dollar short and a day late, then acclimatising yourself to sucking Soylent as you cram for exams makes perfect sense.

Of course, the malnourished students of Ricketts House are an extreme example, but the general tendency's familiar for most of us. The *Lifehacker* site finds an audience for its tips about beating insomnia or prioritising messages in Gmail or whatever else because, actually, most of us now need that kind of information. Saval writes:

> Life-hacking wouldn't be popular if it didn't tap into something deeply corroded about the way work has, without much resistance, managed to invade every corner of our lives. The idea started out as a somewhat earnest response to the problem of fragmented attention and overwork – an attempt to reclaim some leisure time and autonomy from the demands of boundaryless labor. But it has since become just another hectoring paradigm of self-improvement. The proliferation of apps and gurus promising to help manage even the most basic tasks of simple existence – the 'quantified self' movement does life hacking one better, turning the simple act of breathing or sleeping into something to be measured and refined – suggests that merely getting through the day has become, for many white-collar professionals, a set of problems to solve and systems to optimise. Being alive is easier, it turns out, if you treat it like a job.

But what happens when a job for life gives way to a life as a job? Let's return to Marx's alienated worker of the 19th century, a fellow who, condemned to perform monotonous factory work, loathes his labour and comes alive only when 'eating, drinking, procreating, or at most in his dwelling and in dressing-up, etc.'

We know what Soylent does to eating and drinking. But something very similar's occurring with Marx's other 'animal functions.' Take 'dressing up.'

Marx argues that workers, deprived of any creative fulfilment in a labour process shaped by someone else, find opportunities for expression in the clothes they wear. 'What is animal becomes human', he writes, 'and what is human becomes animal'.

Note, he's not suggesting that there's something wrong with dressing up (or eating, etc.); he's highlighting how, barred from controlling the labour by which human society is shaped, the worker can only exercise his will in the brute activities that keep him alive.

'Certainly eating, drinking, procreating, etc., are also genuinely human functions', says Marx. 'But taken abstractly, separated from the sphere of all other human activity and turned into sole and ultimate ends, they are animal functions.'

Now compare Widdicombe's description of how Rhinehart life hacks his wardrobe:

> In an effort to optimise the dressing process, he alternates between two pairs of jeans, and orders nylon or polyester T-shirts from Amazon, wearing them for a few weeks before donating them. When the clothes get smelly, he puts them in the freezer, to get rid of the odor. 'Sometimes, during the day, a couple of hours will do it', he told me. 'I'll wear a towel.'

Consciously eliminating any hint of self-expression from the biological necessity of keeping warm, Widdicombe's removing from his clothing precisely the aspect Marx identifies as human. He's turning dressing into a means to an end, 'optimising it' in the form of the alienated labour from which it once represented an escape. The external compulsion that operates in the workplace has been internalised at home with the pleasure of adornment giving way to a grey, abstract efficiency.

What about procreation, Marx's other 'animal' activity? As it happens, you can find something similar among the life hackers' less-respectable brethren – the so-called 'seduction community'.

The men chronicled in Neil Strauss's best-selling book *The Game* and featured in the VH1 television show *The Pick Up Artist* replace the clumsy happenstance of traditional romance with a Taylorised come-on system based around memorised 'routines'. Essentially, they take the hacks out of the office and into the bedroom (or, at least, the singles bar), deploying an array of pseudo-scientific gambits to more efficiently manoeuvre women into the sack.

Now, the pick-up artists (PUAs) are ostensibly libertines. Yet in their own peculiar way, they, too, valorise productivity over eros, using a distinctively technocratic vocabulary in the 'field reports' in which they reduce sex to numbers ('A blonde 10 in a two-set'). Symptomatically, by the end of his narrative, Strauss describes himself obsessively collecting the phone numbers of girls he never calls, his carnal interests replaced by an almost actuarial concern with statistics.

Where Marx's workers find solace in the body, the tendency of life hacking is to eliminate biology altogether – not because it's too animalistic but because it's too human. As the economic theorist Philip Mirowski says: 'this is the true terminus of the neoliberal self: [...] to shrug off the surly bond rating of earth; to transform yourself at the drop of a hat or the swallow of a pill, to be beholden to no other body but only to the incorporeal market'.

Yet Soylent also illustrates one way that the fundamentally anti-human ideology of neoliberalism can find a modicum of popular support. In *Labour and Monopoly Capitalism*, Harry Braverman explains that scientific management is, first and foremost, about stripping all control of the labour process from the workforce and concentrating that control with the management. '[Taylor]', he writes, 'asserted as an absolute necessity for adequate management the dictation to the worker of the precise manner in which work is to be performed.'

In precapitalist society, artisans might take pride in a job that required the utmost skill, with functionality combining with creativity in everyday activities. As the anarchist Bob Black notes, the Grecian urns we today showcase in museums were constructed for the entirely mundane purpose of storing olive oil. The production of such an object certainly involved labour – but a labour that allowed the maker to express something of himself in his work.

Quite consciously, the Taylorite managers destroyed whatever craft skills had survived the onset of industrialisation, reducing creative work to a series of routine tasks that were meaningless for those who performed them.

That's why, today, creative labour generally takes place on the weekends, with huge numbers of us devoting our spare time to projects that give satisfaction precisely because they're arduous. Think of the so-called Maker Movement – the enthusiasts who use their own time and money to handcraft all manner of weird and complex objects, simply for the pleasure it brings them.

Perversely, there's an element of this in life hacking.

Rhinehart, for instance, apparently spends his spare time hanging out in Soylent discussion sites, forums where he and other aficionados debate the merits of this or that formula for ridding the world of food. The DIY Soylent enthusiasts are, in that respect, operating like Makers or other backyard hobbyists. They share tips, they argue theories, they conduct experiments – basically, they engage in precisely the artisanal tinkering that scientific management eliminated.

This, then, is the strange paradox of life hacking: simply, in the era of neoliberalism, we can feel most human by eroding our humanity. We creatively derive chemical recipes to remove the need for recipes; we find pleasure in the ingenuity with which we eliminate pleasure from our wardrobe.

In his discussion of Soylent, 'Let's embrace the end of food', the left-wing writer Bhaskar Sunkar notes that 'the line between dystopia and utopia is a thin one' – and, certainly, in the Reddit forums where ordinary folks discuss their food replacment formulas, we can glimpse something of the human desire for an unalienated life.

Yet that doesn't alter the profoundly alienated reality from which this self-Taylorism stems, which is why Sunkar's mistaken to identify Soylent as a product with 'a radically egalitarian core'.

His argument – that Soylent might 'facilitate human flourishing and freedom' and 'provide a way out of backbreaking farm work for the first time since the Neolithic revolution' – replicates the error that led Lenin to enthuse about Taylor's work as a resource for socialism.

In reality, Taylorism does not ensure efficiency in general

(a meaningless concept) so much as efficiency within the contours of the capitalist mode of production it buttresses. Indeed, Braverman points out that the 'science' of 'scientific management' is largely bogus:

> It lacks the characteristics of a true science because its assumptions reflect nothing more than the outlook of the capitalist with regard to the conditions of the production. It starts, despite occasional protestations to the contrary, not from the human point of view but from the capitalist point of view, from the point of view of the management of a refractory work force in a setting of antagonistic social relations. It does not attempt to discover and confront the cause of this condition, but accepts it as an inexorable given, a 'natural' condition. It investigates not labor in general but the adaption of labor to the needs of capital. It enters the workplace not as the representative of science, but as the representative of management masquerading in the trappings of science.

Or, as he puts it elsewhere, Taylorism is not 'science of work' but rather:

> a science of the management of others' work under capitalist conditions. It is not the 'best way' to do work 'in general' that Taylor was seeking ... but an answer to the specific problem of how best to control alienated labor – that is to say, labor power that is bought and sold.

Exactly the same can be said of Soylent, a product designed not to feed people but to feed people under capitalist conditions, something entirely different.

It's not simply that no genuine nutritionist has ever suggested that humans could or should subsist entirely on blended mush. It's also that Soylent presumes and promotes an order in which working people possess no agency whatsoever but simply embody a labour power to be grudgingly replenished with spoonfuls of sludge.

The socialist answer to world hunger begins not with protein powder but with the working-class creativity that the Taylorist project seeks to eliminate, using that tremendous resource to reshape the planet.

In a more libertarian moment, Lenin illustrated how a new world might function by declaring that every cook could learn to govern. It's a symptomatic example, echoing Marx's point about alienation. What would happen, we might ask, if the creativity now expressed in private activities like cooking found a public and social expression? What possibilities would open up if, instead of replacing meals, we replaced social structures; if, instead of hacking our lives, we hacked our society?

In the 1973 science fiction movie *Soylent Green*, Charlton Heston eventually discovers that his world subsists on recycled human flesh; that, as he puts it, 'Soylent Green is people!' Rhinehart's ability to appropriate that slogan exemplifies the brazenness of a 21st-century capitalism that increasingly no longer bothers to hide the Gothic horrors on which it depends.

It's not food we need to replace. It's the entire rotten system.

In the battle for the Right, the market always wins

In response to the London riots of 2011, right-wing columnist Andrew Bolt posted a clip of Enoch Powell's 'Rivers of Blood' speech, alongside a link to the full text.

That's the infamous rant in which Powell warns of how, soon, 'the black man will have the whip hand over the white man,' and then reads out a description of black kids as 'wide-grinning piccaninnies'.

Bolt's enthusiasm for what the *Times of London* – not exactly a leftie rag – called, as far back as 1968, 'an evil speech', is vile ('wide-grinning piccaninnies' – really? *really*?), even by his standards. But there's something else going on.

A classical scholar and one-time Professor of Ancient Greek, Powell was not a Fox News–watching Tea Partier, but a defender of capital C culture, Oxbridge elitism and inherited privilege, who dressed up his bigotry with quotes from Virgil.

Well, the world that Powell knew – the strata that he

represented – has been, in the past forty years, nearly wiped out: not by black people, but by the market.

Today, there are very few conservatives – indeed, very few politicians of any stripe – who have not embraced the radical free doctrine known as neoliberalism. And what makes neoliberalism distinctive is its virulent hostility to any authority or values other than the market.

Take, to choose an example at random, the study of Ancient Greek. For a High Tory like Powell, the classics constituted timeless aesthetic excellence, and that in itself justified their survival. In the neoliberal university, such rhetoric simply doesn't compute. Is there a market for Roman poetry? No? Well, that's why, all over the world, classics departments are underfunded.

The past weeks have highlighted an important fault line in politics today: the relationship between neoliberalism and neoconservatism. It's a relationship often misunderstood, since many politicians, especially during the Bush years, embraced both simultaneously. Conceptually, though, neoliberalism and neoconservatism are very different.

Neoliberalism is a market philosophy. It's based on amoral self-interest, a definition of the citizen as a rational profit maximiser. Neoconservatism, by contrast, obsesses about morality. Neoliberalism worships only market forces but neoconservatism usually has a close relationship with Christian evangelism.

For neoliberalism, people are fundamentally consumers; neoconservatism rails against empty materialism. Neoliberalism encourages desire of all kinds, with sexuality merely another sphere into which the markets must be introduced.

Neonconservatism, on the other hand, frets about the nuclear family and denounces gay marriage. Neoliberalism encourages capital to flow around the world, while neoconservatism guards the borders and speaks anxiously against immigrants.

What does that mean in practice? Bolt and others have, predictably enough, blamed hip-hop and gangsta chic for turning British kids into looters. That's a quintessentially neoconservative response: emphasising culture and values, with a nasty (and characteristic) racial tinge – many of those rappers are, don't you know, the kinds of blackity black men who apparently now hold the whip hand over Whitey.

But here's the thing: in the real world, hip-hop spread across the planet, not as the result of nefarious plotting by left-wingers or multicultural elites, but because of the free market policies embraced by the Right (and the rightward-moving social democratic parties).

Rap is big business, a major source of revenue for otherwise struggling multinational music corporations. The lyrics of commercial hip-hop – the stuff that Bolt objects to – reflect that orientation, with an entrepreneurial focus on branding, an obsession with conspicuous consumption, and a narrative emphasis on the dog-eat-dog scramble to the top.

In neoliberal theory, the laws of supply and demand regulate morality and aesthetics just as surely as they regulate everything else. What sells is, by definition, good, and vice versa. Snoop Dogg and Virgil compete in the same market, and the cash register duly decides whether the Doggfather's rhymes are better or worse than the *Aeneid*.

That's neoliberalism – the system championed by, more

than anyone, Liberal former prime minister John Howard, Andrew Bolt's favourite politician. And that's why hip-hop, not folk music or Bach, provides the soundtrack to young people's lives.

The contradiction between neoconservatism and neoliberalism also explains the otherwise mystifying self-pity that prevails in the right-wing blogosphere, an ongoing boo-hooing seemingly at odds with the Right's electoral successes. John Howard was in power for thirteen years, George Bush served two terms, the Tories are ruling Britain – and yet, somehow, the commenters on Bolt's blog understand contemporary politics as one sorry tale of decline. Families keep falling apart, racial ghettoes fester, Christian values are flouted, young people aren't respecting their elders, horses aren't wearing clothes ... yes, yes, you know how it goes. Whatever the topic, the subtext is the same: the more the Right succeeds, the worse everything gets.

In his *What's the Matter With Kansas?*, Thomas Frank attributes the peculiar pity-party that is contemporary conservatism to an ongoing bait-and-switch. It goes like this. Conservative activists, often ordinary people from struggling backgrounds, get whipped into a lather by demagogic neocons over, say, the amount of smut and blasphemy screening in the movies. These activists duly campaign for conservative candidates, who, once elected, implement the neoliberal economics to which the Right is fundamentally committed.

Thereafter, the free market does what the free market is supposed to do: namely, freeing up corporations to make money. Hollywood, of course, knows it will sell more tickets to crass sex comedies than upright Christian narratives, and so, lo and behold, crass sex comedies are what it delivers.

In other words, the crusade against cinematic decadence results in ... more cinematic decadence.

That's why Irving Kristol, the key figure in the establishment of neoconservatism, famously gave only two cheers for capitalism, withholding the third one on the basis that 'consumer societies are empty of moral meaning if not forthrightly nihilistic'.

So there's something fundamentally silly about, say, the *Australian* columnist Greg Sheridan complaining about 'unemployed youth, with no tradition and no real education, with enough money more or less but not many prospects, with no source of moral authority and no help in understanding any basis for right and wrong, nothing to control an impulse ... '

Tradition? Moral authority? Impulse control? As Kristol realised, the market is inherently opposed to all of that – and, for the past decades, the Right and the free market have been synonymous.

But if neoconservatism and neoliberalism are contradictory, they're also, in some respects, complementary, which is why so many conservatives oscillate back and forth between them.

During the Howard–Bush years, foreign policy provided an obvious convergence. Neoliberals liked, at least for a while, how the War on Terror promised to open up closed economies to the market, while neoconservatives applauded the martial values instilled by permanent war. They could, therefore, work together in denunciation of anti-war activists.

In some ways, that opposition to the Left is still what holds free marketeers and neocons together.

The neoliberal Right hates not only trade unionism but any notion of collectivity, since such ideas are fundamentally opposed to the individualism of the market. That's why hard-headed economists can tolerate a certain amount of neocon frothing about issues they don't regard as terribly important.

Most neoliberals are quite prepared to allow gays to get married. But if a campaign can be built about traditional marriage, well, why not let the fundos do it, if, by letting them rant, you can keep a right-wing government in power?

Neoconservatism is equally cynical. Where Enoch Powell no doubt believed his own hateful rhetoric, quite genuinely seeing Western culture as under threat from those he regarded as lesser races, the Murdoch empire – as Andrew Bolt surely knows – does very nicely out of gangsta culture. Why, James Murdoch – Rupert's son and (until their recent spat) heir apparent – cut his teeth establishing Rawkus Records, which was ... wait for it! ... a hip-hop label, responsible for titles such as *Super Thug Killa Rap EXCLAMATION* – precisely the kind of album the neocons carry on about.

Neoconservatism is, in that respect, a tidy racket for those on the inside, in which they play their readers for chumps, again and again and again – urging them on into culture war skirmishes, while the free market parties for whom they gormlessly vote denude everything they hold dear. Does, for instance, anyone think that, once in power, an Abbott government will do anything whatsoever to prevent market forces from continuing the slow destruction of the country towns that drives so much rural conservatism?

But those whom the gods wish to destroy, they first make mad, as Powell famously said. And there's nothing objectively madder than the activists engaged in a constant and frenzied struggle against a culture – indeed, a world – created by the neoliberal politicians they support.

Journey to the west

'One of my pet gripes about modern society [is] the way in which serious issues and events are converted into bizarre forms of celebrity.'

That's a quote *by* Mark Latham but it might equally be a quote *about* Mark Latham: former Labor leader, political theorist (how many other MPs have written a book as ambitious as *Civilising Global Capital*?), newspaper pundit, and now resident contrarian on *The Verdict*. In case you've missed it, that's Channel 9's new tabloid version of the ABC's *Q&A*, a show so desperate for controversy that last night it resuscitated 1990s race-baiter Pauline Hanson to opine on, of all things, marijuana policy.

Not so long ago, Latham mocked domestic violence survivor advocate Rosie Batty for getting 'wheeled out at business functions to retell the story of her son's murder'. Today, he's earning a crust by trolling on demand: 'Will drop pants for food', as Krusty the Clown once said.

Spectacle aside, Latham's new incarnation highlights his dependence on the identity politics he so regularly denounces. Consider a fairly stock Latham rant from August

2015. In this case, he's attacking anti-racists over the Adam Goodes affair, but you can find almost identical Latham sprays aimed at feminists, same-sex marriage campaigners and other predictable targets.

He writes:

> The elites, enjoying the luxury of high incomes and cosmopolitan interests, have subdivided Australia according to questions of race, gender and sexuality. They live their lives through the prism of these identities and expect others to do the same. When suburbanites refuse to comply (instead, prioritising practical concerns about living standards and service delivery) they are vilified by the elites as racist, sexist and homophobic. Identity politics is the standard currency of Australia's outrage industry: the holier-than-thou moralisers that denigrate anyone who steps outside the boundaries of political correctness ... The outrage industry is one of the reasons why Australian politics has entered an era of gridlock.

Now compare Latham's own behaviour on *The Verdict* on the week the panel turned its collective wisdom to Liberal senator Eric Abetz's use of the word 'negro.' Latham, of course, didn't see a problem.

'Back in the '70s and '80s', he said, '"negro" was actually a respected, dignified alternative to really racist terms like "nigger" and "darky". So I must have missed the memo somewhere in the '90s or more recently as to when "negro" became unacceptable. I'm happy to make my weekly donation to Australia's outrage industry by saying "negro, negro, negro"'.

(In passing, let's note that you could defend 'nigger' and 'darky' on a similar basis, given both terms were once standard usage in white newspapers.)

But, in his subsequent remarks to host Karl Stefanovic, Latham gave a fairly standard piece of curmudgeonly back-in-my-day bigotry a distinctive tweak.

'Well, Karl, I could walk through any street in western Sydney and no one would find "negro" offensive. And who are these unelected, self-appointed people who've decided that we all need to speak like them?' With that, he grounds his critique in an assertion of identity, using a methodology entirely familiar to every campus radical.

In almost everything he writes or says, Mark Latham presents himself as the incarnation of western Sydney – or, when he's in a more expansive mood, the outer suburbs in general. He uses that to deploy a 'prolier-than-thou' moralism against his many and varied enemies, countering the more customary triad of race, gender and sexuality with an aggressive assertion of class.

It's the last step that makes Latham so distinctive and (paradoxically) so representative of his era. In the past, a certain kind of Left intellectual might have expressed gender through the analogy of class (think of Engels' assertion that 'within the family ... the wife represents the proletariat'). Latham, however, treats class as gender – or, at least, as an oppression to be understood in terms popularised by the feminist movement of the past several decades. In other words, he associates himself with an identity systemically denied expression, thereby framing his opponents as exclusionary, even censorious.

'This is how I talk in the western suburbs of Sydney in the pub, with my mates at sporting events', he explained at his notorious Melbourne Writers Festival event. 'And if you don't like it you can fuck off.'

In the Goodes article, Latham blasts those who, he says, live through the prism of their identity. But that's exactly what he's doing himself. By referring to western Sydney, he snatches the mantle of victimhood and wields it against others. When activists object to the term 'negro', Latham counters by identifying himself as an outsider and shouting 'check your privilege!'

Now, to the extent that the gambit works, it's because it touches on a genuine issue. The voices of ordinary suburban people *don't* get heard in the forums to which Latham has access – and everyone knows it. WEB du Bois noted that African Americans were always asked how it felt to be a problem. Something similar might be said of the inhabitants of Western Sydney, who are eternally discussed (especially at election time) and yet rarely asked to speak.

That's why – at, say, a writers' festival or similar event – Latham can pose as the brave outsider by mocking feminists: he's speaking, you see, on behalf of the excluded. You might object that there's something a little odd about a career politician and widely published intellectual wrapping himself in the garb of a humble suburbanite. Latham's book from 2014 contains an extensive index entry for 'Henderson, Gerard' (pp. 60, 67, 70, 74, 76, 79, 80, 104, 138, 163–7, 173, 224, 258–60, if you're interested); a preoccupation not exactly characteristic of your average proletarian.

Yet arguments about whether Latham does or does not authentically represent the suburbs only raise more important questions about what 'authenticity' and 'representation' mean in this context.

As it happens, in a recent *Verdict* episode, Latham himself explained that not all western Sydneysiders were created equal.

'It pains me to say in Western Sydney there is a Muslim problem', he said, and then continued: 'So, the best thing the Federal Government can do is get these people out to work. In many ways it is not just a question of stopping radicalisation. How do we promote normality, normalisation in Western Sydney so people are making a positive contribution to society?'

Again, the Muslim residents of the locality are probably far more 'normal' (if by that we mean closer to the statistical mean for income levels, housing, etc.) than Latham himself, a man who, with his parliamentary pension and all, can't exactly be short of a quid. But, of course, the transformation of a region with a couple of million varied inhabitants into a single, stable identity necessitates exclusions.

Latham's performance of 'outsiderness', his establishment of his political persona, relies on a set of markers that hold his identity together with their very familiarity. Latham becomes a 'battler' through the aggressive assertion of 'battler' traits (outspokenness, ocker masculinity, whiteness, etc.), a process that both enables and requires him to marginalise other ways of understanding the suburbs.

You might counter Latham's shtick with the moral

authority of a different 'western Sydney' identity – one based on, say, genuine poverty or religious marginalisation. But that would be susceptible to the same problem, since producing a single category from an unstable multiplicity of people always depends on the exclusion of those who threaten it.

As the American writer Michael Rectenwald has said of identity-based political argument:

> The upshot in political practice is a static pluralism of reified social categories, each vying for more-subaltern-than-thou status on a field of one-downsmanship. While it may be useful for sociologists attempting to describe groups and their struggles with power, as a political theory, it is useless, or worse. This is because, by ending with the identification and isolation of its various constituencies, it in fact serves to sever the connections that it supposedly sought to understand and strengthen. The practical upshot ... is the perpetual articulation of difference, resulting in fragmentation and the stagnation of political activity.

Perhaps that's why identity politics has now been thoroughly adopted by those who most claim to despise it. Every culture warrior rails against identity politics, yet every culture war depends on a very similar strategy, as tabloid pundits construct a victimology around some concocted persona or another. The campaign for the United States Republican presidential nomination provides a perfect illustration: essentially, a contest between professional outsiders competing only on the basis of identity.

As the American writer Malcolm Harris notes in his review of a recent *South Park* episode lambasting political correctness, 'What *South Park* libertarians don't seem to realise is that they've crafted a whole politics around their bruised feelings, which is exactly what they accuse the PC police of doing wrong.' Here in Australia, of course, nobody in the whole country so loudly complains of ill-use as Andrew Bolt and his readers, who are oppressed and censored wherever they turn.

That in itself should give pause to progressives. If the Right can so enthusiastically embrace the politics of identity, perhaps it's time for the Left to rethink.

THE BONES OF THE DEAD

'Drive your cart and your plow over the bones of the dead', advises William Blake in *The Marriage of Heaven and Hell.*

Like a lot of Blake's writing, the line's as cryptic as it is evocative.

At first glance, it suggests an overt hostility to the past.

Progressives often define themselves in simple opposition to what came before. Tradition, custom and heritage: they all seem like weapons for the status quo. When you want to change the world, you think of wresting society free from its accumulated detritus.

Yesterday weighs, as someone once said, like a nightmare on the brain of the living.

Yet Blake's image invokes a much more nuanced attitude than we might first imagine. The farmer ploughs not because she dismisses history but precisely because she doesn't. Working the land doesn't involve destruction so much as transformation, with the cart breaking those old bones so as to nourish the field.

I've written a lot about history over the years. The following section contains a spread of those pieces.

Sometimes, recalling the past provides comfort or inspiration. We look back to find people to emulate; in bleak moments, we reassure ourselves with the knowledge that others endured experiences similar to our own.

More importantly, the past helps us to understand the present moment. By studying it, we can discover how society works. We can turn the case, take off the dial and see how the cogs turn – and then, perhaps, adjust the dial.

In 2014, reports emerged from Syria about the

archaeological destruction wrought by the civil war, with some of the oldest sites in the world pulverised by shellfire and looters. I wrote a piece for the *Guardian* trying to think through how, in the context of so much human suffering, we might think about the relative value of historical treasures.

The wreck of the Dutch merchant vessel *Batavia* culminated in an extraordinary frenzy of mass murder, conducted on tiny coral atolls some 60 kilometres off the coast of Western Australia. For the *Monthly*, I travelled in a tiny plane to the island where archaeologists were uncovering new evidence about one of the grisliest episodes in Australian history. It's a story that sticks in my memory, partly because of the intense loneliness of the wreck site and partly because, in the course of writing it, I got myself more sunburned than ever before in my life.

History never stays settled, with the cultural and political battles of today inevitably impinging on previous periods. Back in 2006, I wrote about a revisionist narrative of the Great Depression, suggesting it told us as much about the present as about the 1930s.

Finally, during the COVID-19 lockdown of 2021, I was struck by the remarkable popularity of dachshunds, seemingly the pet of choice among Australians experiencing forced domesticity. In a piece written for this collection, I recalled the vitriolic campaign waged against the dog during the First World War – and celebrated its new rehabilitation.

Like Blake's farmer, I've tried, in all my writing, to treat the past as a resource, something from which, even in grim times, we can take nourishment.

'Let the slave grinding at the mill', writes Blake in another passage that I love, 'run into the field/Let him look up into the heavens and laugh into the bright air'.

The value of history

The lands of Syria and Iraq gave rise to some of the oldest societies we know: the Sumerians, the Akkadians, the Babylonians, the Assyrians, the Parthians, the Romans and many others. Traces of all of these peoples remain in archaeological sites of the utmost significance.

And now they're being destroyed.

A fortnight ago, satellite imagery revealed the cultural effects of Syria's civil war. 'The buildings of Aleppo, one of the oldest continuously inhabited cities in the world, has suffered extensive damage', explained *Archaeology* magazine. 'The ancient city of Bosra, the ancient site of Palmyra, the ancient villages of Northern Syria, and the castles Crac des Chevaliers and Qal'at Salah El-Din have all been damaged by mortar impacts and military activity.'

So too in Iraq.

Sometimes, the destruction is accidental (if that term means anything in wartime). Sometimes it's deliberate, with the Islamic State systematically levelling ancient religious sites.

After looters rampaged through Baghdad's National Museum in 2003, the archaeologist Francis Deblauwe established the (now defunct) Iraq and Archaeology site, which eloquently expresses what's now once again happening. He wrote:

> War in this cradle of civilization beyond the horrendous, almost invisible casualties – always somebody's husband, always somebody's son – and downplayed 'collateral damage' – always somebody's wife, always somebody's child – inevitably takes its toll on the archaeological heritage as well. After all, this fertile flood plain and surrounding mountains gave birth to agriculture, to writing, to cities, to laws, to the 24 hours in a day, and many more things we take for granted.

Iraq takes its name from Uruk, the ancient city said to have been ruled by Gilgamesh, sometime between 2500 and 2700 BC.

In the epic poem that bears his name, Gilgamesh leaves Uruk, a place he constructed, stricken with grief after the death of his friend. After many adventures, he accepts that only the gods endure forever, and returns with a new appreciation of the city – a human achievement that offers the only immortality humans can expect.

David Ferry's beautiful translation describes Uruk as follows:

> The outer wall
> shines in the sun like brightest copper; the inner
> wall is beyond the imagining of kings.
> Study the brickwork, study the fortification;
> climb the great ancient staircase to the terrace;
> study how it is made…

Uruk's ruins were rediscovered in the 19th century, 250 kilometres south of Baghdad. That means we can, quite literally, study the brickwork and the fortifications and the outer walls upon which Gilgamesh once gazed – and when we do, we confront the same questions about eternity and loss he pondered some 4500 years earlier.

The ancient stones exemplify the persistence of our collective culture, a persistence that provides, as the poem suggests, our sole consolation for the inescapability of our individual deaths. That's why, in *The Seven Lamps of Architecture*, the great Victorian art critic John Ruskin argues that we have a responsibility to such artefacts. He warns:

> They are not ours. They belong partly to those who built them, and partly to all the generations of mankind who are to follow us. The dead have still their right in them: that which they labored for, the praise of achievement or the expression of religious feeling, or whatsoever else it might be which in those buildings they intended to be permanent, we have no right to obliterate.

Great architecture, Ruskin says, belongs to humanity as a whole, and not to 'those mobs who do violence to it'. It's an argument that surely applies to the relics of ancient Mesopotamia, caught between Islamic State fighters and United States strike bombers.

But can we – or, rather, should we – proclaim the rights of the dead when patently we cannot guarantee the rights of the living?

Nearly 200 000 people perished in Syria's civil war. Estimates of deaths from the 2003 Iraq invasion vary from several hundred thousand to over a million, depending on which source you cite. In the midst of almost unimaginable blood and suffering, is it wrong to care about the walls of Uruk?

'I wish to be absolutely clear', writes Deblauwe, 'no epic Sumerian cuneiform tablet, majestic Neo-Assyrian lamassu sculpture or any other Mesopotamian artifact is worth a human life, be it Iraqi, American, British or other'.

The bluntness of that statement, from a man who palpably cares about Sumerian cuneiform tablets, contrasts with the abstraction of Ruskin's formulation, which champions a generalised humanity over the flesh and blood of today's people. Call it the antiquarian temptation: a tendency to privilege a bygone world over the one in which we actually live.

There's a long, disreputable tradition of venerating ancient Rome and Greece while denigrating anyone with the temerity to live in those cities today. When ideologues seized cultural treasures from subaltern populations, they generally did so on the basis that the ignorant locals couldn't appreciate the stuff's value. That's how major British museums built their collections, from the Elgin Marbles to the bones of Aboriginal people.

Yet it's worth thinking about the perceived need for such expropriation.

Why did the Taliban dynamite the Bamiyan buddhas? Like all despots, Mullah Omar and his men made the past into a guarantor of the future. The giant statues represented an alternative system of thought. By blasting away the ancient sculptures, the Taliban proclaimed, 'there are no choices here – and there never have been.'

The absorption of other civilisations' treasures into the British empire spoke to the same need. Consider the incorporation of the diamond known as the Koh-i-Noor into the crown of Queen Elizabeth, an obvious and ostentatious demonstration of Britain's power over India.

Likewise, settler societies such as Australia have always needed to denigrate the achievements of those they displaced, so as to justify the fiction of *terra nullius*. It's a process that continues today. Some archaeologists call the Brewarrina Fish Traps the oldest human constructions in the world – but how many white Australians have even heard of them?

In 1258, Genghis Khan sacked Baghdad, and systematically annihilated its famous House of Wisdom, the first ever university. 'It was so horrible there are no words to describe it', wrote the Persian poet Saadi of Shiraz. 'I wish I had died earlier and not seen how these fools destroyed these treasures of knowledge and learning. I thought I understood the world but this holocaust is so strange and pointless I am struck dumb.'

In her book *The Shock Doctrine*, Naomi Klein records remarkably similar responses to the plunder of the National Museum of Iraq after the United States invasion. 'It was the soul of Iraq', said one local merchant. 'If the museum doesn't recover the looted treasures, I will feel like a part of my own soul has been stolen.' 'Baghdad is the mother of Arab culture', said another man, 'and they want to wipe out our culture.'

I wish I had died. My own soul has been stolen. Can we truly assert that no cultural artifact's worth a human life?

Of course, the question's unanswerable, since valuing the irreplaceable (whether a person or an artwork) constitutes, almost by definition, a category error. Nonetheless, it's clear that the past and its culture cannot be so easily disentangled from the present and its politics.

Klein explains the pillage of Baghdad's museum in terms of the neoconservative attempts to reconstruct Iraq as a deregulated, free market utopia. She quotes the coalition economic advisor Peter McPherson, who saw looting as a DIY privatisation, a legitimate beginning to the downsizing of state assets. 'I thought the privatisation that occurs sort of naturally when somebody took over their state vehicle, or began to drive a truck that the state used to own, was just fine', McPherson explained.

How can you protect a common human heritage when you're innately opposed to collectivity? More importantly, why would you even try?

In the *New York Times*, Ziauddin Sardar discussed the historical destruction taking place in Mecca, where ancient sites have been crudely bulldozed by developers.

'The house of Khadijah, the first wife of the Prophet Muhammad, has been turned into a block of toilets', he says. 'The Makkah Hilton is built over the house of Abu Bakr, the closest companion of the prophet and the first caliph.'

Like the Islamic State militants they fund, the Saudi Salafists despise alternative interpretations of Islam. It's common to call their philosophy 'medieval', but the label misrepresents the entirely 21st-century phenomenon taking place in Mecca. As Sardar argues, the Saudis have turned the 'spiritual heart of Islam [into] an ultramodern, monolithic enclave, where difference is not tolerated, history has no meaning, and consumerism is paramount'.

The same might be said of the Islamic State itself. Its supporters raze ancient sites, not only to wipe out the traditions they represent, but also to capitalise on the thriving market for antiquities in the west, reportedly raising US$36 million alone from the looting of al-Nabuk in Syria.

On the surface, the rich cosmopolitans who buy the stuff and the ascetic fundamentalists who steal it could not be more different. But they share an identical indifference to history as a collective resource for humanity. Do we need, then, a team of George Clooney-style 'Monuments Men', specially trained to guide the United States forces in Iraq and minimise the historical damage they cause?

In 2009, the archeologist Yannis Hamilakis wrote a stinging rebuke to colleagues embedding with western militaries, arguing that they simply legitimised the destruction they sought to forestall. He quoted the Iraqi-born academic Zainab Bahrani: 'The entirety of Iraq is a world cultural heritage site, and there is no way that a strategic bombing can avoid something archaeological.'

Just as recent 'humanitarian' interventions in Afghanistan, Iraq or Libya have culminated in humanitarian catastrophes, efforts by what Hamilakis dubs 'the military–archaeology complex' are unlikely to succeed, since long-term preservation depends upon a relationship between the history of a site and those who inhabit it today.

The great poet and designer William Morris argued something similar during his campaign to spare the ancient buildings of Britain from the ravages of industrialisation. 'Believe me', he explained to supporters, 'it will not be possible for a small knot of cultivated people to keep alive an interest in the art and records of the past amidst the present conditions of a sordid and heart-breaking struggle for existence for the many, and a languid sauntering through life for the few'.

On another occasion, he put it like this: 'If we have no hope for the future, I do not see how we can look back on the past with pleasure'.

The same might be said about Iraq and Syria today. The fight for our collective heritage necessarily involves a struggle for peace and social justice, for it's only when people feel a stake in the world around them that they can appreciate the achievements of the ancients as part of their lives.

Bring up the bodies: New light on the wreck of the *Batavia*

At the University of Western Australia's Centre for Forensic Science in Perth, the skeletons lie on tables, stretched out beside plastic tubs of pelvic fragments, bags of unmatched toes and samples of island sand.

Daniel Franklin, the forensic anthropologist, gestures at one of the skulls, which is grinning at me on its small pillow.

'Just here.'

I look to where he points and see the wound, a little chip in the yellowing surface where a blade has cut through flesh and into bone. It makes the remains seem suddenly human – no longer just an archaeological curio but the corpse of an adult male murdered, along with more than a hundred other men, women and children, in the aftermath of the wreck of the Dutch East India Company vessel *Batavia* off the Western Australian coast, nearly four centuries ago.

The story has been told many times over the years, most recently by Peter FitzSimons in his book *Batavia* and, before him, by Simon Leys (*The Wreck of the* Batavia) and Mike Dash (Batavia's *Graveyard*). But Franklin belongs to the Shipwrecks of the Roaring 40s project, a multi-disciplinary collaboration led by the archaeologist Alistair Paterson and backed by an array of national and international partners, including the University of Western Australia, the Western Australian Museum, the Western Australia Department of Fisheries, and the Netherlands Ministry of Education, Culture and Science. Franklin and the other scientists are reassessing some of Australia's earliest shipwrecks, including that of the *Batavia*, using newly available technology.

I've come to Perth because, for the first time, all the exhumed *Batavia* remains have been gathered together.

'The idea is to get the *Batavia* skeletons in the one place where they can all be studied in association with each other', Franklin explains, 'which we've not done before. Though I'm kind of running out of space'.

He looks ruefully around the room, which is, indeed, uncomfortably crowded with femurs and cracked pelvises and damaged skulls neatly glued back together. The university cleaning staff recently left a note for Franklin, explaining that they are now too scared to dust there.

Franklin's team has just been on a two-week dig near the wreck site and returned with three previously unknown skeletons. That brings the total of *Batavia* bodies unearthed since the early 1960s to thirteen, including six tossed together into a mass grave. Two of the skeletons bear wounds consistent with murder: the one with the sword cut, which Franklin has shown me, and another with a cranium shattered from a blunt blow.

Other skeletons, he says, remain to be unearthed. 'We have teeth of someone we haven't found yet. There is – or there was – someone else there.' It is the coldest of cold cases. One of the darkest episodes in Australian history may, however, have further secrets to reveal.

Retellings of the *Batavia* story rarely avoid the clichés of the Australian Gothic. It contains, after all, every trope of the genre: a small group of European intruders blunder into an eerie and inhospitable landscape to endure privation, insanity and a great deal of Grand Guignol violence.

But less obviously, and just as interestingly, the *Batavia* story is also one of corporate power, involving the richest multinational the world has ever seen.

In the 17th century, the Dutch East India Company (*Vereenigde Oostindische Compagnie*, or VOC) functioned almost as a private state: it waged war (backed by its own military forces), signed treaties, and made and enforced laws. Think of the Weyland–Yutani Corporation from the *Alien* films, and you're pretty close. Recent estimates suggest that the VOC at its height was worth a dizzying US$7.4 trillion dollars in today's money.

In 1628, the VOC commissioned a huge and ultra-modern ship to carry silver to the trading settlements of Java and return carrying spices. The vessel was christened *Batavia* after its destination, the city we now call Jakarta. In

Batavia's *Graveyard*, Mike Dash noted that the life expectancy of Dutch merchants in the Indies was about three years and that 'of the million or so people who sailed with the VOC during the lifetime of the Company, fewer than one in three returned'.

Yet when the *Batavia* left from Texel, Holland, on 27 October 1628 in a fleet of ships, only about two-thirds of the 340 people on board were crew. The others were soldiers and civilian passengers, including twenty-two women. Some of them brought babies; indeed, several of the sailors themselves were still adolescents.

Under the peculiar VOC command structure, the *Batavia*'s skipper, an experienced sailor named Ariaen Jacobsz, served under the *opperkoopman* (senior merchant) Francisco Pelsaert, the official representative of the VOC. That the two cordially disliked each other was only the first of the voyage's many problems.

After rounding the Cape of Good Hope at the southern tip of Africa, the *Batavia* became separated from the rest of its fleet. A fever confined Pelsaert to his cabin. A passenger called Lucretia Jans, the daughter of a wealthy merchant, was sexually assaulted by masked crewmen, one of whom she identified as the boatswain. The obvious tensions brewing within the *Batavia*'s intensely hierarchical social structure might have dissipated, but in the early morning of 4 June 1629, the ship – still a month out of Java – struck Morning Reef on the Houtman Abrolhos, some 60 kilometres off the coast of Western Australia.

According to his record of the voyage, Pelsaert immediately denounced Jacobsz, yelling, 'What have you done, that through your reckless carelessness you have run this noose around our necks?'

Some sailors and soldiers, convinced they were doomed, broke into the stores to carouse and loot. 'You have been masters here long enough', one yelled. 'Now I [will be master] for a while.'

Around forty people drowned over the next days, while a chaotic evacuation sent 180 mostly low-ranking sailors, soldiers and their families to a tiny speck of land they named *Batavia*'s Graveyard (today's Beacon Island). Most of the officers, including Pelsaert and Jacobsz, disembarked on a different, even smaller coral atoll.

A third group remained stranded on the disintegrating wreck. Their number included the *onderkoopman* (junior merchant) Jeronimus Cornelisz, a former apothecary and apparent heretic. Very soon he would become the worst mass murderer in Australian history.

In the Western Australian Museum's Shipwreck Galleries in Fremantle, I stand, slightly awed, beside a section of the *Batavia*'s hull, dredged up from Morning Reef where it was located in 1963.

It's only a fragment, a portion preserved underneath the huge stone portico carried as ship's ballast, but it's breathtaking nonetheless: substantial enough to evoke the majesty of the three-masted, four-decked vessel looming some 12 metres out of the sea at its stern.

I've come to meet the museum's Jeremy Green, another Roaring 40s researcher, and probably Australia's greatest expert on the *Batavia* and its archaeology. Over a cup of coffee near the harbour, he tells me, in his faint British accent, how he left Oxford for Australia in 1971, back before anyone really knew how to explore shipwrecks scientifically.

'All of the technology and techniques were developed in the '70s – unlike in terrestrial archaeology, where they were developed a century or more earlier. Even in the '80s there were no courses in maritime archaeology.'

The *Batavia* had remained lost for centuries, partly because in 1840 the British vessel the *Beagle* (yes, Darwin's *Beagle*) misidentified wreckage from a different Dutch craft. It was only in 1956 that the Perth writer Henrietta Drake-Brockman realised Pelsaert's descriptions matched the northern islands of the Houtman Abrolhos rather than those in the south. Then, in 1963, a fisherman, Dave Johnson, led divers to waters where he'd glimpsed an anchor beneath his boat.

The discovery spurred a new interest in marine heritage. Western Australia came to lead the world in legislating to protect heritage sites. Staff from the museum eventually worked on seven European shipwrecks, learning not only how to locate and recover artefacts, but also how to preserve them away from the water.

'When we started', says Green, 'basically no one had done an excavation of a Dutch East India Company ship – or any shipwreck in Australia. Most people thought – we thought! – that there wouldn't be anything down there'.

I'd seen the results in the Shipwreck Galleries – the massive ship cannons, the navigational instruments, the distinctive Bartmann jugs, the huge portico façade that was being transported to become an entrance to the city of Batavia. The significance of these old finds is growing as technology develops. Though Pelsaert recovered most of the VOC's treasure following the wreck, the divers of the 1960s and 1970s still found a large number of coins. Today, that bullion can be analysed for its physical composition as well as its face value, with metallurgical research revealing precisely where in South America a particular piece of silver originated. The results build knowledge of commodity circulation in the first phases of capitalism, when precious metals moved from the New World to Spain, and from Holland to the Indies.

The wood from a wrecked hull tells a different story of early globalisation. By the 17th century, massive population growth had depleted the ancient forests of Europe. Where, then, did merchants in Amsterdam find the old-growth timber required for an empire in the age of wood and sail? Historians pondering this have two possible sources of dateable high-quality wood. They can sample the frames of a Rembrandt painting or, if they prefer not to damage a Dutch Master, they can analyse a VOC shipwreck in Western Australia.

As well as re-examining older finds, the Roaring 40s team also wants to launch new investigations, especially into the wreck survivors' camps: the very first European occupation of Australian soil.

'They'd have had a fire', Green tells me, 'and there would have been stuff dropped around it. The cooking utensils: they wouldn't necessarily have taken everything home with them. Their diet, their everyday life – are there traces of that still there?'

But, for the time being, there are the skeletons.

'At 2 pm the day before the forensics were due to fly out, we found this body with crossed hands', Green says. 'We obviously weren't going to finish excavating that day, so we decided to leave it and come back at about six in the morning. So we were excavating away and suddenly Dan [Franklin] says, "There are three femurs here". And we realised that there was another body underneath.'

Talking with Franklin in Perth, I'd contrasted it, rather optimistically, with the mass grave into which bodies had been unceremoniously dumped. Surely the crossed arms meant that the corpse had been given a proper burial, that the person had been interred with a certain respect?

Franklin shook his head. They'd found a man and a woman, dumped on top of each other. He specialises in criminal forensics as well as archaeology, and knows a crime scene when he sees one.

'Just saving space', he said. 'If you have your arms out, the killers have to dig a bigger hole.'

'Oh', I said, looking down at the bones.

'It looks nice and peaceful, but it's probably about fitting more bodies in a limited space.'

The murders began slowly.

The survivors soon realised that the coral atolls had no fresh water. After a brief search nearby, the *opperkoopman*, the skipper, the officers and their wives commandeered most of the remaining supplies and all of the salvaged boats. They, a party of nearly fifty, embarked on the 3000-kilometre journey to the Dutch outposts in Java, leaving behind the great majority of *Batavia*'s passengers and crew.

Pelsaert rationalised his decision as agonising but necessary: someone, he argued, had to go for help. But to the 200 or so people stranded on Beacon's barren shores, the disappearance of the officers seemed a flat-out abandonment. They dubbed the smaller atoll 'Traitors' Island'.

In Pelsaert's absence, Jeronimus Cornelisz, who had washed ashore from the disintegrating wreck, became the VOC's most senior representative. He seemed to decide immediately that his own survival depended on thinning out the population. To that end, he took personal charge of the remaining supplies, and set the carpenters to building makeshift boats. He then ordered forty-five men, women and children to cross to the nearby Seals Island (today's Long Island), assuming they would simply die there, thus sparing Beacon's resources. Similarly, he instructed twenty of the surviving soldiers, under the command of Wiebbe Hayes, to explore the distant Wallabi Group of islands and signal if they found water; he expected they wouldn't.

On Beacon itself, Cornelisz ordered executions of those caught stealing from the stores. The first killings both established his own power and blooded those who would do his bidding. Gradually, his thugs moved from punishing thieves to exterminating the sick and the superfluous, initially through surreptitious drownings and then in a more open campaign of slaughter.

In the month of July, they killed more than a hundred people. The descriptions we have of those weeks are almost dizzyingly brutal. A baby was slain to stop it crying, a boy decapitated to test a sword blade. The wife and five of the six children of the Calvinist minister Gijsbert Bastiaensz were exterminated for no reason whatsoever.

Cornelisz and his men took to wearing gaudy clothes from the wreck, parading in what Pelsaert later described as 'silk stockings, garters with gold laces, and ... suchlike adornments.' They resolved that should a rescue ship appear they would seize it so as to continue their new lifestyle as pirates. In the interim, the younger women were kept as sex slaves, with Lucretia Jans installed in Cornelisz's own tent.

The others on the island faced a choice of either joining the extermination or dying from it. Some, like the cabin boy, Jan Pelgrom, pleaded to be allowed to murder. The survivors later spoke of the 18-year-old patrolling the tiny island, waving his sword and shouting, 'Who wants to be stabbed to death? I can do that very beautifully!'

The end of Cornelisz's grim regime began when he and his men spied smoke coming from West Wallabi, the agreed signal that Hayes' expedition had located water. Inadvertently, Cornelisz had sent the soldiers to die in a place far more hospitable than Beacon Island itself, with bounteous game and wells that one man later described as 'sweet as milk.'

Hayes's unanticipated survival transformed the tiny community. Terrified survivors paddled over to West Wallabi, telling of the horrors they'd endured.

Cornelisz knew he had to destroy Hayes, an obvious threat to his power. His forces had the muskets salvaged from the wreck, but they lacked the military training of their opponents. The first boat they sent to West Wallabi was repelled with a shower of missiles.

Next, Cornelisz tried diplomacy. Accompanied by his most loyal followers, he rowed over to West Wallabi to negotiate personally. It was a fatal mistake. As soon as the discussions began, Hayes simply took Cornelisz prisoner and executed the men with him.

On Beacon, Cornelisz's followers regrouped before staging another attack on West Wallabi to free their leader. This time they used their monopoly on firearms to pick off the defenders. For a while, it seemed they might prevail, for Hayes's rocks and clubs provided no real counter to the muskets. Then, unbelievably, in the midst of the battle, a sail appeared on the horizon.

It was Pelsaert, making an improbable return from Java in the *Sardam*, with orders to retrieve the *Batavia*'s silver and its survivors (more or less in that order). He rescued Hayes and subdued the remaining Cornelisz loyalists.

And then, only a short distance from where *Batavia* had wrecked, he started on the torture.

In Geraldton, 420 kilometres north of Perth, I charter a small plane for the 60-kilometre journey out to the Abrolhos Islands. The prospect fills me with some horror, particularly when I realise that the Geraldton Air Charter consists of a shed, a car park and a few tiny aircraft of the sort a nervous flyer like me associates with TV reports about the premature deaths of amateur aviators.

While we wait for take-off, I pace around outside, telling myself to be calm. A short trip in a light plane! Why, in the 17th century, Dutch adolescents had joined the *Batavia* on its voyage to the other side of the world!

Yeah, says the voice in my head, *and how'd that work out?*

Three other passengers are buckled up inside the Airvan, electricians heading out to service the tiny fishing community on nearby Pigeon Island. The man beside me unfolds a tabloid newspaper, as if on a regular morning commute – which, in a sense, he is.

And, of course, it's fine. Better than fine, even, for underneath us the sea glows like opal, and I forget to be nervous, admiring the phosphorescent green of the water running over coral.

Twenty minutes later, we are circling Morning Reef, and over my headphones the pilot identifies the wreck site.

'Look', he says. 'You can see the wedge where the boat struck.'

Indeed you can: a faint V-shape in the coral, the traces of a 1200-tonne ship hitting at full speed.

We circle again and touch down, surprisingly lightly, at East Wallabi Island, on a dirt landing strip amid grey scrub and sand. At the pier, the electricians meet with a fishing vessel, while the pilot and I jump on the Department of Fisheries boat to Beacon Island.

The first surprise is the distance. In the accounts I have read, the *Batavia* survivors make nothing of crossing from one island to another on rafts and homemade boats. But it's 8 kilometres from East Wallabi to Beacon – and, on the water, you feel each kilometre, even in a high-tech patrol vessel.

The second surprise comes at Beacon Island itself. We clamber out of the Fisheries boat's inflatable dinghy on to the coral, near a sign warning of the protected archaeological site. When you imagine castaways on the proverbial desert island, you think coconut palms and jungle. But Beacon resembles an actual desert, an outback vista of bone-white reef fragments and scraggly grey-green shrubs. There isn't even a real beach, just an embankment of broken coral limestone leading down to the water. No trees, no grass and no animals.

We do a circuit in about ten minutes, stopping at the cairn commemorating the wreck and then again where the fishermen's huts have been demolished for the archaeological dig.

Most of the island is yet to be excavated, and researchers say as many as eighty bodies may still lie there. I struggle to imagine Beacon with 200 sunburnt, injured and thirsty people landing upon it. They must have been, almost literally, on top of each other – even by the end, when there were fewer than fifty of them.

Jeronimus Cornelisz was, it seems, an Anabaptist and a follower of Johannes van der Beeck (known as Torrentius), a Dutch painter tortured for heresy. Torrentius scoffed at heaven and hell, contrasting such airy promises with the more immediate pleasures of the flesh. Many thus imagined Cornelisz's reign on Beacon as the implementation of a Torrentian creed – a prolonged exercise in libertinage, fuelled by salvaged liquor and the sudden possession of *Batavia*'s treasures. Maybe so. Traversing Beacon's bleak shores, it seems to me flatly impossible that the island could have been at all comfortable, much less pleasant.

We stand at the end of the atoll and look out to the reef where the *Batavia* sank, some 2 kilometres away. The light changes, lending the water in the shallows a viridescence that takes my breath away.

In his book about the rediscovery of the *Batavia*, Hugh Edwards called Beacon an 'island of angry ghosts'. If there are ghosts here, they aren't manifesting themselves to me. We've been, quite possibly, walking over the graves of murdered men (hell, murdered families), but the atoll is affectless and empty, even in its moments of beauty.

Almost all that we know about the *Batavia* killings comes from Pelsaert's journals, in which he recorded incidents from the voyage and documented his investigation once he returned to the wreck site. As official documents, the journals possess narrative authority; perhaps more surprisingly, they're often remarkably intimate.

For instance, Pelsaert includes a letter that Cornelisz sends to Hayes during their negotiations, a note in which the *onderkoopman* asks Hayes to hand over 'Lucas the steward's mate, Cornelis the fat trumpeter, Cornelis the assistant, deaf Jan Michielsz, Ariaen the gunner, squinting Hendrick' and others. We sense, through the nomenclature, the relationships between men forced into prolonged proximity, necessarily familiar with one another's idiosyncrasies.

There are even fragments of dialogue. We hear Cornelisz explaining why a sailor called Jacop Hendrix must die. 'He is half lame', he says. 'He also must go, he might become a babbler now or later.'

Amid such detail, it's easy to forget that Pelsaert's account derives in large part from confessions extracted under torture. Seventeenth-century Dutch law required defendants in capital cases to own up to their crimes. That sounds remarkably liberal – except that those who wouldn't confess were generally tortured. Afterwards, they were meant to confirm that they'd spoken honestly. If they changed their answers, they were put to the question once more.

Cornelisz initially denies all culpability for the murders. 'Everything that has been done is not my fault', he insists, naming others whom he said had directed the slaughter. Almost at once, the gloves come off, as Dick Cheney might say.

In 2015, we understand more about torture than the writers who rediscovered the *Batavia*'s history in the more civilised days of the past century. There's a certain queasy familiarity about the transcripts now, not least because Pelsaert's trip to the dark side involved waterboarding.

'The Commander', writes Pelsaert, 'proposes to bring to torture the above mentioned Jeronimus [Cornelisz] in order to learn from him the straight truth, as he tries to exonerate himself with flowery talk.'

The Dutch water torture entailed a cloth fitted around the defendant's neck and face, into which liquid was then poured until he either swallowed or choked, or both. It was notoriously unbearable.

'Having started to torture him a little', Pelsaert continues, '[Cornelisz] requests a postponement, for he wished to tell ... what he knew'.

In the days that followed, Cornelisz alternated between denial and confession, with the admissions becoming more detailed and extensive as the torture continued. The other men behaved likewise, gradually incriminating themselves and one another, so that an increasingly detailed narrative about their collective crimes emerged over the course of repeated torture sessions.

Of course, that they had killed was never really in question. But Pelsaert needed not simply to establish criminality but also to attribute responsibility for the disastrous collapse of a commercial venture, in the context of a company famously intolerant of its staff's failings.

For instance, Ariaen Jacobsz, the *Batavia*'s skipper, had successfully navigated a 9-metre open longboat loaded with nearly fifty passengers (the officers and their wives who had so quickly deserted *Batavia*'s Graveyard) more than 1500 kilometres from the coast of Western Australia to Indonesia. This was an extraordinary – almost unparalleled – feat of seamanship. But, after arriving safely in Java, Jacobsz was immediately thrown in gaol for mismanaging the *Batavia*. His boatswain was tortured and eventually executed, having been blamed, presumably by Pelsaert, for the shipboard attack on Lucretia Jans.

Pelsaert himself escaped punishment in Java but he returned to the wreck site under an obvious cloud, having lost the VOC's ship, the VOC's crew and the VOC's treasure. His voyage on the *Sardam* represented a last chance to redeem himself, which was why he spent considerable time sending divers to retrieve silver from the wreck. Naturally, the particular confessions the accused made mattered a great deal.

Further, the commercial imperatives of the case could not be untangled from its theological implications, for the Dutch understood God and the Company as entirely complementary. In his investigation, Pelsaert sought 'to turn from us the wrath of God and to cleanse the name of Christianity from such an unheard of villain.'

The aggregated confessions portray Cornelisz as an 'Epicurean villain', an almost demonic seducer. Even the assault on Jans seemingly had been part of a plan he'd conceived with the skipper to seize the *Batavia*, a scheme only derailed by the collision with Morning Reef. Once on Beacon, Cornelisz had inducted others into his 'gruesome opinions' and the murderous impulses that derived from his heresies.

All of that may well have been true. But the *Batavia* confessions, like most admissions generated under torture, tell a story very close to what the torturers wanted to hear.

To the end, Cornelisz ('more evil than if he had been changed into a tiger') remains a mystery to the modern reader and, I suspect, to Pelsaert himself.

From Beacon Island, we take the inflatable back to the Fisheries boat and then head to West Wallabi. The sun glints on the water, and I realise that I'm already burnt. A school of flying fish races us for a while, darting impossibly above the waves like birds.

Almost immediately we are passing Long Island, a sliver of land running about 1.5 kilometres, less than 200 metres across at its widest. The survivors named it Seals Island – and I can see a trio of the creatures, turning their whiskery noses to the buzz of the engine.

The recent excavations here uncovered bags of nails, fastenings, bolts and other fittings in an area about the size of a room. These are the remnants of a scaffold.

After Pelsaert's investigation, it took some time before the inevitable death sentences were carried out, not least because the ship's carpenters had to erect a suitably robust gallows and anchor it somehow to the island's coral base. Hence the detritus Alistair Paterson and his team found, the legacy of that grim construction.

Cornelisz did all he could to prolong his life, anxiously asking when he would be hanged. 'Tut! Nothing more?' he said, when told the date, only a few days hence. 'How can one show repentance of life in so few days? I thought I should be allowed eight or fourteen days.'

He requested time to be baptised and to 'bewail his sins'. He asked to be taken to Batavia to speak with his wife. Eventually, he prophesied a miracle to deliver him from the gallows, and then apparently tried to poison himself. The dose, though it affected his stomach, wasn't fatal.

On the appointed day, the seven other condemned men begged that Cornelisz might be executed first, apparently because they feared he might yet escape. Like most of the defendants, the *onderkoopman* was mutilated before the hanging. His hands were chiselled off beneath the scaffold, the traditional penalty for those who defrauded the VOC.

'[He] could not reconcile himself to dying or to penitence', says Pelsaert. Cornelisz screamed at the council and his fellow condemned (and they back at him), promising he would seek justice with them in the afterlife. 'And so he died stubborn.'

It's easy to forget that Pelsaert's sentences were, for the time, relatively lenient. One of the few ringleaders transported all the way to Batavia was later broken on the wheel – that is, his limbs were pulverised with a hammer until they could be bent around a cartwheel in a ghastly crucifixion. By contrast, on the islands, some of the lesser offenders were simply flogged or dropped from the ship's yardarm (a customary, and usually non-fatal, sailor's punishment).

Pelsaert's mercy manifested itself most dramatically in the case of Jan Pelgrom, the cabin boy who had yearned to kill. Pelgrom was sentenced to death, but on execution day he broke down in tears and begged to be spared. Pelsaert commuted his sentence to banishment.

Thus, on 16 November 1629, Jan Pelgrom and a man called Wouter Loos were set down on the 'Southland', probably at Wittecarra Gully in today's Kalbarri National Park, a hundred or so kilometres north of Geraldton.

Pelsaert wanted them to survive, even flourish – he thought they might gather information of value to the VOC. So they were landed near a water source and given a boatload of gear, including trinkets for barter, along with suggestions as to how to befriend the natives.

Did that happen? We don't know, for Pelgrom and Loos disappeared from history. Intriguingly, in the late 1930s, the anthropologist Daisy Bates wrote of the 'flat heavy Dutch face, curly fair hair, and heavy stocky build' of some local people in the area, and drew a connection with the marooned men – though this is a conclusion that's treated with great scepticism nowadays.

Nonetheless, it's fascinating that in 1629 everyone

involved accepted that the survival of the men – the first permanent European settlers – depended upon a certain kind of racial assimilation: namely, the absorption of the two whites into black civilisation. That's a strikingly different way to think about interaction between colonists and Indigenous people in the predawn of modern Australia, and it would be nice to believe that black society provided some sort of redemption for two men implicated in such horrors in the white world.

Inland at West Wallabi, we unexpectedly encounter one of the reasons why Cornelisz sending Hayes to what they called the 'High Islands' had been so wrongheaded: a tammar wallaby, bounding out from under a bush.

The *Batavia* survivors called the wallabies 'cats' and feasted upon them: much better food than at Beacon. They were, said Pelsaert, 'creatures of miraculous form, as big as a hare'. It's a description that perfectly evokes men reaching the very limits of the known world, a liminal space of wonders and terrors and miraculous cats.

After another ten minutes, we come to the fort.

It isn't anything much, or at least it doesn't seem to be: a square structure of stacked coral, open to the air and with walls waist-high. The construction is similar to that used by fishermen elsewhere on the islands, employing the only solid material available as a kind of natural brick. Yet these are the walls that Wiebbe Hayes laid out in 1629 as he prepared to fight off Cornelisz's men.

Over the years, the building has been tampered with:

built up for photos and plundered by souvenir hunters. Still, when Alistair Paterson's team excavated near its base, they found sufficient Dutch material to be confident of its authenticity.

'Tiny book clasps', he told me in Perth, 'that we think come from a Bible, bits and pieces of military clothing, and lots and lots of butchered bone'.

It is, then, the oldest example of Western architecture in Australia.

We are sufficiently far inland that the ocean is no longer visible, and its absence – we could be absolutely anywhere – makes the tiny fort feel lost beneath the sky: a little scrap of Europe, built by desperate men impossibly far from home.

Paterson has compared the islands (Beacon in particular) to Stonehenge: sites where our knowledge will keep changing the more archaeology that is done. Daniel Franklin thinks he could spend at least another six months on the skeletons alone, working out which countries they'd come from, how well they'd been nourished, whether they'd endured any particular illnesses or injuries. Jeremy Green wants to search Beacon for the cooking and sleeping areas.

Their research could, perhaps, put names on some of the bones, matching skeletons with the individuals in the diaries. From small discoveries, like the musket balls Paterson had shown me, which had been in the pockets of the recently discovered adolescent skeleton, they may also learn a great deal more about the everyday life of the castaways in the months after the wreck.

So does such work matter? It seems to me that it does.

Pelsaert's diaries have provided irresistible material for

novelists, dramatists, poets and librettists; the narrative has been told and retold in popular histories. Yet somehow the *Batavia* has never captured the Australian imagination – at least, not to the extent you might expect.

Ned Kelly, Squizzy Taylor and Chopper Read are household names, but who, in the eastern states particularly, has heard of Jeronimus Cornelisz, much less Wiebbe Hayes? Perhaps, perversely, the problem lies in the story's significance. It's a tale of firsts, after all. As an apothecary, Cornelisz was the first practitioner of Western medicine in what became Australia (even if he used his skills simply to make poisons); the battle on West Wallabi could be seen, with only a slight stretch, as the first European military engagement; the trials represent the first criminal prosecutions under a European legal code. And maybe that is the difficulty. Perhaps we don't want to think about the *Batavia* as a Western origin story.

The traditional narrative of white Australia posits the coming of the First Fleet as an almost natural development, the inexorable result of the British Empire's growth. By contrast, the *Batavia* story, and contemplation of the Dutch presence in Australia prior to 1788, sets both England and the Australian continent itself on a different axis. It remaps the regional geography around Jakarta, and Amsterdam becomes more significant than London. We're pushed into a multivalent history in which there are more actors and the outcomes feel somehow less preordained. The specific way that white settlement unfolded loses some of its inevitability.

And that seems to me to be a good thing. When the past opens up, so does the future. The world of the *Batavia* is undoubtedly strange to us and will surely remain so, no matter how many skeletons we find. Nonetheless, the story we tell about the lives saved and lost in that desperate episode almost 400 years ago illuminates, in some ways at least, the stories we tell about ourselves today.

Depression? What Depression?

Since Keith Windschuttle's *The Fabrication of Aboriginal History*, it's become something of a patriotic duty for historians to iron out unpleasant creases from Australia's past, to the extent that one awaits the enterprising scholar who will launch *Those Lucky Convicts* or *Happy Days on the Somme*.

David Potts might not be a history warrior by inclination – economically, for instance, he channels Clive Hamilton rather than Milton Friedman – but *The Myth of the Great Depression* certainly seems to have been cooked in Windschuttle's overheated ideological oven.

Which is a pity, because the book begins with an intriguing premise. Throughout the 1960s and 1970s, Potts interviewed survivors of the Depression and noticed that, alongside deprivation and misery, many recalled moments of joy and pleasure. It's in this sense he decries the 'myth' of the Depression. Most of us think of the era only in terms of wretched victims rotting on the dole when, actually, the struggle to survive provided many with a sense of purpose, even a happiness, absent from more prosperous times.

Yet, by pushing this idea to the limit and then beyond, Potts has transformed an interesting thesis into a polemic far more unbalanced than the orthodoxy he seeks to correct.

It is one thing to argue that most Australians avoided the extremes of the Depression, to suggest that unemployment only peaked at 25 per cent rather than the much higher figures often quoted, and to point out that wages maintained much of their value. But only the most determined Pollyanna would celebrate 'the long walks and ... carrying and cart-pushing' forced upon impoverished shoppers as 'another boost to good health' or emphasise that families foraging in the bush for food saw gathering blackberries and mushrooms as 'a significant pastime and a pleasure'.

While Potts wants to focus on people overcoming adversity, his relentless accentuation of the positive makes him occasionally sound as if he's denying they faced much in the way of adversity at all. The jobless men who went gold fossicking found it, he says, 'recreational, led on by hope and adventure, and undertaken in beautiful places', while those reduced to selling door-to-door could find themselves transformed into successful small businessmen. 'A lad who collected shell grit at Point Stephens, for backyard poultry owners in Sydney, did well enough to pay for loading equipment, a new road and a new boat.'

Even impoverished farmers – when they were 'freed in interviews from any disposition to complain for gain' – admitted that they were really rather happy in bush hovels. 'One man described his "wattle and daub home" as "very comfortable", and another his "slab home" with bark roof and an earthen floor as "quite snug" ... A Queensland woman settler [...] described her shack and her kerosene-case furniture as "lovely".'

Where George Orwell reported with sympathy on the desire of the poor not to eat 'dull wholesome food but something a little bit tasty', Potts is made of sterner stuff. 'Dripping', he explains, 'is not a significant nutritional change from butter nor particularly distasteful (especially when mixed with meat juices). One girl reported, 'We loved dripping . . . It was a real treat'.

And if there was no dripping to be had, well, 'going without food intermittently for two or three days, or five or 10, or even a degree of persistent hunger, does not damage the body or health'.

Though Potts wants to take seriously the subjective experience of ordinary people, his quest for the silver lining in every Depression-era cloud leads him to identify with an officialdom openly sceptical about the poor: he shows far more enthusiasm, for instance, about the charity networks (despite their 19th-century paternalism) than the jobless who sought money instead of meal tickets.

Though he discusses the methodological problems implicit in oral history, nothing he says counters the obvious charge that middle-aged men and women, looking back from the safety of the Long Boom, would naturally recall their youth with nostalgia. Here's a woman called Ellen Howcroft reminiscing about her mother and father:

> Really, they didn't work – they slaved ... but we were very happy and they were good people ... I feel sorry for the kids now, even though they've got everything.

Are we to conclude that she enjoyed the drudgery and genuinely believes the rising generation would benefit from a spot of slavery – or is it more sensible to think she simply misses her parents and the childhood she spent with them?

David Potts writes well, and his book contains valuable information that will be debated by scholars. It's just a pity that *The Myth of the Great Depression* emerged in an era that encourages public historians to abandon nuance for polemical fervour.

The dachshund at war

The Dachshund is a German dog—
A low-down, Hun-like creature—
A sort of animated log,
With no redeeming feature.[1]

The poem entitled 'The Freak' appeared in multiple Australian newspapers during the First World War, part of a sustained patriotic attack on a breed known in German as the *teckel* and in English as the dachshund.

From the perspective of a century later, the denunciations offer a glimpse into the often-forgotten xenophobia that descended upon Australia during the First World War. The campaign helped redefine the dachshund in the English-speaking world – and then, perhaps, laid the basis for its renewed popularity in a very different era.

In 1914, *Lone Hand* magazine responded to the declaration of hostilities with the song 'Sons of Australia':

With Britain's other gallant sons
We're going hand in hand,
Our War-cry 'Good old Britain boys',
Our own dear motherland.[2]

As the lyrics made plain, local patriots understood themselves as fighting for England, the country 'where our fathers first drew breath.' Yet with the battlefields of Europe so very far away, Australians – particularly those disinclined to enlist – struggled to think how they might immediately demonstrate their loyalty to 'good old Britain.' People of Germanic descent living within Australia provided an initial and obvious target.

In August 1914, the government required local Germans to register with their nearest police station. Initially, officers could make their own assessment as to whether those before them were 'reputed to be anti-British', but the regulations quickly became stricter and more encompassing.

Today, the Anzac mythos presents the Great War as a fight for freedom. In reality, within a few months of hostilities, parliament passed the War Precautions Act, stripping away all manner of traditional liberties. The Act gave the authorities unparalleled power, including the ability to censor the press, outlaw protests and monitor dissidents.

So-called 'enemy aliens' were subjected to particular restrictions. They could be prevented from owning motor vehicles – presumably, on the basis that cars provided a dangerous mobility. They could be forbidden from possessing telephones, cameras, homing pigeons or any other equipment a spy might purchase. More importantly, they could also be imprisoned, with subsequent amendments allowing a military intelligence officer to detain someone without trial if they judged them a 'possible danger'.

By the end of the war, nearly 7000 men and women had been incarcerated in eleven facilities described officially as 'German concentration camps'.[3]

The crackdown was urged on by the newly formed Anti-German League, whose members pledged publicly 'not to deal with Germans or to buy from shops which employ Germans'.[4] It was also supported by an often-hysterical press.

'The Germans are beasts', explained an editorialist for the *Sunday Times*. 'Only as beasts can they be made to understand. Use the whip, and for every blow dealt to a defenceless British subject in the Kultured land of Germany, let us strike a hundred blows here.'[5]

Yet, precisely because mass internment had been so rapid and so all-encompassing, finding flesh-and-blood Germans on whom to rain blows became increasingly difficult. As a result, the patriotic agitation took a cultural turn.

'I am a true born Australian of nearly 70 years of age', explained one correspondent to a Queensland newspaper, 'and with my fellow countrymen I think it is high time that we Britishers demanded that everything German should be torn down; that towns and districts with German names should be renamed with something Australian'.[6]

The renaming of places could proceed easily enough. An eastern Riverina community unlucky enough be known as Germanton publicly 'express[ed its] indignation at the conduct of Germany in the war' and announced it would henceforth be called 'Holbrook'.[7] Townsville's German

Gardens became the Belgian Gardens; Melbourne's Bismarck Street stood forth as Kitchener Street; Weinberg Road transformed into the more dinkum Wattle Road; and so on.[8]

But the imperative to tear down 'everything German' proved more ticklish. What, precisely, did it mean?

Australians wanting to demonstrate fidelity to the 'dear old motherland' necessarily confronted the awkward ties between the establishment in Britain and aristocratic Germany. The 1840 marriage between Queen Victoria and Prince Albert of Saxe-Coburg and Gotha brought a Prussian dynasty to the English throne, something that made distinguishing the Saxon and Anglo-Saxon particularly fraught. In both countries, a hereditary elite ruled; in both countries, leaders espoused a similar mix of militarism, imperial power and social hierarchy.

When war broke out, King George had hastily distanced himself from his first cousin Kaiser Wilhelm by adopting the surname 'Windsor' rather than the embarrassingly Germanic 'Sachsen-Coburg-Gotha.' Yet, in some ways, the gesture did not draw a sharp line between the two enemies so much as demonstrate the alarming fluidity of national identities.

In February 1915, the *Bulletin* tackled the matter head on with a competition promising a half-guinea prize to the best response to the question, 'What is a German?'[9]

None of the answers proved particularly satisfactory. One of the published replies came from a certain SA Perry, who wrote his response in rhyme:

> Arrogance, treachery, cruelty, lust,
> Murder and arson and sullen mistrust;

All these, personified, is he. So why
Ask to define him? Useless to try.
What is a German? Answer comes, pat:
A German's a German! Leave it at that.[10]

But that was precisely what those committed to culture war could not do. By 1916, the more excitable elements of the press came to worry that mass incarceration had detained only the most overt Germans, leaving at large a nefarious element dangerous precisely because it couldn't be detected. 'German spies everywhere!' warned a *Border Chronicle* headline. 'Designs on Australia!'[11]

With a protean foe so difficult to locate, dachshunds – overtly foreign and yet handily local – proved an irresistible target. The dogs were, after all, as unambiguously German as one could hope. Dachshunds first appeared in the historical record in the game master Johann Friedrich von Flemming's book *The Complete German Hunter* in 1723.

When two Prussian officers formed the German Dachshund Club in 1888, they cemented the association between the so-called *teckel* and an aristocracy much wedded to the traditions of the hunt. The affection of Kaiser Wilhelm – or, as local journalists styled him, 'Balmy Bill of Berlin' – for his dachshunds Wadl and Hexl was well known, with the Australian press circulating a passage from journalist Henry Fischer describing the pair unkindly as 'biting snarling little brutes with jaws measuring half the length of their smooth bodies, and a corresponding penchant for people's calves, skirts and petticoats'.[12]

Abhorring the *teckel* duly became a patriotic

responsibility. In 1916, the novelist Ethel Turner (best known for her classic *Seven Little Australians*) published a children's book entitled *John of Daunt*. In the book, Turner describes her protagonist, little Ian, encountering a 'dachshund of a most pronounced type'. The dog, she tells us, possesses a 'body … a yard, at least, in length', so that it 'looked a live, distorted cylinder supported on ridiculously inadequate and crooked legs'.[13]

The family servant invites the precocious boy to contemplate 'the kind of dog Germans keep' – and then warns that the monster wags its tail whenever a British battleship sinks. Ian determines to administer it poison, an ambition that he pursues (albeit unsuccessfully) through a considerable portion of the remaining narrative.

The analogy Turner made between the dachshund's warped body and the German's twisted soul appeared again and again during the war years. The second verse of 'The Freak' described the dog in precisely this fashion, explaining that:

> It walks on inconspicuous legs,
> All body (like its nation),
> And represents the very dregs
> Of canine degradation.

The 'degradation' of the dachshund was often highlighted through a contrast of breeds said to be more British and thus nobler. For instance, when, in 1915, Melbourne's Government House raised money for the war effort with a 'patriotic dog parade', the *Argus* described the event as 'bulldog versus dachshund'. With some 1700 animals assembled, the crowd roundly applauded the English dogs – but, as the reporter gloated, 'the unfortunate dachshunds won little attention from an unsympathetic public'.[14]

Editorialists and cartoonists regularly made the same comparison, presenting the war as pitting, in the words of one recruiter, 'men of the bulldog breed' against 'curs of the cringing dachshund tribe'.[15] But the contrast necessitated a reinterpretation of precisely the traits that had led German militarists to value the dog.

Von Flemming, for instance, had described the '*dachs kriecher*' (badger crawler) or '*dachs krieger*' (badger warrior) not as deformed but as perfectly designed, with short legs and big paws for digging out badger or fox burrows and a missile-shaped body to wriggle down tunnels.

Prior to the First World War, the dachshund's tenacity was almost proverbial – and not just in Germany. In the 1891 *American Book of the Dog*, William Loeffler praised large and small dachshunds alike as 'equally savage in their attacks'. Dachshunds, he said, looked 'more like demons than dogs', as they emerged from badger burrows with 'eye and ears red and full of dirt, the tongue dry and hanging near the ground, their breath short and quick, and bleeding from the wounds made by their enemy'.[16] He lauded one dachshund that 'had been victor in nearly fifty battles [with badgers]' and 'whose ears were nothing but fringes [and] whose chest, neck and whole body showed one scar near another'. When the creature eventually succumbed to its traditional enemy, 'every hunter within many miles felt this loss deeply, for these men looked upon the dog as a dead hero'.

In the same year that Loeffler published his panegyric to dachshund ferocity, the English novelist Marie Louise Ramé ('Ouida') wrote of her abhorrence for what she called 'the squat, clumsy, deformed dachshund'.[17]

Yet her objections were notably different to those raised after 1914. When she judged the poor dachshund 'as ugly as he is out of place on the cushion of a carriage or a boudoir', she wasn't impugning its character nor its courage. On the contrary, she was suggesting that, as a little killing machine, it did not make an appropriate home companion.

The wartime campaign entirely reversed her argument. Once the conflict began, the Australian press presented the dachshund not as a hunting dog wrongly classified as a pet but as a pet preposterously imitating a hunter. In that way, the *teckel* could illuminate the necessary distinction between an English ruling caste and its German equivalent.

The British aristocracy, the argument went, had been refined and ennobled like the bulldog by a carefully preserved bloodline. The German rulers, however, mirrored their dogs: degraded and deformed by overbreeding. Like the stumpy dachshund, they fancied themselves as something they were not, ludicrously posturing as cultured and brave despite their cowardice and weakness. On that basis, a wartime poet mocked what he called 'The Dachshund Fleet', explaining:

> The German fleet is like a dog
> That runs out, then 'renegs;'
> Then rushes, howling home again
> Its tail between its legs![18]

Both the yappy dachshund and the posturing German warranted stern measures. In 1918, for instance, a joke circulated in the press: a gag featuring a cultivated lady talking to her chauffeur:

'Was that a dog you just ran over, Jenkins?' she asks.

'Yes, madam,' he replies.

'Oh, Jenkins! How can you be so careless!'

'I wasn't careless, madam,' says the driver. 'It was a dachshund.'[19]

Of course, not everyone believed dachshunds should be run over by cars. Even at the height of the campaign, the animals retained their defenders.

In February 1915, a dog-lover wrote to the papers suggesting the persecution was misplaced. He floated the idea that dachshunds originated not in enemy Germany but in allied France, from where they'd been foully kidnapped by Teutonic noblemen. Unfortunately, the argument rather suffered from his admission that 'we do not find this theory supported by any authority we have consulted.'[20]

Another dachshund supporter tried versifying from the perspective of an unjustly vilified dog:

Only a faithful dachshund,
(What in the world have I done?)
Quite a naturalised Briton,
Never, most certain, a Hun.

Not a bomb on a baby.
Have I dropped from the sky,

Hymns of hate are beyond me,
So are the ways of a spy

While you're so kind to Germans,
Wandering happy and free.
Why must you turn your anger
On a poor little dog like me?[21]

The suggestion that a hatred for German *teckels* got in the way of hatred for actual Germans did not, however, prove particularly persuasive, simply because so many patriots were demonstrably able to combine both.

Indeed, the anti-dachshund crusade raged, not only in Australia, but throughout the empire. In his memoir, the novelist Graham Greene recalls seeing the dogs 'stoned in the High Street' in Britain during the First World War, while the historian James Hayward suggests that the numbers of the dogs plummeted so precipitously that, when the conflict ended, the bloodline could only be replenished through imported stock.[22]

On face value, the outbreak of a second and even more destructive war against Germany might have seemed likely to have finished the dachshund once and for all in the British dominions. Yet that wasn't the case at all. On the contrary, it might even be argued that the Second World War helped the public rehabilitation of the breed in the English-speaking world. Certainly, in Australia, the little dogs did not come in for the same sustained abuse during the war against the Nazis.

A letter in the *Adelaide News* in 1939 exemplifies the difference between the two conflicts. In it, a correspondent styling himself as 'Maximillian' writes in on behalf of something called the Loyal British Dachshunds' Association. Maximillian explains how the Australian dogs in his organisation 'bitterly resent[ed] the unpatriotic role assigned to them in numerous cartoons'. His dachshunds were, he said, 'faithful and courageous, and will defend this land valiantly should the need arise'.[23]

One might wonder as to precisely the circumstances (an invasion of badgers, perhaps?) under which Maximillian imagined the nation might press its sausage dogs into service. Nevertheless, in standing up for his dogs, he was nowhere near as isolated as the dachshund supporters of the First World War had been.

A few years later, the *KCC Kennel Gazette* in Melbourne explained publicly that the dachshunds, these 'staunch little companions', had become 'thoroughly Anglicised and [...] Australianised', and so 'any antipathy to them is not only unfair but ridiculous'.[24] Along similar lines, a Tasmanian writer calling himself 'Mundoora' declared hostility to dachshunds 'hardly fair' – and then reiterated the old theory that the dogs were more French than German.[25]

Naturally, the dachshunds' national origins remained precisely the same as they'd always been. If Mundoora's rejection of any association with Germany seemed suddenly credible, that was less to do with the dogs themselves than with the regime to which they were linked.

Like the Kaiser, Hitler loved dogs. But he wasn't an

aristocrat and didn't particularly care for badger-hunting dachshunds. Hitler admired wolves – and showered affection on Blondi, a German shepherd akin to the dogs guarding the concentration camps.

During the Second World War, an accusation that the Nazis were over-bred lapdogs strained credulity. National Socialism explicitly rejected the buttoned-up propriety of the hereditary upper class, replacing it with an animalistic brutality based on survival of the fittest. Accordingly, the dachshund-as-Germany trope lost its potency: sausage dogs manifestly did not belong in Hitler's world of industrialised genocide. That's perhaps why the very traits propagandists once mocked became the basis for a renewed embrace of the breed.

The novelist PG Wodehouse – famously, a dachshund owner himself – provides a neat illustration of how the post-war affection for the dog rested on the Great War denunciations.

In the 1960 novel *Jeeves in the Offing*, Wodehouse's dim-witted protagonist, Bertram Wooster, warns the butler Jeeves that the estate in which they are staying contains a dachshund, an animal who 'when you first meet him will give you the impression that he plans to convert you into a light snack between his regular meals'.

Though harmless, the dog must, Bertie explains, feign ferocity because he's been named 'Poppet'.

'One can readily appreciate', he says, 'that when a dog hears himself addressed day in and day out as Poppet, he feels he must throw his weight about. His self-respect demands it'.

'Precisely, sir', replies Jeeves.

'You'll like Poppet. Nice dog. Wears his ears inside out. Why do dachshunds wear their ears inside out?'

'I could not say, sir.'

'Nor me. I've often wondered.'[26]

During the First World War, loyalists had sought to distinguish a (good) upper class in the English-speaking nations from a (bad) upper class in Imperial Germany. Picking quarrels like an angry dachshund, the Kaiser revealed himself as an ill-bred menace against whom bulldog Britishers needed to fight.

But by 1960, the old privileged caste based on hereditary privilege had lost its significance in both England and Germany. The humour in the Jeeves stories stems, at least in part, from anachronism, with Wodehouse chronicling the romantic adventures of a clique rendered endearingly ludicrous by the passage of time. Naturally, his ridiculous characters own ridiculous dogs. Like the 'mentally negligible' Wooster himself, the dachshund cuts a comical figure because of the gulf between appearance and reality. He blusters like a German autocrat; he wears his ears inside out and answers to the name 'Poppet'.

'In an expanding universe', the English humorist Quentin Crisp once explained, 'time is on the side of the outcast. Those who once inhabited the suburbs of human contempt find that without changing their address they eventually live in the metropolis.'[27]

The almost racialised demonisation of Germans during the First World War no longer makes sense, with the contours of discrimination shifting almost beyond recognition. The very people against whom Australian nationalists most fervently distinguished themselves (Germans, but also Italians, Greeks, etc.) now feature as part of a European heritage allegedly menaced by Muslims and other new targets.

The dachshund remains, if anything, more freakish than ever. Nearly a quarter of all the dogs develop intervertebral disc disease, a form of spinal osteoarthritis that can cause stiffness, pain, incontinence and paralysis. Fanciers pay big dollars for dachshunds with a distinctive dappled coat, even though dapples crossed with other dapples produce 'double dapples': animals with a propensity for blindness, deafness and other ailments.

Nonetheless, despite their health problems, dachshunds are enjoying an unprecedented popularity, not least because of their outsized presence on social media. Take Crusoe the Dachshund: a dog that boasts nearly 4 million followers across the various socials, a YouTube channel with a billion views, some 900 000 fans on Instagram, and several best-selling books. Crusoe's empire – both a parody and an example of online celebrity – rests on kitsch images and videos in which he waddles, on his inconspicuous legs, in various absurd costumes.

During the COVID-19 lockdown, Australian embraced dachshunds in record numbers, so that, for a while, it seemed like almost every second walker during the mandated exercise hour strode along with an animated log on a lead. In a very different international crisis, many of us took some consolation in seeing 'the dregs of canine degradation' enjoying their redemption.

Notes

A slave state

1 Johanna Marie and Stephanie Doole, 'Queensland Mayor Issues Historic Apology over Blackbirding Slavery of Pacific Islanders', ABC, 30 July 2021, <www.abc.net.au/news/2021-07-30/queensland-mayor-sorry-blackbirding-south-seas-slavery/100333302>.

2 'The Importation of Stock', *Adelaide Observer* (SA: 1843–1904) (SA, 18 April 1885), <nla.gov.au/nla.news-article160737617>.

3 Edmund Barton, 'Pacific Islands Labourers Bill' (1901).

4 Edmund Barton, 'Immigration Restriction Bill' (1901).

5 Ernest Renan, 'What Is a Nation?', 1998.

6 Jane Lydon, *Anti-slavery and Australia: No Slavery in a Free Land? Empires and the Making of the Modern World, 1650–2000* (Routledge, New York, 2021), 23.

7 Calvert, Camden and King conducted seventy-seven voyages, taking some 22 000 slaves to the Caribbean. See Kenneth James Cozens, 'Politics Patronage and Profit: A Case Study of Three 18th Century London Merchants' (Greenwich Maritime Institute, n.d.), 75.

8 Lydon, *Anti-slavery and Australia*, 44.

9 Clare Anderson, *A Global History of Convicts and Penal Colonies* (Bloomsbury Publishing, London, 2020).

10 Lydon, *Anti-slavery and Australia*, 22.

11 Freg J Stokes, 'Australia, a Counterrevolutionary Colony', *Jacobin*, 9 February 2020.

12 Interview with Ben Fordham, 2GB, 11 June 2020.

13 Katharine Murphy, 'Scott Morrison Sorry for "no Slavery in Australia" Claim and Acknowledges "Hideous Practices"', *Guardian*, 12 June 2020, <www.theguardian.com/australia-news/2020/jun/12/scott-morrison-sorry-for-no-slavery-in-australia-claim-and-acknowledges-hideous-practices>.

14 Cassandra Pybus, *Black Founders: The Unknown Story of Australia's First Black Settlers* (UNSW Press, Sydney, 2006), 5.

15 Pybus, *Black Founders*, 34.
16 Pybus, *Black Founders*, 43.
17 Emma Christopher, 'An Illegitimate Offspring: South Sea Islanders, Queensland Sugar, and the Heirs of the British Atlantic Slave Complex', *History Workshop Journal* 90 (25 February 2021): 238, <doi.org/10.1093/hwj/dbaa018>.
18 Vivienne Parsons, 'Scott, Thomas Alison (1777–1881)', in *Australian Dictionary of Biography*, 18 vols. (National Centre of Biography, Australian National University, Canberra), <adb.anu.edu.au/biography/scott-thomas-alison-2644>.
19 Christopher, 'An Illegitimate Offspring', 237.
20 Editorial, 'War with America', *Argus*, 1 March 1862.
21 Terry Smyth, *Australian Confederates: How 42 Australians Joined the Rebel Cause and Fired the Last Shot in the American Civil War* (Random House Australia, Sydney, 2015), 26.
22 Raymond Evans, Kay Saunders and Kathryn Cronin, *Race Relations in Colonial Queensland: A History of Exclusion, Exploitation, and Extermination* (University of Queensland Press, Brisbane, 1993), 150.
23 Christopher, 'An Illegitimate Offspring'.
24 Marilyn Lake, *Faith: Faith Bandler, Gentle Activist* (Allen & Unwin, Sydney, 2002), 2.
25 Clinton Fernandes, *Island off the Coast of Asia: Instruments of Statecraft in Australian Foreign Policy*, 2018, 13, <search.ebscohost.com/login.aspx?direct=true&scope=site&db=nlebk&db=nlabk&AN=2045403>.
26 Georgie Arnott, 'Australia's Deep Connection with Enslavement', *Age*, 16 June 2020.
27 CR Moore, 'Queensland Sugar Industry from 1860 to 1900' (James Cook University, Townsville, 1974).
28 Christopher, 'An Illegitimate Offspring'; Doug Hunt and KH Kennedy, 'By Bye Blackbirder: The Death of Ross Lewin', *Journal of the Royal Historical Society of Queensland*, 19, no. 5 (n.d.).
29 Alex McKinnon, 'Blackbirds: Australia's Hidden Slave Trade History', *Monthly*, July 2019, <www.themonthly.com.au/issue/2019/july/1561989600/alex-mckinnon/blackbirds-australia-s-hidden-slave-trade-history>.
30 Philip Gavin Griffiths, 'The Making of White Australia: Ruling Class Agendas, 1876–1888', 2006, 157.
31 Griffiths, 'The Making of White Australia', 317.
32 'The "Hopeful" Martyrs', *Queensland Figaro and Punch*, 21 April 1888.
33 'Slave Stealing and Slave Dealing', *Brisbane Courier*, 3 February 1868.
34 Christopher, 'An Illegitimate Offspring', 246.
35 CJ Coventry, 'Links in the Chain: British Slavery, Victoria and South Australia', *Before/Now* 1, no. 1 (2019): 35.
36 Griffiths, 'The Making of White Australia: Ruling Class Agendas, 1876–1888', 153.
37 Editorial, *Brisbane Courier*, 28 July 1880.
38 Evans, Saunders and Cronin, *Race Relations in Colonial Queensland*, 174.

39 Nicolas de Condorcet, *Outlines of an Historical View of the Progress of the Human Mind, Being a Posthumous Work of the Late M. de Condorcet* (Philadelphia, 1796), 122.
40 Henry Reynolds, *Truth-telling: History, Sovereignty and the Uluru Statement* (NewSouth Publishing, Sydney, 2021), 21.
41 Henry Reynolds, *The Other Side of the Frontier: Aboriginal Resistance to the European Invasion of Australia* (UNSW Press, Sydney, 2006).
42 'Prominent Topics', *Advocate*, 4 March 1905.
43 Reynolds, *Truth-telling*, 179.
44 Henry Reynolds, *Forgotten War* (NewSouth Publishing, Sydney, 2013), 146.
45 Reynolds, *Truth-telling*, 182.
46 'Editorial', *Queenslander*, 1 May 1880.
47 'Letters to the Editor', *Queenslander*, 8 May 1880, 594.
48 'Letters to the Editor', *Queenslander*, 22 May 1880.
49 'Queensland Parliamentary Debates' (1880).
50 'Jackey and Australian Slavery', *Evening Journal*, 16 December 1889.
51 Evans, Saunders, and Cronin, *Race Relations in Colonial Queensland*, 152.
52 Lyndon Megarrity, '"White Queensland": The Queensland Government's Ideological Position on the Use of Pacific Island Labourers in the Sugar Sector 1880–1901', *Australian Journal of Politics & History* 52, no. 1 (2006): 4.
53 Megarrity, '"White Queensland"', 5.
54 'Coloured Labour Question', *Evening News*, 4 January 1884.
55 Griffiths, 'The Making of White Australia: Ruling Class Agendas, 1876–1888', 329.
56 Geoffrey Blainey, *A Land Half Won* (Macmillan, Melbourne, 1980), 201.
57 *Brisbane Courier*, 21 August 1886, p. 4.
58 'A Northern Queensland Slave State', *Warwick Argus*, 23 June 1885.
59 'Separation and Slavery', *Daily Northern Argus*, 12 March 1888.
60 Helen Irving, ed., *The Centenary Companion to Australian Federation* (Cambridge University Press, Cambridge, 1999), 95.
61 Timothy Kendall, 'Within China's Orbit? China through the Eyes of the Australian Parliament', 2008, 12.
62 Alfred Deakin, 'Immigration Restriction Bill' (1901).
63 Irving, *The Centenary Companion to Australian Federation*, 108.
64 George Reid, 'Immigration Restriction Bill' (1901); Samuel Mauger, 'Immigration Restriction Bill' (1901); James Ronald, 'Immigration Restriction Bill' (1901).
65 See Marilyn Lake, 'The White Man under Siege: New Histories of Race in the Nineteenth Century and the Advent of White Australia', in *History Workshop Journal*, vol. 58 (Oxford University Press, 2004), 41–62.
66 Henry Bournes Higgins, 'Immigration Restriction Bill' (1901).
67 '*A White Australia: An Object Lesson from America*', *Toowoomba Chronicle and Darling Downs General Advertiser*, 23 November 1901.
68 'Official Record of the Debates of the National Australasian Convention' (1898).
69 Alfred Deakin, 'Immigration Restriction Bill'.

70 'The Kanaka's Point of View', *Brisbane Courier*, 12 October 1901.
71 Alex McKinnon, 'Blackbirds'.
72 'The Kanaka Union' (18 April 1906), *Daily Mercury* (Mackay, Qld: 1906–1954), p. 2 <nla.gov.au/nla.news-article171570125>.
73 Clive Moore, '"Good-Bye, Queensland, Good-Bye, White Australia; Good-Bye, Christians": Australia's South Sea Islander Community and Deportation, 1901–1908', *The New Federalist* 4 (1999): 22–29.
74 Moore, 'Good-Bye, Queensland'.
75 Kanaka Petition (7 February 1902), *Telegraph* (Brisbane, Qld: 1872–1947), 4, <nla.gov.au/nla.news-article173570746>.
76 *Bulletin*, 27 December 1906.
77 'Deportation of Kanakas', *Evening Telegraph*, 25 July 1908.
78 Edmund Barton, Pacific Islands Labourers Bill.
79 Edmund Barton, Pacific Islands Labourers Bill.
80 James Ronald, Immigration Restriction Bill.
81 'Journeys to Sugaropolis: The Australian South Sea Islanders story of the Gold Coast region', City of Gold Coast, 2013, 24.
82 Ben Doherty, '"Full Truth": Descendants of Australia's "Blackbirded" Islanders Want Pioneer Statues Amended', *Guardian*, 24 August 2017.

What if we found a thylacine?

1 Simon Bevilacqua, 'Look a Tiger in the Eye', *Mercury*, 7 September 2016.
2 Kearney, Nicole, '"If It Lives, We Want It": Exploring the Acclimatisation Society of Victoria's Role in Australia's Ecological History', *Biodiversity Heritage Library* (blog), 25 January 2018.
3 'Alleged Mainline Thylacine Sightings', *Natural Worlds* (blog), n.d., <www.naturalworlds.org/thylacine/history/extvssurv/mainland/alleged_mainland_sightings_1.htm>.
4 'Thyla Seen Near CBD?', *Age*, 19 August 2003.
5 Andrew Rule, 'Tiger Tales: It's Out There Somewhere ... Or Is It?', *Age*, 1 June 1997.
6 'They've Seen ... Heard Blood-Curdling Screams', *Argus*, 5 December 1955.
7 Nicholas Shakespeare, *In Tasmania* (Vintage, Sydney, 2005), 313.
8 'The Huijdecoper Journal', State Library of New South Wales (blog), 14 April 2014, <www2.sl.nsw.gov.au/archive/discover_collections/history_nation/voyages/rich_lands/voya_huydecoper.html>.
9 David Owen, *Thylacine: The Tragic Tale of the Tasmanian Tiger* (Allen & Unwin, Sydney, 2003), 83.
10 Nicholas Clements, *The Black War: Fear, Sex and Resistance in Tasmania* (University of Queensland Press, Brisbane, 2014), 12.
11 Clements, 44–45.
12 Shakespeare, *In Tasmania*, 311.
13 Clements, *The Black War*, 163.
14 Owen, *Thylacine*, 114.
15 'Tiger Extermination', *Mercury*, 21 August 1884.
16 Owen, *Thylacine*, 131.

17 Owen, 152.
18 Bevilacqua, 'Look a Tiger in the Eye.'
19 William James, *On a Certain Blindness in Human Beings* (Penguin, London, 2009).
20 Amanda Lohrey, *Quarterly Essay 8: Groundswell: The Rise of the Greens*, 2002, 12.
21 Jon Mooallem, *Wild Ones: A Sometimes Dismaying, Weirdly Reassuring Story about Looking at People Looking at Animals in America* (Penguin, New York, 2014), 1.
22 Barry W Brook et al, 'Resolving When (and Where) the Thylacine Went Extinct', preprint (*Zoology*, 19 January 2021), <doi.org/10.1101/2021.01.18.427214>.

Revolving on wheels

1 Helen Pidd, 'Keir Hardie's Cycling Club Jettisons Socialism', *Guardian*, 14 June 2021.
2 'Cultural Changes: Bicycles, Bloomers, and the New Woman', *Cleveland Plain Dealer*, September 1895.
3 'Cultural Changes: Bicycles, Bloomers, and the New Woman.'
4 Cited in 'Social Movements and the Bicycle', Thinking About Cycling blog, <thinkingaboutcycling.com/social-movements-and-the-bicycle/>.
5 Sue Macy, 'The Devils Advance Agent', HistoryNet website, 27 September 2017, <www.historynet.com/devils-advance-agent.htm>.
6 Steven E Alford and Suzanne Ferriss, *An Alternative History of Bicycles and Motorcycles: Two-Wheeled Transportation and Material Culture* (Lexington Books, Lanham, 2016), 148.
7 Stephen Kern, *The Culture of Time and Space 1880–1918* (Harvard University Press, Cambridge, Mass, 2001), 111.
8 Frank Dumont, *The New Woman's Husband: A Satire in One Scene* (The Penn Pub. Co., Philadelphia, 1906), <catalog.hathitrust.org/Record/012436062>.
9 Adrienne LaFrance, 'How the Bicycle Paved the Way for Women's Rights', *Atlantic*, 26 June 2014, <www.theatlantic.com/technology/archive/2014/06/the-technology-craze-of-the-1890s-that-forever-changed-womens-rights/373535/>.
10 Zachary Mooradian Furness, *One Less Car: Bicycling and the Politics of Automobility* (Temple University Press, Philadelphia, 2010), 19.
11 'The Project Gutenberg EBook of Bicycling for Ladies, by Maria E. Ward', <www.gutenberg.org/files/62227/62227-h/62227-h.htm#Page14>.
12 Ellen Gruber Garvey, 'Reframing the Bicycle: Advertising-Supported Magazines and Scorching Women', *American Quarterly* 47, no. 1 (1995): 66–101, <doi.org/10.2307/2713325>.
13 Garvey, 'Reframing the Bicycle.'
14 Furness, *One Less Car*, 28.
15 'Women on the Move: Cycling and the Rational Dress Movement', Cycle History website, 30 January 2015, <cyclehistory.wordpress.

com/2015/01/30/women-on-the-move-cycling-and-the-rational-dress-movement/>.

16 'A Public Service Announcement from 1896', Forgotten Stories website, 26 November 2012, <forgottenstories.net/2012/11/26/a-public-service-announcement-from-1896/>.

17 'Since 1878 – Our Journey from the Bicycle Touring Club to Cycling UK | Cycling UK', <www.cyclinguk.org/article/cycling-guide/journey-bicycle-touring-club-cycling-uk>.

18 Tom Hughes, 'Victorian Calendar: April 5, 1899 – Turned Away at the Inn', Victorian Calendar (blog), 28 March 2011, <victoriancalendar.blogspot.com/2011/03/april-5-1899-turned-away-at-inn_28.html>; Michelle Higgs, 'Lady Harberton, Cycling and the Rationals Scandal' <blog.britishnewspaperarchive.co.uk/2014/08/28/lady-harberton-cycling-and-the-%E2%80%98rationals%E2%80%99-scandal/>.

19 LaFrance, 'How the Bicycle Paved the Way for Women's Rights.'

20 'A Wheel within a Wheel, by Frances E. Willard – A Project Gutenberg EBook', <www.gutenberg.org/files/60356/60356-h/60356-h.htm>.

21 Nick Clayton, *A Short History of the Bicycle*, 2016, <nls.ldls.org.uk/welcome.html?ark:/81055/vdc_100034692478.0x000001>.

22 David V Herlihy, *Bicycle: The History* (Yale University Press, New Haven, 2004).

23 Richard Harmond, 'Progress and Flight: An Interpretation of the American Cycle Craze of the 1890s', *Journal of Social History* 5, no. 2 (1971): 235–57.

24 Alford and Ferriss, *An Alternative History of Bicycles and Motorcycles*, 27.

25 AB Paterson, 'Mulga Bill's Bicycle', *Sydney Mail*, 25 July 1896.

26 'A Wheel within a Wheel, by Frances E Willard – A Project Gutenberg EBook.'

27 *History of the Russian Revolution*, vol. 3.

28 Herlihy, *Bicycle*, 264.

29 Alford and Ferriss, *An Alternative History of Bicycles and Motorcycles*, 133.

30 'The Wheels of Chance; a Bicycling Idyll, by H.G. Wells', <www.gutenberg.org/files/1264/1264-h/1264-h.htm#link2H_4_0001>.

31 JA (John Alexander) Hammerton, ed., *Mr. Punch Awheel: The Humours of Motoring and Cycling*, 2009, <www.gutenberg.org/ebooks/29022>.

32 Martin Wright, 'Robert Blatchford, the Clarion Movement, and the Crucial Years of British Socialism, 1891–1900', *Prose Studies* 13, no. 1 (1990): 74.

33 Wright, 75.

34 'The Clarion Scouts', WCML, <www.wcml.org.uk/our-collections/creativity-and-culture/leisure/clarion-movement/the-clarion-scouts/>.

35 'The Clarion Cycling Club', WCML, <www.wcml.org.uk/wcml/en/our-collections/the-clarion-cycling-club/>.

36 David Prynn, 'The Clarion Clubs, Rambling and the Holiday Associations in Britain since the 1890s', *Journal of Contemporary History* 11, no. 2/3 (1976): 65–77.

37 Robert Tressell, *The Ragged Trousered Philanthropists* (BoD–Books on Demand, 2018).

38 'The Salvation Army Bicycle Brigade for Riverside Drive', *New York Journal*, 23 August 1896.
39 Hannah Arendt, *Men in Dark Times* (Houghton Mifflin Harcourt, New York, 1968), 9.
40 Furness, *One Less Car*, 34.
41 Furness, 36; 'Socialist Cycling Scouts', *Socialist*, October 1919.
42 Furness, *One Less Car*, 25.
43 Robert Blatchford, *Merrie England* (Clarion office, 1896).
44 Eric Hobsbawm, *Interesting Times: A Twentieth-Century Life* (Pantheon, New York, 2007).

The dachshund at war

1 'The Freak', *Northcote Leader* (Vic.: 1914–1918) (Vic., 4 December 1915), <nla.gov.au/nla.news-article126170591>.
2 'Sons of Australia', *The Lone Hand*, 1 October 1914.
3 Gerhard Fischer, 'German Experience in Australia During WW1 Damaged Road to Multiculturalism', *Conversation*, 22 April 2015.
4 'Anti-German League' (16 September 1915), *Sydney Morning Herald* (NSW: 1842–1954), p. 9, <nla.gov.au/nla.news-article15613954>.
5 'The Huns Have Done This', *Globe and Sunday Times War Pictorial* (Sydney, NSW: 1914–1917) (Sydney, 15 May 1915), <nla.gov.au/nla.news-article100568490>.
6 'The German Element', *Northern Herald* (Cairns, Qld.: 1913–1939) (Cairns, Qld., 3 March 1916), <nla.gov.au/nla.news-article147502137>.
7 Michael Lech, 'Germanton or Holbrook?', Text, Sydney Living Museums, 21 March 2017, <sydneylivingmuseums.com.au/ww1/germanton-or-holbrook>.
8 'List of Australian Place Names Changed from German Names', in Wikipedia, 1 August 2021, <en.wikipedia.org/w/index.php?title=List_of_Australian_place_names_changed_from_German_names&oldid=1036538819>.
9 'What Is a German?', *Bulletin* (John Haynes and J.F. Archibald, 18 February 1915).
10 'What Is a German?', *Bulletin* (John Haynes and J.F. Archibald, 8 April 1915).
11 'German Spies Everywhere', *Border Chronicle* (Bordertown, SA: 1908–1950) (Bordertown, SA, 7 January 1916), <nla.gov.au/nla.news-article212858921>.
12 'Balmy Bill of Berlin', *Truth* (Brisbane, Qld.: 1900–1954) (Brisbane, Qld., 15 November 1914), <nla.gov.au/nla.news-article203041361>.
13 Ethel Turner, *John of Daunt* (Ward, London, 1916), 89.
14 'Patriotic Dog Parade', *Argus* (Melbourne, Vic.: 1848–1957) (Melbourne, Vic., 22 March 1915), <nla.gov.au/nla.news-article1504745>.
15 'Recruiting.', *Daily News* (Perth, WA: 1882–1950) (Perth, WA, 19 February 1917), <nla.gov.au/nla.news-article81059894>.
16 George O Shields, *The American Book of the Dog: The Origin, Development, Special Characteristics, Utility, Breeding, Training, Points of Judging, Diseases,*

and Kennel Management of All Breeds of Dogs (Rand, McNally, Chicago, 1891), 224.

17 Ouida, 'Dogs and Their Affections', the North American Review (1821–1940) 153, no. 418 (1891): 312.

18 'The Dachshund Fleet', *Independent*, 7 June 1916.

19 'Knew What He Was Doing', *Ballan Times* (Vic.: 1914–1918) (Vic., 14 November 1918), <nla.gov.au/nla.news-article119546183>.

20 'The Dachshund', *Leader* (Melbourne, Vic.: 1862–1918, 1935) (Melbourne, Vic., 6 February 1915), </nla.gov.au/nla.news-article91365909>.

21 'Topics of the Times', *Daily Telegraph* (Launceston, Tas.: 1883–1928) (Launceston, Tas., 18 May 1915), <nla.gov.au/nla.news-article151958847>.

22 Graham Greene, *A Sort of Life* (Bodley Head, London [1971), 64. James Hayward, *Myths and Legends of the First World War*. (The History Press, Stroud, 2011), 38, <search.ebscohost.com/login.aspx?direct=true&scope=site&db=nlebk&db=nlabk&AN=789766>.

23 'What Our Readers Think!', *News* (Adelaide: 1923–1954) (Adelaide, SA, 7 December 1939), <nla.gov.au/nla.news-article131989274>.

24 'Don't Despise the Dachshund', *Sunday Times* (Perth, WA: 1902–1954) (Perth, WA, 18 May 1941), <nla.gov.au/nla.news-article59153388>.

25 'All About Dogs: Real Origin of the Dachshund', *Examiner* (Launceston, Tas.: 1900–1954) (Launceston, Tas., 16 March 1940), <Nla.Gov.Au/Nla.News-Article92643811>.

26 PG Wodehouse, *Jeeves in the Offing* (Arrow, London, 2008), 115.

27 Quentin Crisp, *The Naked Civil Servant* (Harper Perennial, London, 2007), 2.

Publication details

A slave state
Written for *Provocations*

A queer bushranger
Monthly
November 2015

The threshold of another trembling world
Overland
27 November 2012

Today's elites are gods
Originally published as 'By every meaningful measure today's elites are gods. This should make us angry.'
Guardian
21 January 2013

A place of punishment
Originally published as 'A place of punishment: *No Friend but the Mountains* by Behrouz Boochani'
Sydney Review of Books
21 September 2018
What days are for
Guardian
24 November 2014

Len Lawson: Australia's most infamous comic artist
Monthly
October 2019

The perfect combination of art and science
Guardian
20 October 2019

U2, Apple and the strip-mining of punk rebellion
Baffler
18 September 2014

The Magic Pudding
Guardian
25 October 2015

Live in the moment
Overland
12 July 2016
Fangs for the memories
Age
17 April 2010

What if we found a thylacine?
Written for *Provocations*

Australia's oldest things
Guardian
14 July 2019

The art of losing
Guardian
2 December 2019

Where have the Christmas beetles gone?
Originally published as 'The humming of Christmas beetles was once a sign of the season. Where have they gone?'
Guardian
23 December 2019

On the Collins Street Falcons
Crikey
7 October 2019

Revolving on wheels
Written for *Provocations*

'When the burning moment breaks': Gun control and rage massacres
Overland
6 August 2012
Memory and the anti-politics of ANZAC
Overland
24 April 2012

When settlers dream
Jacobin
8 September 2014

Theatre of war
Overland
Summer 2007

Unholy enthusiasm
Meanjin
Autumn 2010

What's the end game for Australia's border policy?
Guardian
5 May 2016

The death of Sisto Malaspina
Guardian
26 Oct 2018

Soylent, neoliberalism and the politics of life hacking
Counterpunch
19 May 2014

In the battle for the Right, the market always wins
Drum
19 August 2011
Journey to the west
Monthly
13 November 2015

The value of history
Guardian
7 Oct 2014

Bring up the bodies: new light on the wreck of the *Batavia*
Monthly
April 2015

Depression? What Depression?
Age
29 July 2006

The daschund at war
Written for *Provocations*

Acknowledgments

Every book is a collective production and one like this more than usually so. My thanks to:

- Sam Wallman for the amazing art, the bicycle rides and the friendship;
- The always enthusiastic and supportive Martin Shaw from Shaw Literary;
- Harriet McInerney, Emma Hutchinson and everyone at NewSouth Publishing;
- Jocelyn Hungerford for her scrupulous and intelligent copyediting;
- The editors who commissioned, fact-checked, tweaked, massaged and otherwise improved the raw versions of these articles, including Jason Steger (*Age*); Alexander Cockburn and Jeffrey St Clair (*Counterpunch*); Dan Woods and Meg Watson (*Crikey*); Jonathan Green (*ABC Drum*); Gabrielle Jackson, Adam Brereton, Alyx Gorman, Lucy Clark, Bridie Jabour, Svetlana Stankovic and Josephine Tovey (*Guardian*); Bhaskar Sunkara (*Jacobin*); Sophie Cunningham (*Meanjin*); Nick Feik and Patrick Witton (*Monthly*); Jacinda Woodhead, Alex Skutenko and Giovanni Tiso (*Overland*); and Catriona Menzies-Pike (*Sydney Review of Books*).

The project was supported by the Head of School Investment Fund at the School of Culture and Communication at the University of Melbourne, where I work in the Centre for Advancing Journalism. More than anything, thanks once more to my partner Stephanie Honor Convery, always my first and best reader.